Retailing Today

JAY DIAMOND

Department of Marketing and Retail
Nassau Community College

GERALD PINTEL

Professor Emeritus
Department of Accounting and Bus
Nassau Community College

Prentice Hall, Englewood Cliffs, N

Editorial/production supervision and interior design: Kim Gueterman
Cover design: Lundgren Graphics, Ltd.
Manufacturing buyer: Ed O'Dougherty

© 1988 Prentice Hall
A Division of Simon & Schuster
Englewood Cliffs, New Jersey 07632

Printed in the United States of America

10 9 8 7 6 5 4 3 2 1

ISBN 0-13-777509-1 01

Prentice-Hall International (UK) Limited, *London*
Prentice-Hall of Australia Pty. Limited, *Sydney*
Prentice-Hall Canada Inc., *Toronto*
Prentice-Hall Hispanoamericana, S.A., *Mexico*
Prentice-Hall of India Private Limited, *New Delhi*
Prentice-Hall of Japan, Inc., *Tokyo*
Simon & Schuster Asia Pte. Ltd., *Singapore*
Editora Prentice-Hall do Brasil, Ltda., *Rio de Janeiro*

Contents

3 ORGANIZING AND STAFFING THE STORE 61

4 BUYING FOR STORES 97

5 MERCHANDISING 127

6 ADVERTISING AND SALES PROMOTION 155

10 RESIDENT BUYING OFFICES AND OTHER RETAIL ADVISORY ORGANIZATIONS 283 _____

Preface

Contemporary Retailing was written to introduce students to the technical and theoretical aspects of retailing through the exploration of retail organizations throughout the United States. The format, a textbook-workbook combination, enables students to apply what they have learned by participating in a variety of case problems and projects, all of which have been classroom-tested.

The content of the book has been designed to explore the current pertinent practices of retailing and to give insight into the many career opportunities afforded students.

Each chapter is organized to provide not only the important retailing principles but also a variety of features that are motivational for further exploration. An *opening vignette* provides the reader with a specific store or business experience; it is followed by *learning objectives*, which indicate what will be accomplished upon the reading of each chapter. At the conclusion of each chapter's main text is a section, *small store adaptation*, that describes how the principles used by the giants of industry may be applied to the small retail outlet. A *career opportunities* feature, at each chapter's end, provides information relevant to the specific tasks found in that chapter. A variety of questions—*completion, true or false, multiple choice,* and *discussion* reinforce comprehension of the material presented, as are a variety of *case problems* and *projects*. Numerous photographs, drawings, and charts are incorporated to highlight the text.

A teacher's manual, providing answers to all of the questions and case problems, as well as sample tests, is available.

The authors thank Robert Cole, Abraham & Straus, for providing illustrative materials; Ellen Diamond, for her photography; and Winnie Garrahan and Mary Cole, for the typing of the manuscript.

Jay Diamond

Gerald Pintel

Introduction to Retailing

SOARING TO NEW HEIGHTS

Recent years have witnessed enormous changes in the world of retailing. All across the United States merchants have taken the initiative to improve their positions in an ever increasing competitive marketplace. Department stores and chains have gone to the suburbs to meet the needs of the customer who doesn't find it convenient to shop downtown. Downtown shopping areas have improved their locations by putting giant roofs over their stores and have, in effect, created malls in the middle of the cities' heaviest traffic areas. The enclosed malls, once a one-floor operation, have moved skyward to multilevel structures as outlying real estate has soared in price, thus making the one-level mall less practical in terms of profitability.

The latest and most daring adventure in retailing, which promises to overshadow anything that has yet taken place in retailing, is the new and exciting Herald Center in New York City (see Fig. 1–1). Situated in the highest traffic location in the United States stands a towering reflective glass eleven-story structure. Herald Center's uniqueness has been spearheaded by Stanley Marcus, chairman emeritus of the world-famous Dallas-based Neiman-Marcus Co.

Unlike other retail centers, Herald Center expects to become a tourist attraction as well as a place for New Yorkers to shop. Situated next to the flagship store of Macy's, New York, it is also surrounded by such landmarks as Madison Square Garden and the Empire State Building, the garment center, and the Broadway theatrical district. Never before in the history of retailing have so many international shops and restaurants competed for space. More than 200 of the world's prestigious shops occupy Herald Center. The cream of retailing—such as Ann Taylor, Charles Jourdan, Yves St. Tropez, Guy Laroche, Dunhill Alfred of London, St. Remy, Tannery West, Marimekko, and Escada—are represented. Various restaurants at the top of the structure in a double-level atrium and the United Nations Food Fair feature the finest in international cuisine.

Customers are transported from one floor to the other by the city's first glass-walled exterior elevators, from which they can see much of the city, to selling floors each having an individualistic character. The theme of Herald Center is New York, New York, with each of its ten levels depicting an area that epitomizes New York City. Greenwich Village features shops with brick and brownstone facades as well as sidewalk cafés. Fifth Avenue is resplendent in travertine and brass and offers high-fashion merchandise. Central Park is a haven for sports enthusiasts and boasts a working, antique carousel. Madison Avenue's merchandising concept centers upon art, antiques, fine linens, and periodic auctions for customer participation. Wall Street, Broadway, Columbus Avenue, Herald Square, the United Nations—all feature equally exciting fare that is relevant to their areas.

In this carefully planned, climate-controlled, exquisite setting, Herald Center is expected, in little time, to take its place among New York's tourist attractions and to become one of the most profitable, quality-oriented merchandise centers in the world.

FIGURE 1–1

Photo courtesy of Herald Center, Inc. Used with permission.

LEARNING OBJECTIVES

Upon completion of this chapter, the student should be able to

1. Write a brief essay on the growth of retailing in the United States, including the reasons for change.

2. Describe six different types of retailing.

3. Discuss the concept of off-price retailing.

4. Identify several merchants of distinction and describe their operations.

5. List five current trends in retailing and discuss the impact they are making in retailing.

6. Prepare a brief paragraph on five future retailing concepts.

One need only scan the newspapers and business-oriented periodicals to sense the excitement of today's retailing. Articles abound with words and phrases that were only dreams a few years ago or, indeed, were totally unknown. Licensing, off-price merchandising, private labels, and electronic shopping are just a few of the terms that surface in most discussions about retailing.

We live in a time where intuition and long hours are insufficient to ensure retail success. Those were the trademarks of yesteryears' merchants. Although both still play an important part in the success of most of today's operations, other factors are considered more important. Retailing has become a sophisticated industry complete with all the trappings of other businesses. Competition demands the constant analysis of the past so that the future can meet and beat competitive forces.

In this chapter, and throughout the text, the latest innovative practices of the retail world will be examined to ensure the reader the experience of understanding the "game" of retailing as it is presently being played.

LOOKING BACKWARD

Before one can satisfactorily grasp the sophistication of contemporary retailing, it is advisable to take a backward glance to see how it evolved to its present-day status. Although many of the early practices are no longer valuable in their original forms, some are still in evidence today, refined perhaps, in stores throughout the country.

American retailing as we know it today, with its sophisticated research methods and such decision-making devices as the computer, had its meager beginnings in the early sixteenth century at the trading post. At that time, currency was not used to make purchases; instead, goods from European markets were exchanged for the pelts of fur trappers and produce grown by farmers.

In the mid-eighteenth century this first retail institution began to expand its operation to better serve the needs of the colonists. A greater variety of merchandise was needed by the settlers, and the trading post gave way to the general store. This retail store operated on a cash basis, a departure from the barter system of the earlier retailer. The merchandise assortment was extensive, with offerings of foodstuffs, yard goods, feed for cattle, manufactured goods from Europe, shoes, and such animal supplies as harnesses. The merchandise was not carefully organized as it is in retail stores today. A haphazard nondepartmentalized arrangement was typical.

Figure 1–2 shows a typical general store that is found today primarily in rural areas. Although the emphasis is not on cattle feed and

FIGURE 1–2

Photo courtesy of Ellen Diamond. Used with permission.

supplies any longer, this form of retail operation is still frequented on a daily basis by people for much of their household needs. Remember that not every community is conveniently located within the trading areas of supermarkets, department stores, and malls.

In the middle of the nineteenth century a great variety of goods was being produced in the United States, so much so that the general store was unable to carry all the offerings of manufacturers. This necessitated the beginning of specialization in retailing and the introduction of the limited line store. This type of store carried a wide variety of one kind of merchandise. Shoe stores, women's specialty shops, jewelry stores, and groceries are examples of limited line stores. Today the limited line store—or specialty store, as it is commonly referred to—still enjoys an important place in retailing. The early specialty shops were generally individual proprietorships (individually owned). Many of them have grown into large, well-known retail empires and enjoy the distinction of having started the chain organization. A number of these great merchants are discussed later in this chapter.

The chain organization, the first venture into large-scale retailing in the United States, began in the latter part of the nineteenth century. It is generally defined as two or more stores similar in nature and having common ownership. Many of those operators of successful limited line stores opened second, third, and more units in other areas. Among the early chain organizations were J. C. Penney Co.; A&P, the food giant; and F. W. Woolworth Co., The "5 & 10 cent store."

At the end of the nineteenth and the beginning of the twentieth century the department store, a departmentalized retail store carrying a wide variety of hard goods and soft goods, became popular. Essentially, the department store brings together many limited line operations under one roof, with common ownership. This institution differed from the general store in that it presented an orderly arrangement of many types of merchandise, in contrast to the disorganized presentation of goods in the general store. The offerings of the department store—in addition to the typical hard goods such as furniture, appliances, and tools and the soft goods such as wearing apparel, clothing accessories, and piece goods—often include departments specializing in groceries, baked goods, gourmet foods, pets, optical goods, travel arrangements, entertainment information and sales, and so on. The luxury of one-stop shopping is available to the department store customer. Branch stores, smaller units of the department store, carrying a representation of the main store's offerings, have become popular as people have moved to the suburbs. Today in the retail field few new department stores are being established; instead, we are witnessing a great expansion of the established stores through additional branches.

In an effort to better serve the needs of those people unable to patronize existing retail institutions, either because of their distance from the stores or their lack of time to buy in person, the mail-order retailer began to attract attention. At first, in the late nineteenth century, little was available to the mail-order customer. Extensive catalogs, which since then have enjoyed great popularity, were prepared and sent to customers, and the mail-order business became an important part of retailing. Montgomery Ward & Co. and Sears, Roebuck and Co. were early mail-order houses. Today, even with mass transportation and with the extensive chain organization and the branch store, mail-order retailing continues to flourish.

An extension of mail-order retailing was the catalog store. This afforded the consumer the same type of purchasing as mail-order retailing but also provided the services of the store attendant to answer questions about the merchandise. Some of these units had on hand sample merchandise for customer examination. Figure 1–3 shows an example of such a store that is still in operation today.

The supermarket, a large departmentalized food store, became popular in the late 1930s. In addition to a large variety of foodstuffs, they carry an abundance of miscellaneous items such as drugs, toys, men's, women's, and children's accessories, plants, and hardware. As the department store provides one-stop shopping for the consumer, the supermarket affords the luxury of purchasing all one's food needs at one location. No longer does the shopper have to make separate trips to the grocer, butcher, baker, and produce dealer. Although the great majority of supermarkets are chain organizations, many independent markets are in operation.

Another major innovation in retailing is the discount operation. Unlike the conventional retail store with all of its services, the discounter offers limited service in exchange for lower prices. This method of merchandising is not restricted to one type of retailing organization, but is found in chain, department, and specialty store operations. Although it no longer enjoys the favorable status it once did, the discount store is still in operation and is the forerunner to another present-day operation, off-price retailing.

FIGURE 1–3

Photo courtesy of Ellen Diamond. Used with permission.

RETAILING TODAY

Having looked back to the past and examined the twists and turns taken by retailers, one finds that some of the operations of the past have virtually disappeared while others continue to flourish. No longer are the trading posts of pioneer retailing in evidence, nor are the general stores enjoying the widespread success they once had. Rather, it is the giants of the industry that are capturing the vast majority of the consumer's dollar. A scan of newspapers quickly calls to one's attention that retailing belongs to the large retailer. Remember, though, that the field still has small retailers that function successfully and continue to turn profits. By examining both large and small retailing institutions and operations separately, one can see retailing as it is being played today. Also dominant in today's retailing world are the nontraditionalists, whose structures will be examined.

The Small Retailer

The small retail business, as defined here, grosses under $100,000 annually. Typically, there is little job specialization. The store owner is generally responsible for the overall management and merchandising tasks. The owner buys, sells, sets work schedules, plans sales promotions, secures personnel, and so forth. The "larger" small retailer, doing business at the $100,000 level, has more specialized personnel working in the organization. There might be a person responsible only for merchandising duties, which include the entire buying-selling cycle. A part-time display person might be hired for window decoration. A store manager would be responsible for overseeing the physical layout of the store and supervising personnel.

The majority of small retail stores are individual proprietorships, that is, they are owned by one person. However, included in the group are partnerships and corporations. The general store and the specialty store are the two major types of small stores, with the latter accounting for almost all small retailing institutions.

In addition to the typical small retail establishments, another trend in retailing on a small scale is gaining momentum. Flea markets, both the outdoor and inside variety, are flourishing. They provide opportunities for those who wish to retail but have chosen not to take the traditional store route.

The General Store

The age of specialization, the success of the chain organization, movement to urban and suburban communities, the automobile, and the continued growth of the mail-order house are some factors that have contributed to the decline of the general store.

In rural areas, the general store, which features a wide variety of unrelated merchandise, is still in operation. Management of the operation is generally haphazard. The sophisticated tools and aids of today's modern retailers are rarely employed. The proprietor purchases merchandise that is so varied as to include cracker barrel goods and ready-made apparel. The knowledge of such owners in any single area is so limited that they lack the ability necessary to make the right decisions. How can one person have the product knowledge for so diversified an inventory? The limited floor space doesn't allow for wide assortment within each merchandise classification.

The general store has the questionable distinction of being the most mismanaged type of retail organization. Retailers, although reluctant to agree on many things, usually concede that the general store will never regain its popularity.

The Specialty Store

The limited line store—or the specialty store, as it is usually referred to today—is an establishment carrying one line of merchandise. Stores specializing in jewelry, furs, shoes, hardware, groceries, baked goods, and broader classifications such as women's clothing or men's accessories are examples of the specialty store. The majority of successful small retailers operate specialty stores. Some of the factors that have led to the success of this type of organization are personalized service, wide assortment of merchandise in a limited classification, and knowledgeable buying.

The chain organization is the major competitor of the small specialty store. The chain is actually a retail organization with many units carrying specialty merchandise. The chain's ability to offer lower prices due to greater buying power, and its wide advertising to the consumer, poses the greatest threat to the small retailer.

In an attempt to meet the "unfair" competition of the chain, many small merchants have united informally. The combining of small orders to qualify for quantity discounts, particularly in groceries, small hard goods, and staple menswear such as shirts and other accessories, has enabled the small merchant to become more competitive. As of late, advertising, an area that the small retailer often avoids because of its costs, has become popular as a group activity. Where one merchant would spend a large sum for an advertisement, the group now shares the costs. A complete listing of all the stores involved in the advertisement indicates to the consumer those offering the advertised merchandise. In both group-buying and group-advertising activities, noncompeting stores are generally involved.

More formal groups of small retailers are the voluntary chain and the cooperative chain. The voluntary chain is usually organized by a wholesaler who enters into contractual arrangements with the individual retailers, requiring that all purchases be made from the wholesaler. In addition, promotional plans, point-of-purchase display arrangements, advertising materials, merchandising advice, counter and shelf arrangements, and location selection are typical aids provided by the wholesaler. The cooperative chain differs in that the retailers join together and operate their own warehouse. They, too, are involved in many group activities that tend to lower the cost of individual operations and increase individual efficiency.

In retailing today, with the giant chain and department store organizations, small retailers can more effectively compete through group activities such as group buying and advertising, which reduce costs to the individual member. Of paramount importance in the field is knowledgeable advice on management and merchandising. Whereas the large retailer can afford the luxury of specialists, the small merchants, through their combined efforts, can avail themselves of an exchange of ideas. One store owner may be expert in designing store layouts; another might excel in the buying activity; still another might have a talent for preparing advertising copy. This exchange of information and ideas provides the specialized knowledge so necessary for success in retailing. Because the merchants are not direct competitors, this free exchange can be open and beneficial to all.

Because the nature of some small stores dictates a different type of management, retailing today still includes completely independent retailers that are not involved in any group arrangement. Others find this type of arrangement well suited to their needs.

Flea Market Operations

Once located primarily off back roads and in less than carefully manicured fields, flea markets have moved into the cities and suburbs.

Operating under conditions that are not considered ideal by traditional retail standards, flea markets and their devotees continue to increase in number. While the typical "off the beaten path" flea market is still thriving today, as evidenced in Figure 1–4, some flea market operators rival big business.

Racetrack parking lots, drive-in movies, and abandoned warehouses and stores are just a few of the places where flea marketing thrives. Not only are the locations different from where earlier flea markets flourished but so is the merchandise offered for sale. In these recent ventures no longer will one find accumulated "treasures" but rack upon rack and counter upon counter of the latest in fashion with names like Izod, Polo, Gant, Converse, Gloria Vanderbilt, Jordache, and others in plentiful supply and at bargain prices.

The early flea markets were established as places where people were able to dispose of the "treasures" they accumulated. Once having accomplished this, they usually were out of business. Today, however, the flea market is not an arena for this purpose, but a regular format for individuals to conduct retail businesses. For a modest fee, approximately $20 a day, an individual can set up shop. So successful has this format become, that acquiring a space has been as difficult as gaining a desirable location in a traditional shopping area. Stalls are generally leased for a one-year period.

Merchants at flea markets specialize in a particular type of merchandise, much the same as the specialty store. The main feature is price. Returns and refunds are usually as liberal as those in the traditional retail establishments. So effective is flea market retailing that it has caused

FIGURE 1–4 Flea Market

Photo courtesy of Ellen Diamond. Used with permission.

considerable concern for retailers who are located near them. Where the large retailer has generally had the advantage over the small retailer, it is the flea market independent that is actively and successfully competing with the large retail companies.

Boutiques

Recent years have seen significant growth among small retailers in the form of boutique merchandising. Typical of these operations is high-priced merchandise, one-of-a-kind items, a lack of depth in sizes and colors in particular styles, unique designs, and so on. Unlike specialty stores, which carry a broad range of specific merchandise such as shoes, the boutique is an operation that assembles a wide variety of related merchandise. For example, a high-fashion women's boutique might feature some dresses for streetwear, evening separates, jewelry, handbags, activewear, and so forth. Each classification would be represented by a few pieces, more or less guaranteeing the purchaser a certain degree of exclusivity. These stores are popping up all over the country in fashionable areas and are proving to be excellent outlets for producers of unusual and high-priced merchandise.

The Large Retailer

Today retailing is dominated by the large organization. The department store, chain organization, supermarket, and mail-order house provide the majority of retail sales.

The Department Store

The department store is a departmentalized retail institution that offers a large variety of hard goods and soft goods, provides numerous customer services, has large sales volume, and employs a great number of people specializing in various tasks. Its organization is discussed in detail in Chapter 3.

The merchandise assortment varies, depending on the size of the store. Organizations such as Macy's and the Allied Stores offer enough types of merchandise in a range of prices for a consumer family to satisfy just about any of its needs. Such merchandise as men's, women's, and children's clothing, apparel accessories, musical instruments, sporting goods, toys, furniture, hardware, perfumes, toiletries, gourmet foods, liquor, floor covering, bedding, draperies, and appliances are among those in the inventory. A Macy's shopper can buy anything from an iguana to a painting by Joan Miró, from a set of Tom Swift books to fresh beluga caviar.

In many stores, optical goods, beauty salon services, precious jewelry, religious articles, meat and poultry, silverware, and other commodities are available through leased departments. These departments are operated by independents or independent chain owners, generally because the nature of the goods or services warrants unusual specialized ability. The department is usually leased on a square foot basis or for a percentage of sales. Department stores have found that a greater profit

FIGURE 1–5

Macy's	May Department Stores	Batus
Macy's, New York	May Co., California	Marshall Field, Chicago
Macy's, New Jersey	Hecht's, Washington, D.C.	Frederick & Nelson, Seattle
Macy's, California	Famous Barr, St. Louis	Ivey's, Carolinas
Allied Stores	Kaufmann's, Pittsburgh	Ivey's, Florida
Jordan Marsh, New England	May Co., Cleveland	*Carter Hawley Hale*
The Bon, Seattle	Meier & Frank, Portland	
Sterns, New York, New Jersey,	G. Fox, Hartford	Broadway, Southern California
Long Island	M. O'Neil, Akron	Emporium-Capwell, San
Maas Brothers, Tampa	May-D&F, Denver	Francisco
L. S. Ayres, Indianapolis	Strouss, Youngstown	John Waxmaller, Philadelphia
Jordan Marsh, Florida	May-Cohens, Florida	Thalhimer's, Richmond
Joske's, Houston, Dallas,	*Associated Dry Goods*	Weinstock's, Sacramento
San Antonio	Lord & Taylor, New York	Broadway Southwest, Phoenix
Miller & Rhoads, Richmond	J. W. Robinson's, Los Angeles	
Donaldson's, Minneapolis	Sibley, Lindsay, Curo, Syracuse	
Millers, Knoxville	Joseph Horne, Pittsburgh	
Reads, Bridgeport	Denver Dry Goods	
Blocks, Indianapolis	Hahne & Co., Newark	
Federated Department Stores	Goldwaters, Phoenix	
Bloomingdales, New York	Robinson's, Florida	
Abraham & Straus, Brooklyn	Stewart, Kentucky	
Burdine's, Miami	Loehmann's	
Foley's, Houston	*Mercantile Stores*	
Rich's, Atlanta	Gayfer's, Mobile	
Lazarus, Columbus	McAlpin, Cincinnati	
Sanger Harris, Dallas	Castner-Knott, Nashville	
Shilleto/Rike's, Cincinnati	Jones Store, Kansas City	
Filene's, Boston	Joslin's, Denver	
Goldsmith's, Memphis	Gayfer/Montgomery Fair,	
Boston Store, Milwaukee	Montgomery	
	Bacon/Roots, Louisville	
	J. B. White, Augusta	
	Lion, Toledo	

The figure includes some of the department stores owned by the largest ownership groups. All of the stores listed are among the top 100 department stores. The list includes only department stores; many of the ownership groups are involved with chain stores as well.

for the store can be realized in this way than if they operated these departments themselves. An important reason for offering these specialized goods and services is to provide the customer with convenient one-stop shopping.

The greatest variety of customer services offered in retailing is in the department store. Free delivery, giftwrapping, charge accounts, return privileges, extended credit plans, and meeting rooms for clubs are among the usual services. Unusual ones include personal shoppers for foreign-speaking people, baby sitting while parents are shopping, special hours for children shoppers before holidays, and tickets for theatrical and sporting events.

Department stores may be individually owned, belong to ownership groups such as the Allied Stores Corp., or be chains such as Macy's, which has a nationwide organization of more than ninety stores in several regional divisions. Figure 1–5 shows the leading ownership groups.

Branches and twigs. With the increase in the number of families moving from the cities to the suburbs, the almost hopeless traffic congestion, the shortage of adequate parking facilities, and the development and growth of shopping centers, department stores have opened units away from the city. The branch is a store, usually smaller than the main store, carrying a representation of the parent store's merchandise. It is geared to the needs of the community in which it is located. Some branch stores have exceeded the sales volume of the main store.

Twig stores, relatively rare in retailing today, are very small units belonging to a department store, which, unlike the branch, carry only one classification of merchandise. For example, a department store might operate a shop in a college town featuring merchandise worn on the campus.

The Chain Store

The chain store may be defined as a centrally owned and managed organization with two or more similar units each carrying the same classification of merchandise. The merchandise categories include drugs, hardware, shoes, restaurants, jewelry, variety goods, groceries, baked goods, and other goods and services. For example, S. S. Kresge is a variety chain; A&P, a supermarket chain; J. C. Penney, a general merchandise chain; Edison Brothers, a shoe chain; and Lerner Shops, a women's clothing chain. Each unit in these chains is similar to the other units.

Whereas the department store has the main store as its base of operations, the chain organization operates from central headquarters, a location that houses merchandisers, buyers, personnel administrators, advertising executives, and so on. Large chains have regional offices in addition to central headquarters. The units of the chain are generally charged with the responsibility of selling merchandise, and the central team is the decision-making body of the organization. Store managers do not formulate policy; instead, they carry out the policies of the central staff.

In addition to functioning centrally in the areas of buying and merchandising, chains occasionally are centrally involved in other than the usual areas. For example, Lerner Shops, a large women's specialty chain with stores throughout the United States, has at its main offices in New York City a display department that plans window displays centrally. Windows are arranged with merchandise, photographed, and distributed for duplication by each store. Supplementary materials and directions for ease of execution are included with each photograph. In this manner, all stores are assured of having similar high-quality displays. As a result, the company projects a uniform image and has control over the individual stores' displays. Further, display costs are decreased because high-salaried display persons are not needed to execute the displays in each store; a store manager can easily follow the simplified plan.

The trend indicates that chains will grow larger and the individual units will increase in size.

Supermarkets

The supermarket is a large, departmentalized, self-service organization selling primarily food and other merchandise. The merchandise assortment has grown from the usual grocery, meat, poultry, and produce categories to include hardware, toys, hosiery, drugs, books, greeting cards, and so on. A supermarket may be independently owned, belong to a voluntary or cooperative chain, or be part of a regular chain organization. The greatest number of supermarkets belong to the third category. Emphasis on lower prices, customer parking facilities, and one-stop food shopping are some of the more important factors that lead to their success. A&P, Safeway, and Kroger Co. are among the largest supermarket chains.

The Mail-Order Retailer

Selection of merchandise from a catalog, ordering through the mail, and delivery by similar means are the major characteristics of the mail-order house. The merchandise offering of some mail-order houses is so large and diversified that rarely can one find as wide an assortment in a "merchandise-stocking" store. In addition to those retailers that sell exclusively by mail, a large percentage of the total sales of department and specialty stores can be attributed to this method of retailing. L. L. Bean, The Vermont Country Store, Spiegel, and Sears, Roebuck are leading mail-order retailers. Sears presently enjoys the status of being the world's largest retailer. The more than 140,000 items sold by Sears include mink stoles and sculpture priced as high as $39,500. With the exception of food, liquor, and automobiles, almost any article can be bought from Sears.

Although the chain has moved retail stores closer to the people and in some cases made buying through catalogs not as necessary as it once was, mail ordering has not disappeared. Perhaps the increasing number of women in the work force results in less time for shopping and encourages mail-order purchasing. As is evidenced by the great sales volume of mail-order houses, this form of retailing is still important.

The Catalog Store

A companion business to the mail-order retailer is the catalog store. This method of retailing involves stocking merchandise in "warehouse" stores where customers either come in for immediate receipt of goods or may order, through a catalog, from their homes. The main feature of catalog retailing is price. At considerably lower prices than traditional retailers charge, consumers can purchase appliances, precious jewelry, housewares, cameras, and so on. One such company, a giant in the field, is Consumers Distributing with stores throughout Connecticut, New Jersey, New York, and California. Like traditional retailers, Consumers Distributing offer such services as charges, gift certificates, refunds, and exchanges.

Through a combination of in-store purchases and mail order, the catalog store is continuing to grow and has become a major force in large-scale retailing.

The Nontraditionalists

Thus far in our discussion the various retail operations that have been examined have taken the conventional route to satisfy customer needs. Save for the flea market sellers, the others have used and continue to use an approach that could be considered conventional retailing. The last few years have seen an explosion in the industry and the birth of new approaches to what is believed to be a viable, untapped market of purchasers. Throughout the country retailers have been setting up shop as off-price merchants or as outlets for overproduction of manufacturers' goods. In the off-price arrangement, the store is independent of the manufacturers; the outlets are usually owned and operated by the manufacturers.

Off-Price Retailers

The popularity of off-price retailing, which provides customers with brand names, designer labels, and fashion merchandise at 20 to 50 percent below the regular price, is quite evident when one examines the enormous success of Marshall's, Hit or Miss, Brannam Stores, and Syms.

Figure 1–6 focuses on the ten off-price leaders in retailing, based on recent sales. At the time of this writing, it is estimated that the off-price industry will make an even greater impact by significantly increasing the number of units throughout the country.

A question that seems to be gaining more attention today is, "How will off-price retailing eventually affect the traditional retailer?" Many traditional merchants fear serious competition from the off-pricers. Most agree that the new merchandising concept is something to be reckoned with.

The element that seems to be a key factor in the survival of traditional retailing is timing. Stores throughout the country like Macy's, Bloomingdale's, Saks Fifth Avenue, Neiman-Marcus, and Jordan Marsh

FIGURE 1-6   The Off-Price Leaders in Retailing

Company	Affiliation	Sales in Millions	Number of units
Marshall's	Melville Corp.	$830	137
T. J. Maxx–Hit or Miss	Zayre Corp.	525	353
Loehmann's	Associated Dry Goods	260	61
Pic-A-Dilly	Lucky Stores	165	250
Syms, Inc.	No affiliation	147	8
Burlington Coat Factory	No affiliation	128	31
J. Brannam	F. W. Woolworth	85	30
T. H. Mandy	U. S. Shoe	80	52
Dress Barn	No affiliation	32	49
Ross Stores	No affiliation	15	6

provide their customers with goods early in the season. Their customers want the merchandise before it is to be worn, and often, price is not a serious consideration. These companies buy early, at the top price, but provide their customers with early availability. On the other hand, the off-price store must wait until the traditionalist receives the goods and for the manufacturer to cut prices for quick disposal of the remaining inventory. By that time, the traditional retailer has had sufficient time to sell. Customers of traditional stores want the goods early, with a "penalty" of a higher price; off-price customers are willing to wait for the "bargain."

Can the two coexist? So far the answer is yes. Evidence is in the fact that companies like Lord & Taylor, Abraham & Straus, Sears, and Penney's are operating traditional stores as well as discount or off-price operations.

Manufacturers' Outlets

Rare is the situation where a producer can guarantee the sale of all of the merchandise produced. Even in the best of times, manufacturers experience excess inventory through stores' cancellation of orders, slow sellers, production of the "wrong" colors, and the like. Many of these companies dispose of their overproduction to the much heralded off-price merchants.

The last few years have seen a wave of outlets open that belong to manufacturers that sell directly to the public. Names like Liz Claiborne, Dexter Shoe Co., Mikasa, Waterford, and Totes are featuring merchandise that they sell in their own outlets. Places like Secaucus, New Jersey, and Reading, Pennsylvania, have become enormous centers for such merchandising. In Freeport, Maine, a tiny village on the coast, there are enough "names" to satisfy the most discriminating of shoppers. There for the asking are individual manufacturers' outlets that feature their own prestigious brands—Ralph Lauren's Polo, Anne Klein, Cole-Haan shoes, Dansk—all at up to 60 percent below normal retail prices.

So popular is the concept that directories are available that list the locations of these outlets all across the United States.

MERCHANTS OF DISTINCTION

No matter what the field, there are those who deserve special attention and recognition. Retailing, too, has its own stars. Although the list can be argued, as can any "top ten" or "best," the following choices are those of the authors.

No list could be complete without *Macy's*. Recent figures for the New York Division alone shows nineteen units, 6,988,000 square feet, and a sales volume of $1,290,000,000. Alone, its main store at Herald Square covers more than 2 million square feet, more than 175 selling departments, and more than 400,000 items and is the world's single largest store. About ten years ago, the company began an ambitious transition from "middle of the road" retailer to today's image as fashion innovator in "top of the line" merchandising. Where other stores, once well known, have halted their operations because of failure, Macy's has met every challenge and competitive situation. Its overall operation is national in structure with divisions based in such areas as New Jersey, San Francisco, and Kansas City. In more than ninety units across the country, it regularly shows up to be a retailing giant.

Service, competitive pricing, and innovation are the key factors contributing to the store's success. About three dozen comparison shoppers check competitors' prices, and if Macy's are higher for the same merchandise, the price is lowered. Its own bureau of standards puts merchandise through rigid laboratory tests to make certain the needs of the consumer are met. Personal shoppers are made available to satisfy any customer's unusual requirements. The Thanksgiving Day Parade was a Macy's first, an official opening for the Christmas season. This organization was even the inspiration for a well-known motion picture, *Miracle on 34th Street*.

Perhaps no other store caters to a wealthier clientele or carries the unusual merchandise assortment found in *Neiman-Marcus*. Its reputation was built by the free-spending customer. His and hers Beechcraft airplanes, a seven-passenger $149,000 plane, and a four-place $27,000 craft, respectively, were featured in a Christmas book. Later, a genuine Chinese junk (boat) made in Hong Kong was offered F.O.B. Houston. Eleven of them were sold. The store even offered an Aegean cruise for ten on a chartered yacht. Continuing with its offer of unusual merchandise, the 1980 Christmas Book featured such items as a Martin D-45 guitar priced at $9,500, and the latest his and hers gifts, a pair of young ostriches for $1,500 to keep or give to one's favorite zoo. In order to increase its volume, the company has embarked on a program of opening units throughout the United States and, in addition to its unique merchandise, has added merchandise that would appeal to a less affluent market.

Filene's of Boston is one of the world's largest specialty shops. It operates two separate kinds of retailing enterprises under one roof. The unusual part of the organization is the basement operation. Other retailers have bargain basements and budget basements, but none has the unique system of merchandising developed by Edward Filene. Merchandise is reduced weekly for thirty days, and at the end of this period whatever is unsold is given to charity. Separate buyers operating in all of the world's fashion centers purchase for the basement store. Merchandise from world-famous retailers and leading manufacturers are purchased and sold with the original labels; Neiman-Marcus and Saks Fifth Avenue labels are found in the basement at fractions of their original selling prices. Stores that have overstocked because of a bad season or manufacturers that overproduced look to Filene's to help them. This unusual merchandising policy sells so much merchandise that less than 1 percent is given away to charity.

It should be noted that Filene's tried to expand its basement operation on Long Island. The successful innovative practice in Boston faltered there, and units are presently running as typical off-price merchandisers. As of this writing, the results are not yet in as to the success of Filene's merchandising philosophy for Long Island. Even the most successful and unique retail organizations don't always carry forth their plans in a profitable manner.

Henri Bendel, the store with the "street of specialized shops," features eight small shops with separate windows on the main floor to give the customer the feeling of individual, specialized retail operations. Each boasts a different decor. This different approach, inaugurated by Geraldine Stutz, transformed a losing business into a financially sound one.

Brooks Brothers, the oldest men's shop in the United States, boasts a clientele of former presidents, statesmen, business executives, authors, and so on. Its meticulous, conservative merchandise and the personal service given to customers are chiefly responsible for this continued success. While other retailers have employed the newer scientific methods of merchandising, the century-old traditions of Brooks Brothers are still successful.

The Limited Stores is a retail organization that merits distinction. At present, its 560-unit specialty apparel chain is making a great impact on the public through extensive use of private label merchandising. This philosophy has curtailed competition and has made the chain extremely profitable. Not satisfied to rest on its laurels, The Limited has entered into a licensing agreement with Kenzo, one of the hottest names in fashion. The Kenzo collection, created exclusively for The Limited, provides fashion excitement at an affordable price. This successful venture, following on the heels of private labeling, has separated The Limited from other chains and has catapulted the organization into the forefront of retail excitement.

Sears, *Roebuck*, known as the mail-order retailer to millions, is an organization that continuously tries new concepts to maintain its level of appeal. Not totally satisfied with its image of the private brand reputation it has built over the years in housewares and appliances, Sears set out on a fashion merchandising emphasis that incorporated the likes of a Cheryl Tiegs Collection to help alter its image. Soon after the emphasis was on 100,000 square foot plus stores that had more of the traditional department store concept of featuring brand name fashion merchandise. The latest from Sears is opening stores with 14,000 to 35,000 square feet. With these new ideas and concepts, Sears hopes to touch all bases in consumer attention. From every indication it will continue to be one of the greatest of merchants.

Many other famous retailers are worth investigating, but we will mention only their names and their distinguishing features.

Tiffany's, the world-famous jeweler, boasts jewelry and silver treasures ranging in price from a few dollars to more than $100,000; *Lane Bryant* caters to the customer generally forgotten, the full-figured woman; *Castro Convertibles* manufactures and retails the "bed hidden within the sofa"; and *Bergdorf Goodman* is the wealthy client's retreat on Fifth Avenue in New York City, where haute couture is commonplace.

No other period in history has seen the number of innovations and trends being explored by today's merchants. Through investigating these trends, one can realize how diversified retailing has become.

Franchising

In the arrangement known as franchising, an organization (the franchisor) that has developed a successful retail product or service sells to individuals (the franchisees) the right to engage in the business, provided they follow the established pattern. Because of the expertise of the franchisor, the probability of success for the individual opening such an operation is greater than if that entrepreneur ventured into a completely new independent enterprise. Most retailers agree that inexperience and incompetence account for the great majority of retail store failures. The franchisor offers such services as location analysis, tested managerial techniques, knowledgeable merchandising, training plans, financial instruction, and counseling in other pertinent areas. With these services provided by the franchisor, the risk of failure is greatly reduced.

Franchising got its major start in 1898 in General Motors; today it accounts for more than 10 percent of the gross national product through 500,000 outlets. Carvel, Howard Johnson, Chicken Delight, International House of Pancakes, AAMCO Automotive Transmissions, Rexall Drug Co., Hickory Farms, and Baskin-Robbins 31 Flavor Stores are examples of franchise operations that bring to the consumer a variety of goods and services.

Owning a franchise is often the best route to success, particularly for a person lacking experience. However, this type of business has its drawbacks. For one thing the lump sum payment required to get into business is likely to be high. While a franchise for Augie's, Inc., Industrial Catering truck is only $1,000, a Good Taco Co. restaurant can run as high as $1.5 million. In addition, most franchisors require royalty payments based on sales. This has the effect of reducing the profit margin of the franchise compared to that of a conventional outlet. Perhaps the biggest complaint of franchisees is the dictatorial direction of the parent company. When disputes arise, and they often do, the individual franchisee feels like a pigmy against the giant corporation. To overcome this, some franchisees like the Midas Dealers Association, which represents some 1,400 dealers, have been able to exert considerable power. When Midas decided to expand, the association was able to protect its members' territories. Chapter 2 fully explores franchising as a means of helping one enter into his or her "own" retail business.

Multilevel Malls

All over the country two-level and three-level malls have become commonplace. The anchor stores in these multilevel malls generally have entrances to their stores at each level to benefit favorably from the traffic generated on each floor.

An innovation in multilevel shopping centers is Herald Center in New York City. It boasts ten levels featuring shops rarely found in enclosed shopping centers. Each floor is based on a theme and features a variety of merchandise in unique shops from around the world, many at price lines never before found in malls; restaurants designed for every appetite; and attractions such as a carousel to amuse the children. It is expected to eventually "outtrump" the famous multilevel "shopping mall" of New York's internationally acclaimed Trump Tower, a six-story enclosed shopping extravaganza.

Warehouse Outlets

Since the start of the 1980s, warehouse outlets have opened in record numbers throughout the United States. Most operate on a no-frills basis. Wal-Mart Stores, Inc., opened three stores in 1983 with many more planned. Zayre & Co. is presently testing the concept in New England. The Warehouse Club in Niles, Illinois, broke every marketing rule in 1983 by opening in an out-of-the way location in less than attractive surroundings. Annual sales for the first year of operation approached $25 million. Whereas such stores as R. H. Macy & Co. are seeking to appeal to the more affluent customer, warehouses are seeking to fill the void with bargain prices aimed at the less traditional shopper. Secaucus, New Jersey, and Reading, Pennsylvania, are two areas that boast warehouse centers featuring scores of such outlets. It is expected that this form of retailing will soon become a major force in business.

Private Labeling

For many years, a significant number of retailers have concentrated their merchandising efforts on filling their shelves with nationally advertised and easily recognized brands and labels. With the recent success of the off-price merchants, these retailers have experienced difficulty in achieving the high markups associated with the manufacturers' labels. In an effort to counteract the adverse effects caused by selling the well-known brands off-price, many major retail organizations have developed private label programs.

Under this concept, stores make arrangements for manufacturers to produce goods strictly for the particular store's own use, to be identified by the store's "private label." In that way the consumer's ability to comparison shop is eliminated. As one major retailer stated, "Private label is our number one option for coping with off-pricers."

The trend has been steadily increasing, with many stores adding more private label goods to their merchandise mix. Dayton's private label Boundary Waters has been setting records. Such giants as Carter Hawley Hale, Associated Dry Goods, Allied Stores, Macy's, and Saks are just a few that have gone all out in introducing private label programs for their stores.

Licensing

Using a well-known name has taken retailing by storm. Spearheaded by the Halston–J. C. Penney marriage, retailers have joined forces with designers and celebrities to stock their shelves and racks with "familiar" names. Some stores have gone the Penney's route with exclusive license arrangements, while others have opted for designer labels on everything from chocolate (Bill Blass) to children's wear (Guy Laroche) on a nonexclusive arrangement. It seems that the consuming public has become so preoccupied with "names" that it will be motivated to buy and pay more for such merchandise.

Such "brands" as the Dynasty Collection, Kenzo for The Limited, Cheryl Tiegs for Sears, Jaclyn Smith for K-Mart, Cacharel for the Federated Stores, Gloria Vanderbilt bed linens for K-Mart, Levi Strauss, the Perry Ellis America Collection, and Liz Claiborne's domestics line are just a few of the latest in licensing.

FUTURE RETAILING CONCEPTS

Not yet in actual operation, but more than merely dreams, are many new concepts that retailers will be using in the near or distant future. The expected changes necessitated by both increases in operational expenses and shortages in qualified personnel may be any or all of the following.

Automatic Fund Transfer Machines

Living in a cashless society is not a myth any longer, but a theory that is going into practice. Diebold, Inc., a North Canton, Ohio, based company that manufactures automatic teller machines for banks, is experimenting with a similar machine for retailer use. The device, called a convenience center, is a computer terminal that would automatically transfer money from a customer's personal bank account to the store's account. It would involve the use of a personal card, much like the bank cards now used, to complete the transaction. This system would enable the retailer to gain immediate access to the customer's bank account for the entire purchase when authorized by the customer's signature. It would eliminate the time needed to gain the dollars now generated by store credit cards and third-party cards. It could encourage the customer who is fearful of carrying cash to make cash purchases easier.

Shopping by Computer

More than $500 million has been spent by companies in the research and development of systems that would enable customers to shop at home. American Bell as well as IBM are busily engaged in this area. American Bell is experimenting with the Video Frame Creation Terminal, which will enable artists to draw detailed color pictures with a quality similar to the home video games. These computerized networks would permit the shopper to buy a store's current offerings without leaving the house.

Joint Training Centers

Aware that it is expensive to train retail personnel properly and dangerous to place untrained people on selling floors or in other store areas, merchants are beginning to talk about the creation of cooperative training centers. The plan is not really farfetched and is operational in the advertising field. In this way, stores could continue to have trained employees while reducing their expenses.

Main-Street Mall Conversion

It is obvious to knowledgeable merchants that consumers are flocking to malls for the conveniences they offer. Small merchants that occupy locations on main streets are, in surprising numbers, discussing the conversion of their locations into malls. In Miami Beach, Florida, merchants on the famed Lincoln Road have done so and have convinced the city to close the area to automobile traffic. Retailing seems to be moving ever closer to developing areas resembling the giant enclosed malls. It is expected that merchants will alter their shopping streets not only to prohibit auto traffic but also to provide interstore connections for easier access. This will eliminate to some degree the need for complete enclosure under one roof, while affording the shopper the luxury of shopping in climate-controlled areas.

Employee Sharing

As impossible as it might seem to many retailers, there are indications that a sharing of employees, particularly salespeople, might become a reality. The arrangement is conceivable for two reasons. First, peak sales hours are not the same in all stores—sales personnel in one store may not have much to do, while at the same time another store desperately needs help. Thus an employee-sharing plan could be arranged to accommodate two or more employers' needs. Second, with the costs of transacting business becoming increasingly higher, this new arrangement could minimize expenses while maximizing profits. It might be suggested that part-time employees working exclusively for one retailer could accomplish the same goals as would be found in an employee-sharing plan. Most experienced retailers will agree, however, that those guaranteed full-time work for which they can earn a full salary are more committed than are part-time employees.

These innovative ideas, along with many others that will eventually be put to the test, will continue to assist retailers in the challenges they face in the future.

SMALL STORE ADAPTATION

Most textbooks on retailing are totally consumed with the problems and practices of the major retail organizations. Their focus is almost exclusively on how these operations function on a day-to-day basis and in what manner they deal with both expected and unforeseen business situations.

Although the vast majority of retailing is attributed to the large organizations, we have learned that there is still potential for the individual who seeks opportunity as an independent merchant. For this reason, each chapter in this book features a concluding section on Small Store Adaptation that addresses ways in which small stores can benefit from and make use of the presented materials. For example, advertising and sales promotion are often considered too costly for small retailers. Many suggestions are offered, and at minimal cost, to those with very limited promotional budgets. Through this chapter end feature, we hope to dispel the misconceptions of those who believe small retailers simply cannot apply the theories and applications available to their large store counterparts.

CAREER OPPORTUNITIES

Close inspection of classified advertising throughout the United States indicates the enormous opportunities available to those pursuing a career in retailing. Unlike many fields where career opportunities are restricted to particular geographic locations, retailing has no such boundaries. Not only are there opportunities in every part of the country, but the variety of job titles is greater than most industries can boast. Finally, the preparation to achieve success in retailing is significantly less than that which is required in fields with comparable salary potential. While it is generally agreed that formal education is paramount to success in the industry, the level of study is not as stringent or restrictive as for such areas as accounting, engineering, or medicine. Discussions with many directors of personnel indicate that many retailing and retailing-related positions will be satisfied with an associate's degree or a certificate of competency. The consensus is that such personal qualities as initiative, enthusiasm, intelligence, and imagination are imperative for success.

Employment is available in both large and small organizations, with, for obvious reasons, the larger retailer providing the greater opportunity. The job titles are numerous in department stores, chain organizations, specialty stores, and retail-related institutions such as resident buying offices and reporting services. It should be understood that different organizational structures employ different job titles, but the tasks performed by all retailers are virtually the same. For example, some companies prefer sales associate to salesperson even though the basic requirement is selling. The majority of the store organizations, as well as

**FIGURE 1–7 Job Prospects, 1980s—Selected
Categories**

Job Classification	Percentage Change
Engineers	+ 22.5
Math specialists	+ 28.1
Computer specialists	+ 30.8
Teachers	− 3.7
Buyers, purchasing agents	+ 44.3
Administrators	+ 18.7
Advertising personnel	+ 42.4
Keypunch operators	− 26.7
Billing clerks	+ 59.9
Sales managers, retail	+ 54.0

some resident buying offices, are grouped under four major divisions, with each offering a number of specific jobs. Merchandising, advertising and sales promotion (sometimes called publicity), store operations (often referred to as store management), and control make up the four classifications.

In this text, specific career opportunities will be examined in detail in those chapters that are appropriate to the particular job. For example, buying careers are discussed in Chapter 4, Buying for Stores, and the service manager in Chapter 9, Customer Services.

Figure 1–7 gives a general overview of specific retail and retail-related job classifications and how they compare to other fields for the 1980s as projected by the U. S. Labor Department's Bureau of Labor Statistics. It is safe to assume, from examination of the figure, that those pursuing retailing careers need not fear unemployment.

KEY POINTS IN THE CHAPTER

1. Retailing began at the trading post and has developed into an industry that today offers customers many different types of establishments for their purchasing needs.

2. The small retailer, challenged by the giants in the field, has made significant advances through the operation of flea markets and boutiques.

3. Large-scale retailing continues to dominate the field with significant expansion through branch store openings for department stores and new units for the chain organizations.

4. With the increased number of women in the work force, mail-order retailing is bigger than ever.

5. The concept of off-price retailing has taken the market by storm. Merchants that use this method of operation are able to offer customers designer labels and fashion merchandise at 20 to 50 percent below the regular retail price.

6. Numerous manufacturers have opened retail outlets to dispose of their overproduction. Labels such as Polo, Mikasa, Dansk, Anne

Klein, and Liz Claiborne are available at these producer-owned outlets and are enjoying enormous success.

7. Many merchants of distinction are prospering in the United States. Such organizations as The Limited, Neiman-Marcus, Filene's, Sears, and Macy's continue to flourish because of their unique and creative methods of operation.

8. Warehouse outlets are springing up throughout the country, appealing to those customers who are willing to forgo service for lower prices.

9. Private labeling is a significant trend for retailers that wish to gain a degree of exclusivity and counteract the inroads made by the off-price retailers.

10. The future of retailing promises such concepts as automatic fund transfer machines and shopping by computer, both of which are expected to increase sales.

Worksheet 1

COMPLETE THE FOLLOWING STATEMENTS

1. A _____ is a centrally owned and managed organization with two or more similar units each carrying the same classification of merchandise.

2. A limited line or _____ is an establishment carrying one line of merchandise.

3. In an arrangement known as _____, individuals buy the right to market a successful retail product or service provided they follow an established pattern.

4. Small units, belonging to a department store, that carry only one classification

   of merchandise are called _____ stores.

5. A companion business to the mail-order retailer is the _____

   _____ which services customers in person rather than by mail.

6. The latest fast-growing retailing is taking place in _____

   _____ where business is transacted at a modest fee in a makeshift arena.

7. Many large retailers are competing with off-price merchants by developing

   _____ programs.

TRUE OR FALSE

_____ 1. A general store carries a wide assortment of merchandise.
_____ 2. Job specialization is a characteristic of the small retailer.
_____ 3. A voluntary chain is organized by a group of retailers.
_____ 4. Branch stores differ from twig stores only in size.
_____ 5. Chain stores employ centralized buying.
_____ 6. Trends indicate that chains will grow larger and individual units will decrease in size.

_____ **7.** Franchising is a relatively new concept.

_____ **8.** Small-scale retailing is on the increase with the emergence of flea markets.

_____ **9.** In comparison to other fields, the 1980s hold the greatest promise for individuals aspiring to retailing careers.

_____ **10.** Selling via cable television and advertising a product on conventional television are one and the same.

MULTIPLE CHOICE

_____ **1.** A small retailer offering a wide variety of goods in a specific classification for cash is known as a

(a) trading post
(b) specialty store
(c) chain store
(d) twig store

_____ **2.** The success of the specialty store is due to

(a) personalized service
(b) wide assortment of merchandise
(c) knowledgeable buying
(d) all of the above

_____ **3.** Department stores are responsible for the management of

(a) franchised outlets
(b) branch stores
(c) leased department
(d) all of the above

_____ **4.** The following is a characteristic of a warehouse outlet

(a) expensive fixtures
(b) out-of-the-way locations
(c) slow delivery
(d) high prices

_____ **5.** Similar to the mail-order retailer, but offering customers immediate merchandise, is the

(a) warehouse outlet
(b) catalog store
(c) leased department
(d) twig store

DISCUSSION QUESTIONS

1. Which was the first retail store to operate on a cash basis, and what were some of its other characteristics?

2. Define the department store, and describe how it differs from a limited line operation.

3. Discuss the difference between branch and twig stores.

4. How can the discounter afford to sell merchandise at prices lower than the conventional retail organization?

5. If customers can have all their merchandise needs satisfied under one roof in department stores, how do you account for the success of specialty stores?

6. Discuss group activities and their importance to small retailers.

7. What is central management and which type of organization employs this system?

8. Describe some of the drawbacks to owning a franchise.

9. Name two types of nontraditional retailing and briefly discuss their operations.

10. How does the Neiman-Marcus Christmas catalog differ from other stores' catalogs?

11. Explain private label merchandising and discuss why retailers are embracing the concept.

12. Discuss the term "licensing."

CASE PROBLEM 1

After ten years as the merchandise manager of home furnishings for David's, Inc., a giant retail mail-order house in Dallas, Elayne Shenker has decided to leave her position and establish her own mail-order firm. At David's, her merchandise responsibilities include glassware, dinnerware, silverware, lamps, rugs, clocks, and other accessories for the home. Her present annual salary is $65,000. Her duties consist primarily of supervising the various home furnishing buyers in their determination of quantities and styles, visiting markets, and budgeting and approving merchandise requests.

Shenker has commitments from several vendors for the financial backing needed to open her own company. Her initial plan is to open an operation similar to David's, but on a smaller scale. Her consumer market would be the same. David's has customers throughout the United States, with about 50 percent in the Southwest. Its only competition at this time is Alan's, Inc., which carries the same type of merchandise.

1. Do you believe that the type of backers Shenker will use are advantageous? Discuss fully.
2. Is Shenker's background sufficient to open an operation of this type? What, if anything, does she lack?
3. Is it likely that Shenker will be able to compete with David's? Discuss.

CASE PROBLEM 2

For the past five years, Helen's Boutique has been in operation in the suburbs of a major city. Each year since its opening, the store's sales have increased 20 percent because of the tremendous, continuous shift in population from the city to this suburban area and the consequent increase in business. Requests for merchandise other than what it carries are being received. These items include men's and children's clothing, major and small appliances, furniture, carpeting, and accessories for the home.

Management has been discussing the possible expansion of its specialty operation into a larger boutique to include men's and women's clothing, or conversion into a small department store. The department store could accommodate the recent requests for hard goods and soft goods that are not presently stocked. Adjacent to the boutique, which is a one-story building of 6,000 square feet, is a two-story structure with 10,000 square feet. (The rent is fair.)

1. What factors should management consider before making any decision on expansion?
2. Would Helen's Boutique be better off by enlarging as a ladies' boutique, enlarging to include only men's, women's, and children's wear, or enlarging to a department store structure? Defend your answer.

PROJECT 1

Prepare a brief report on a store in your area that has been in operation twenty-five years or longer. If you are unable to obtain information directly, through interviews or store literature, select a famous store from the sources available in the library.

1. Type of store
2. Merchandise carried
3. Price range
4. Clientele
5. Innovations
6. Reasons for continued success

PROJECT 2

Visit any five of the following types of retail stores, observe the operation, and complete the blank columns in the following table.

1. Supermarket
2. General store
3. Small specialty store
4. Large specialty store
5. Department store (main store)
6. Department store (branch)
7. Twig store
8. Mail-order store
9. Chain store
10. Boutique
11. Off-price store
12. Manufacturers' outlet

	Type of Store	Type of Store	Type of Store	Type of Store	Type of Store
Merchandise carried					
Price range					
Service or self-service					
Services offered (list)					
Display (outstanding, appealing, poor, etc.)					
Store appearance (orderly, attractive, poor, etc.)					
Store location (downtown, shopping center, etc.)					
Other distinctive features (list)					

CHAPTER 2

Small Store Organization and Operation

FROM RAGS TO RICHES

Although it might not be everyone's cup of tea, being in business for oneself is the American dream for countless people. The competitive climate of contemporary retailing generally dampens the chances of the small business hopefuls' quest for success. Whether it is truly the enormous competition from the retailing giants, or the inexperience of the novice, or a combination of both factors is something that can be debated.

Holding out the offer of success to the individual without significant experience but fortified with some capital, the franchisor has given many people the opportunity of being in their own businesses. Although the topic of "real ownership" is often discussed in regard to franchisees, it may be considered to be "ownership with big brother watching," at least. Those who have invested in franchising, or who have at least explored its potential, have discovered a route for self-employment.

Potential franchisees have, thus far, been making investments primarily in fast food restaurants, ice cream shops, and hotels. Little was available for the person wanting to enter a franchised fashion-oriented retail operation. However, regardless of the pitfalls of franchising, or the doubts expressed by many, an Italian family from Treviso has initiated what seems to be an enormously successful franchise organization.

About twenty years ago, a sister and three brothers set up shop to fill the needs of Italians who wanted natural fiber, colorful sportswear at affordable prices. Preppy rugby shirts, sweaters, pants, and novelties produced and retailed by Benetton have taken the international retailing world by storm. It has become commonplace for men, women, and children to be seen in Benetton attire. Benetton's present-day high technology began in 1966 with the designs of Giuliana Benetton and has grown into a worldwide network that includes 1,000 stores in Italy alone. Producing about 4,000 styles a year in 350 different colors with such sophisticated methods as computer designing directly on video screens with light sensor pens, electronically restocking inventories all over the world in fifteen days, and shipping merchandise with robot arms without the touch of a human hand has made Benetton one of the most desired franchises in the United States today.

At present, there are more than 450 Benetton franchises in the United States. They are found on Fifth Avenue in New York City and in shopping malls throughout the best locations in the country. The line has taken on the prestigious aura that seems to ensure the much-sought-after status demands of enormous numbers of consumers. All the franchises incorporate a look of cleanliness and simplicity with emphasis on orderly color arrangements of the merchandise. Each store looks exactly like the next. The organization has a character all its own and seems to be just what the customer wants.

Whether the individual profits for franchisors in the United States are what were expected will be told in time. If rapidity of growth is a measure of success, then Benetton is a successful franchise. Like the offer of franchising in general, it affords the less experienced potential retailer the opportunity for ownership in an organization that offers immediate customer recognition not available with starting one's own business from scratch.

LEARNING OBJECTIVES

Upon completion of this chapter, the student should be able to

1. Identify three areas of concern in setting up a small store and discuss each in detail.
2. List and describe the important steps in location analysis.
3. Describe two major types of retail locations.
4. Define franchising and discuss its significance in present-day retailing.
5. Discuss three types of franchise arrangements.
6. Contrast the advantages and disadvantages of franchising.

INTRODUCTION

Retailing today is dominated by giants: Macy's, Neiman-Marcus, Lord & Taylor, and their brethren seem to be everywhere. They build magnificent stores, set the fashions, and dominate the media with clever advertising and innovative special events. Their names are household words, and they are still expanding at a breakneck pace. How strange it is, then, to find a statistic that indicates that more than 50 percent of all retailing employees work for small stores and that most of the small retailers employ five or less workers. For years we have been told that the small retailer is doomed, that the giants would take over the world. Every time a Sears or a J. C. Penney moved into a neighborhood, people would shake their heads and sigh for the small retailer that "could not compete" and would be forced out. Despite this, today's retailing scene indicates that the small retailer is not only surviving but actually flourishing despite the rapid expansion of the major chains and department stores.

One of the reasons for small store success is the growth of large shopping centers. Since these areas generally house from two to four major department stores, which are "anchors" of the centers and are the major "draws," many locations are to be found that are ideal for small retail shops. Although these stores must pay high rentals, they benefit from the traffic attracted to the mall by the huge promotional budgets of the principal stores. As a result, the typical mall will be tenanted by a few department stores and units of large chain organizations, with the remainder, successful small retailers.

Another reason for the continued success of small retailers is that they have adapted to the presence of their giant competitors by becoming more specialized. While a 2,000-square-foot store cannot hope to match the menswear offerings of a major department store, it can succeed if it sells only jeans or caters only to men over six feet tall.

There are many other reasons for small store success and they could be discussed at great length. The point is that small store retailing is alive and well. Therefore, it is appropriate for this text to discuss setting up a small store operation.

One route for self-employment is becoming part of a franchised organization. Instead of starting from the beginning, individuals, for a fee, can become part of a well-known retail operation in stores that sell clothing, food, or other consumer products. This chapter explores going into a totally new business as well as franchised opportunities.

SETTING UP A SMALL STORE

In 1886, Richard Sears, who had been selling watches as a railroad station agent, invested $5,000 in a small retail business that later became Sears, Roebuck. Rowland H. Macy started what was to become the world's largest department store with an investment of $10,000. (Incidentally, he had failed with three other stores previously.) Being in business for yourself, and becoming a multimillionaire, is the aspiration of most Americans. But they had better be careful: According to the Small Business Administration 65 percent of small businesses fail within the first five years of operation. Careful planning and soul searching are necessary before a decision to open a small store is made. Some factors to consider include the following:

1. Personal competence
2. Financing
3. Location analysis

Personal Competence

The major reason for small business failure is poor management. Bad management can have many causes, such as poor physical fitness, lack of intelligence, or laziness, but the principal reason for failure due to the inept management is lack of experience. The person opening a retail store must be experienced in that line and in retailing in general. He or she must know where to buy, what to buy, and when to buy. In addition, one must understand the principles of store layout, display, promotion, and all the other areas that go into a successful merchandising operation. In short, the person must be a retailer, and while much of this can be learned in school, there is no substitute for actual on-the-job experience. It is a must. Moreover, it must be specific experience—a successful hardware retailer lacks the experience to open a ladies' sportswear store.

Sometimes people with excellent experience fail because their experience is not well rounded. A highly successful buyer of children's clothing may stock his newly opened store with a perfect assortment of merchandise and still go wrong. Sales supervision, financial control, layout, in fact, all of the other principles of retailing may be neglected while the buyer is out in the market putting together the perfect stock assortment. Often, people who excel in a specific area of retailing tend to believe that their particular function is the only reason for retailing success, and they ignore other areas. It doesn't work that way. Retailing is made up of many functions; some may be more important than others, but none can be ignored. This is a major problem. A small store, with limited funds and available personnel, must depend on the owner to be a jack-of-all-trades. Unfortunately, success as a salesperson doesn't guarantee success as a buyer. Experience, therefore, indeed vital, must be well rounded rather than specific.

Financing: Start-Up Costs

Inadequate financing is another major reason for small business failure. This is a particular problem even for experienced people. Even those with excellent, well-balanced experience rarely have financed a new store, and those who have started businesses before will find that times have changed. Requirements and costs have varied, and starting a new retail business is a brand-new ball game. The person who plans to start a retail operation must resign himself or herself to the fact that outside expertise will be necessary. Estimating financial needs is not a job for an amateur, no matter how gifted.

To begin, the store must be properly designed and decorated. Many contractors are available who would be glad to estimate these costs for the opportunity to eventually get the job. The costs of fixtures and equipment and their installation are another item that dealers will be glad to help with. This may require some legwork, since all the various needs make it unlikely that one dealer will be able to supply everything. Different suppliers will have to be visited for estimates on shelves, lighting fixtures, cash registers, outside signs, and so forth. Extensive planning is required to determine the size and makeup of the opening inventory. The manufacturers or distributors of the merchandise will help with this problem.

There are many other areas for which money must be provided and for which information must be sought. These include deposits for rent and public utilities, promotion costs for the opening, legal fees, accounting fees, and others. To these opening costs must be added sufficient working capital to keep the store going until it can generate enough sales to carry itself. Expenses to be covered include salaries, rent, advertising, delivery, supplies, telephone and other utilities, insurance, taxes (including payroll taxes), interest, and professional fees. The Small Business Administration suggests that the total of these monthly expenses should be multiplied by three to provide sufficient working capital to give the store a fair chance of success.

After the costs of setting up the store and the necessary working capital to run it are added together, the problem of raising the necessary funds arises.

Financing: Raising the Capital

The most common and by far the best source of financing is the savings of the individual or partners. While it is sometimes possible to borrow the entire amount needed, it is generally agreed that at least 50 percent of the start-up money should belong to the owners. Borrowing more than 50 percent of the money will require repayments that are more than a new business can stand.

Of the sources of funds, certainly family and friends top the list. Their interest rates, if any, are fairer than others, and they are unlikely to force a store into bankruptcy for nonpayment. The next most common source available to borrowers are the people he or she does business with. Traditionally, businesses that sell and install fixtures and equipment require a moderate down payment and long-term notes for the balance, often from three to five years. Suppliers of merchandise also readily grant credit to their customers. These generally are short-term loans that must by paid in thirty to sixty days. Commercial banks are the primary source of short-term loans. Such loans, though, are difficult for a new business to get because banks often demand collateral or cosigners for a business with no track record.

Location Analysis

One of the most common causes of failure of new retail stores is management error in the location of the store. Despite a considerable amount of research in this field, the number of retailers that actually do a scientific survey of sites is still very small. It is not the purpose of this chapter to go into the complicated mathematics of scientific site evaluation. Instead, the discussion is limited to the important factors that must be weighed before a decision can be made, first on the general area for a new retail operation and then on a specific site within that area.

Selecting the General Area

A logical approach to store location is to begin by selecting the general area in which the store is to be established. In making this decision, one should carefully analyze the following factors.

Geography of the area. The size and shape of the proposed area must be analyzed to determine the boundaries within which the customer population will fall. The population within this area can then be studied.

Population. Any analysis of future customer demand must begin with an understanding of the nature of the typical customer. Population size and density is generally agreed to be a most important factor affecting retailing success. A detailed study of an area's population should include the following considerations:

1. It is important to know the predominant age of the population. Since young people's needs and wants differ from those of older

people, the success of many types of retail operations depends on the careful analysis of age data.

2. Differences in sex and marital status have much the same effect on retail sales as age differences, and care must be taken to determine any unusual facts concerning the population's sex and marital status.

3. The size of the population may be subject to seasonal variations. This is true of summer resorts. If the area is likely to be affected by such seasonal changes, the information is vital to the location selection.

4. The various religious affiliations, education levels, and national origins of the population must be determined. These differences frequently indicate variations in prejudices, needs, and preferences.

5. The income level of the population can be estimated in many ways. Data on per capita and family earnings are obtainable from the census bureau. Information about the number of telephones and auto registrations per house, and on the value of the dwellings themselves, is available. Since retail volume depends on income level, the investigation of the earning power of the area must be extensive. Such information as the source, stability, and seasonal nature of the income must be determined and weighed before the decision to locate can be made.

6. The buying needs of homeowners are considerably different from those of apartment renters. Although these differences may not be obvious in the buying of food and clothing, they certainly would be important to the sales of major appliances and gardening tools. Moreover, the buying needs of the new homeowner are considerably different from those of the established homeowner.

Characteristics of the area. Certain information about the trading area itself is required.

1. An alert, progressive community whose members are willing to tax themselves for a quality school system and other local improvements will probably attract new families for years to come. Such a community is frequently the home of an active chamber of commerce and other clubs. A test of progressiveness is the rate of new development, both of commercial enterprises and of new homes. Active growth is generally a by-product of progressiveness.

2. Both the quality and quantity of the competition in the area should be judged. The fact that there are several conventional appliance stores might not rule out the introduction of a discount appliance store.

3. The area should have features that attract out-of-the-area customers. Parks, theaters, zoos, and athletic events frequently bring transient retail business into an area.

4. Judgment should be made about the accessibility of the area. The roads should be good, the traffic bearable, and after a fairly fast trip the customer should have no trouble finding a parking space. In

these times of serious road congestion this factor has become of prime importance. In addition to being easily accessible to automobiles, a good shopping area should be fed by public transportation.

5. Proper banking help is important to the retailer. Sound audit control requires the daily deposit of cash sales. In addition, banks are needed to make temporary working capital as well as long-term improvement loans. With the recent wide expansion of commercial banks, lack of banking facilities is rarely a problem.

6. Present-day retailing requires the store to grant its customers speedy credit on demand. To do this, extensive credit checking must be done by outside agencies. It is vital that such credit-checking agencies be available in the area.

7. Those retailers that depend on advertising to promote their merchandise must be certain that the required advertising media are available in the area.

8. The retailing area selected should be within short delivery time of the store's major sources of supply.

9. Many retail customers demand that their purchases be delivered. Facilities for delivery must be available if the store is to offer this service.

10. There must be an adequate labor force in the area to staff the store at a salary level within the store's budget. If the prospective labor force is unionized, union requirements must be studied.

11. Local laws must be studied to determine sales taxes, necessary licenses, days in the week the store may remain open, and so on. In addition, such possible problems as difficulty in obtaining insurance and the local crime rate should be determined.

12. The history of the area should be analyzed to determine current trends. Is the area the same as it was ten years ago? Five years ago? If it has deteriorated, is it likely to continue to do so? Is any improvement likely to continue? Are the characteristics of the population changing? In what way?

It should be understood that a trading area does not have to score perfectly in all of the areas listed. Few successful stores would have that perfect a report. However, each of the factors should be considered before a decision to locate is made.

Selecting the Shopping District

After the general area has been selected, the specific shopping district within the area must be decided upon. Like the decision on the general area, this decision must be based on a considerable body of facts. There are many types of retail locations, and the relative merits of each type must be carefully weighed.

Downtown areas. The central shopping district located in the hub of a large city has usually been the focal point for the strongest retail establishments. It is at this point, where the area's population is at its densest, that the highest volume of sales per square foot of selling space is made. This attracts the retailing giants and the largest department stores. High-promotion stores are characteristic of such areas; the great potential of available customers almost guarantees the success of any worthwhile promotion. Central business district locations are usually at a premium, and the rentals are very high.

Shopping centers. Although downtown central shopping districts are still of great retailing importance, recent years have seen a trend toward decentralization. The downtown stores are being subjected to more and more competition from large regional shopping centers in the suburbs. Many metropolitan department stores have been both adding to and taking advantage of this trend by locating branch stores in suburban shopping centers. The success of the suburban shopping center has been mainly due to the following factors:

1. Since 1945 there has been a massive population exodus from the cities. Because this shift in population has been among the upper- and middle-class families, the disposable income loss from the city to the suburbs has been great. As a result, the per capita income of the city families has declined, while the purchasing power available in the suburbs has skyrocketed. Retailers, anxious to tap this mine of purchasing power, have moved to suburban locations.

2. As a result of the increased use of the automobile, downtown shopping areas are marked by traffic congestion and unavailability of inexpensive parking facilities. These problems greatly favor suburban stores, where traveling and parking are relatively effortless.

3. As the trend toward suburban living continues, nearby suburbia becomes crowded and homeowners are forced even farther away from the city. As a result, many homeowners are simply too far from the city for convenient shopping.

4. Competitive downtown stores are generally so close to one another that the shopper is able to compare quality and price before making a purchase. But comparison shopping has been less important in recent years, partly due to the fact that a few pennies saved by such methods are not important to our inflation-oriented society. Moreover, improved communication techniques, such as television and newspaper advertising, have lessened the importance of comparison shopping.

5. The availability of space in the suburbs has played a part in the increase in retailing activity in the outlying districts. Downtown locations are generally poorly planned, overpriced, and difficult to find. In contrast, suburbia offers building to order, cheaper rents, and a choice of locations.

The Specific Site

Once the general area for store location and the particular type of shopping district within the area have been decided upon, the remaining step is the selection of a specific site. The decision on specific site is a sensitive one, since 100 feet can mark the difference between an excellent and a poor site. Similarly, a successful high-priced men's shop can fail in an area perfectly suited to a low-price operation. Several factors must be considered.

Analysis of the population.   An analysis of the population for a specific site requires more than only a name count. Differentiation must be made between potential customers and disinterested browsers. For example, only one in thousands of commuters may be likely to stop at a men's haberdashery on the way to work, but a far greater number may stop at a coffee shop.

Neighboring stores.   The nearby stores must be compatible if the site is to be a successful one. Many stores do well by locating near department stores and attracting customers whose prime purpose is to shop at the department store. Similarly, women's clothing, accessory, millinery, and shoe stores tend to complement one another, particularly if they appeal to the same economic level. The opposite is also true. A high-priced shop in an area catering to low-income customers is unlikely to be successful. The wrong sort of neighbor may be damaging. A fine restaurant should not be located next to a garage, or a children's shop next to a bar.

Traveling convenience.   If the site selected is in an urban center and if success depends on nonlocal customers, convenient mass transit systems must be available. In suburban retailing locations, the same logic requires good roads and sufficient parking for a successful location.

FRANCHISING

Opening a small retail store is difficult and dangerous. Franchising offers a safer alternative. Statistics indicate that while 65 percent of new businesses are gone in five years, only 5 percent of new franchisees go under in that period. The reason for the success of franchising is that it strengthens the very areas of weakness that cause new business failure. By providing expert know-how in management operation, site selection, financing, and so forth, franchising just about eliminates the major causes of small store failure. Unfortunately, franchising success frequently tarnishes the American dream. The franchisee is not his or her own boss, but must rigidly adhere to the rules and regulations set forth by the franchisor, even when the franchisee disagrees with them. In addition, franchising fees and other costs can have a considerable effect on profits. In other words, going into a franchise operation reduces the risk of failure at the cost of reduced profits and independence.

The possibilities for an individual to become involved in franchising are so varied that a deal can be made for an initial outlay of as little as $12,000 for a modern bridal franchise to as much as $500,000 for a McDonalds. Even the more expensive possibilities can be heavily mortgaged, considerably bringing down the capital requirements.

There is nothing new in the concept of franchising. It is likely that this type of agreement existed in America during colonial times. Rapid growth began after World War II, when industry grew to enormous proportions. In large part this expansion was caused by returning servicemen, some with accumulated savings and many taking advantage of the financing available through the Veterans Administration. They were eager, after years of rigid army discipline, to be their "own bosses."

The major problem faced by these young men was their lack of business experience. Their early mature years had been spent in the service, and most of them had never held full-time jobs. To tap this huge sum of money and vast store of ambition, many established business organizations undertook the franchising of their products. They offered proven products, big business know-how, and financial help in return for a considerable expansion of their profits. The result has been a continuing boom in franchise sales that has increased in volume each year.

Although statistics are not available, it is believed that franchise sales are in excess of $500 billion annually, arising from some 500,000 franchise outlets. Since this represents about 10 percent of all American business, it is obvious that the franchising industry is one of considerable importance to the American economic scene. The amounts indicated do not represent only new franchises. Automobile agencies and gasoline stations, which were franchised before World War II, are responsible for a large share of these statistics. But a glance at the business opportunities section of any newspaper indicates that the franchising boom is still gaining momentum.

Potential franchisees, however, should be aware of the risks involved in this type of venture. To proceed with caution is the best advice a prospective franchisee could follow.

Definition

Because of the great variety of franchising agreements, it is difficult to define a franchise. It is estimated that there are between 2,000 and 4,000 companies offering franchising deals, and each company's contract is different. The broadest definition is one given by the Small Business Administration:

> A franchise contract is a legal agreement to conduct a given business in accordance with prescribed operating methods, financing systems, territorial domains, and commission fees. It holds out the offer of individual ownership while following proven management practices. The holder is given the benefit of the franchisor's experience and help in choice of location,

financing, marketing, record keeping, and promotional techniques. The business starts out with an established product or service reputation. It is organized and operated with the advantage of name and standardization.

This definition contains the great amount of information that a textbook definition should. However, all franchising agreements do not include every item mentioned. For example, many franchisors make their profit by selling the product to the franchisee, and others profit by charging a commission on all franchisee sales. Only careful examination of the particular contract will indicate the particular arrangement.

Types of Franchise Arrangements

While there are numerous franchise arrangements, retail franchises are generally organized in one of the following ways:

Conventional

The conventional arrangement is usually broken down into two types, both involving varying degrees of geographical coverage.

The territorial franchise gives the holder the privilege of enjoying an "override," or percentage, on sales of all the units within a particular area. The area might be confined to a large city, an entire state, or even a section of the country. Frequently the holder also assumes the responsibility of training and setting up the various operators of subfranchisees within the given area. It is not unusual for the operating franchisee never to come in direct contact with the parent organization, but rather to deal entirely with the owner of the territorial franchise.

The operating franchise is held by the independent operator within any given territory who runs his or her own business within the given area allotted by the franchise (often conferred by the territorial franchisor). The operator deals either directly or indirectly with the parent organization.

Coownership

A coownership occurs where a large capital outlay is needed. The franchisor and franchisee share in the investment and then divide the profits. Many firms in the food service industry utilize such plans, including Denny's Restaurants.

Comanagement

Under a comanagement arrangement, the franchisor usually controls the major part of the investment. The investor-manager is allowed to share proportionately in the profits. An increase in sales volume increases the owner-manager's share and thus acts as an incentive to further promote the firm's business. Several motel chains operate on this basis, for example, Travelodge and Holiday Inn.

Service

In a service franchise, the franchisor sets forth prescribed patterns by which a franchise will supply a professional service. Employment agencies and any number of other service businesses fall in this category. An example of a service franchise is Lawn-A-Mat, a lawn preparation company.

It should be noted that many franchising firms do not fall within one specific category. Indeed, most firms offer more than one type of arrangement and exhibit a great degree of flexibility according to the situation. Counteroffers by prospective franchisees are not unusual, especially with regard to the more expensive franchises involving large capital outlays. In addition, some firms are in a constant state of reorganization in adapting their plans to the needs of the market.

How to Find a Franchisor

Finding a franchise deal is relatively simple. With the growth of the franchising industry, there is considerable competition among franchisors in finding interested franchisees. This has led to a great deal of advertising, as evidenced by the business opportunities section of most newspapers, which contain ads for many types of franchises. In addition, various organizations run franchise shows at which prospective franchisees are given an opportunity to discuss deals with a wide variety of franchisors. The *Franchise Annual*, a trade publication, lists scores of franchise opportunities in major cities throughout the country, as does the *Franchise Opportunities Handbook* published by the U. S. Department of Commerce. (See Fig. 2–1.)

Simply examining a list of franchises is insufficient to make a determination as to its value. It is advisable to address such questions as are listed by the U. S. Department of Commerce (see Fig. 2–2) before a decision is made.

Personal Qualifications for Franchisees

Before going into a franchising contract, prospective franchisees should consider their own qualifications. The Small Business Administration suggests that the prospect ask such questions as the following:

1. Are you qualified, in terms of the capital and special qualifications needed, for the deal?
2. Are you willing to accept the franchisor's supervision and to abide by the rules and regulations that the franchisor requires? These can be real problems for independent-minded people who are in business for themselves.
3. Why would you want a franchised business rather than one you can start entirely on your own? Essentially, the franchisee splits the

FIGURE 2–1 Excerpt from Franchising Opportunities Handbook

Franchise Opportunity

Just Pants
201 North Wells Street
Suite 1530
Chicago, Illinois 60606
Hadley Flint, Director of Real Estate/Franchise Development

Description of Operation: Just Pants stores average 2,000 feet with expansion geared to regional shopping malls of 500,000 square feet GLA. Street or strip center locations can be considered if there are existing units in the market. Just Pants stores sell quality branded jeans, slacks, tops and accessories primarily to teenagers, college-aged people and young men and women.

Number of Franchises: 52 (147 units) in 24 states. Areas available in all states except Florida and a few areas currently adequately covered by present licenses.

In Business Since: 1969

Equity Capital Needed: Regional mall $70,000–$130,000. No initial franchise fee. Investment covers: site development, inventory, fixtures and working capital.

Financial Assistance Available: None

Training Provided: Just Pants will furnish a training program consisting of 2 weeks or more of "on-the-job-training" in 2 or more actual operating Just Pants stores plus much additional instruction to the manager with respect to other aspects of the business. The licensee will be responsible for the travel and living expenses and the compensation of the manager while enrolled in the training program.

Managerial Assistance Available: Operating assistance will include advice and guidance with respect to: (1) buying pants and other merchandise; (2) additional products authorized for sale by Just Pants stores; (3) hiring and training of employees; (4) formulating and implementing advertising and promotional programs; (5) pricing and special sales; (6) the establishment and maintenance of administrative, bookkeeping, accounting, inventory control and general operating procedures. Further, Just Pants will advise the licensee from time to time of operating problems of the store disclosed by financial statements submitted to or inspections made by Just Pants. Just Pants will make no separate charge to the licensee for such operating assistance.

Source: U. S. Department of Commerce, *Franchise Opportunities Handbook.*

FIGURE 2–2   Checklist for Evaluating a Franchise

The Franchise

1. Did your lawyer approve the franchise contract you are considering after he studied it paragraph by paragraph?
2. Does the franchise call upon you to take any steps which are, according to your lawyer, unwise or illegal in your state, county or city?
3. Does the franchise give you an exclusive territory for the length of the franchise or can the franchisor sell a second or third franchise in your territory?
4. Is the franchisor connected in any way with any other franchise company handling similar merchandise or services?
5. If the answer to the last question is "yes" what is your protection against this second franchisor organization?
6. Under what circumstances can you terminate the franchise contract and at what cost to you, if you decide for any reason at all that you wish to cancel it?
7. If you sell your franchise, will you be compensated for your good will or will the good will you have built into the business be lost by you?

The Franchisor

8. How many years has the firm offering you a franchise been in operation?
9. Has it a reputation for honesty and fair dealing among the local firms holding its franchise?
10. Has the franchisor shown you any certified figures indicating exact net profits of one or more going firms which you personally checked yourself with the franchisee?
11. Will the firm assist you with:
    a) A management training program?
    b) An employee training program?
    c) A public relations program?
    d) Capital?
    e) Credit?
    f) Merchandising ideas?
12. Will the firm help you find a good location for your new business?
13. Is the franchising firm adequately financed so that it can carry out its stated plan of financial assistance and expansion?
14. Is the franchisor a one-man company or a corporation with an experienced management trained in depth (so that there would always be an experienced man at its head)?
15. Exactly what can the franchisor do for you which you cannot do for yourself?
16. Has the franchisor investigated you carefully enough to assure itself that you can successfully operate one of its franchises at a profit both to them and to you?

FIGURE 2–2 Continued

17. Does your state have a law regulating the sale of franchises and has the franchisor complied with that law?

You—The Franchisee

18. How much equity capital will you have to have to purchase the franchise and operate it until your income equals your expenses? Where are you going to get it?
19. Are you prepared to give up some independence of action to secure the advantages offered by the franchise?
20. Do YOU really believe you have the innate ability, training, and experience to work smoothly and profitably with the franchisor, your employees, and your customers?
21. Are you ready to spend much or all of the remainder of your business life with this franchisor, offering his product or service to your public?

Your Market

22. Have you made any study to determine whether the product or service which you propose to sell under franchise has a market in your territory at the prices you will have to charge?
23. Will the population in the territory given you increase, remain static, or decrease over the next five years?
24. Will the product or service you are considering be in greater demand, about the same, or less demand five years from now than today?
25. What competition exists in your territory already for the product or service you contemplate selling?
    a) Nonfranchise firms?
    b) Franchise firms?

Source: U.S. Department of Commerce, *Franchise Opportunities Handbook.*

profits with the franchisor. Moreover, expansion possibilities are strictly limited by some franchisors.

4. Can you afford to be without income during the training and setting-up period? Going into business is a giant step. Selecting the correct format for oneself adds to the complications.

Advantages and Disadvantages of Franchising

Surveys have found that a large majority of American workers would like to be in business for themselves. Coupled with this information is the fact that three out of five people who begin small businesses fail in the first two years. The two principal reasons for small business failures are lack of business experience and insufficient capital. Franchising helps to alleviate these problems, but there are disadvantages to the operation as well.

Advantages

To understand the advantages of a franchised operation, we must bear in mind that the success of the franchisor depends on the success of the franchisee. Only by having its individual units operate on a solid, profit-making basis can the parent company continue to sell products and make money.

Realizing that lack of management know-how is a principal cause of small business failure, franchisors have developed highly scientific operational systems that they teach new franchisees in training programs that may run from several days to many weeks. Just Pants, for example, offers a training program that consists of two or more weeks of on-the-job training at two or more operating stores. New applicants are taught management, accounting, personnel relations, inventory control, advertising, and so on. In addition, many franchisors offer constant assistance in the form of periodic visits by experts for normal business advice or special problems.

Although the total cost may be high, a franchised business frequently requires a smaller cash investment for fixtures and equipment than a conventionally owned business, thanks to the credit help available from the franchisor. Often the credit resources of the giant franchisor can be used to aid the franchisee. Similarly, operating cash needs are less, since many franchised operations require less diversified inventories, and the terms under which such merchandise is purchased are quite liberal. The enormous purchasing power of the franchisor often results in smaller costs and higher profits for the franchisee. (Some franchisees will argue this point.) Other types of savings are also available because of size, such as insurance, hospitalization, and retirement benefits.

Advertising and promotion, carried on by the home office, although not free, offer benefits far in excess of those available to conventional small businesses. Keenly aware of competition, the parent company maintains a constant program of research and development aimed at improving its product and service. Displays, kits, and other up-to-date merchandise assistance are constantly being prepared by the home office and distributed to the outlets.

Franchisors offer help in record keeping, tax advice, and assistance in the many other areas that frequently plague small businesses. Such assistance is frequently at no cost to the franchisee. Most franchisors offer scientific help in choice of locations, and will often refuse to go into a franchising agreement if the site selected doesn't measure up to their standards.

In short, the prospective franchisee can expect any reasonable help from the franchisor that will increase franchise profits. It is not until it comes to dividing up that total profit between the franchisor and the franchisee that trouble begins to develop.

While the advantages to be derived from operating a franchise are considerable, the franchisee must in one way or another pay for them. The following are some of the major dissatisfactions expressed by many franchisees.

Disadvantages

The costs are too high. Many franchisees feel that the fees, prices for supplies, and other required charges are exorbitant. In many instances, it is felt that profits could be increased if the franchisor could be eliminated. This logic is questionable because it rarely takes the advantages of the system into account.

At the present time there is a class action suit (potentially 2,600 McDonald's Corp. franchisees) charging that McDonald's illegally requires its franchisees to purchase only Coca-Cola rather than a different, perhaps cheaper, cola brand. The suit further charges that franchisees are forced to lease the land and building from a realty company affiliated with McDonald's at an unusually high rent. It will be some time before the suit works its way through the courts. The result will have a considerable impact, since it could lead to other charges in the franchise contract. For example, if the franchisees win, will they be able to sue to change the product or the marketing system as well? Would the resulting change in standards be helpful or harmful to the franchisees? After all, their success is based on customer acceptance of a specific product and system.

Many complaints center around the decisions made in far-off home offices with little or no understanding of the conditions at the local outlets. Thus, policies that benefit the majority of the outlets may be harmful to a few locations. As with many large, centralized organizations, rigidity can be a serious problem.

Although franchisors know that their ultimate success depends on the success of their franchisees, they question the amount of success. There is, after all, a certain amount of profit to be divided up between franchisor and franchisee. How that pie is divided is largely in the hands of the franchisor. Consequently, decisions that affect the profit generally favor the franchisor.

The franchising contract is the source of many complaints. This document is frequently long, complicated, and not fully understood by the franchisee. One of the principal problems is termination of the franchise. Some franchisees complain that their contract can be terminated for two reasons. One, as expected, is failure. The other is success, in which case the franchisor might wish to take over a lucrative location to run it as a company-owned unit. Even in cases in which the contract states that termination can only be effected for "good cause," the problem of defining "good cause" is difficult. What constitutes late payment—one day, one week? What about poor management? Who is to decide? Some states have passed legislation to control termination, but efforts to pass a federal law have failed. Since no legislation can specifically cover all possible causes of termination, it is likely that the courts will continue to be an important factor in this area.

SMALL STORE ADAPTATION

The very title of this chapter, and the nature of its subject matter, speak directly to small store organizations. Whether they are independent or part of a franchise, they significantly face problems that are encountered and dealt with by the major retailers.

The very key to the success of the small merchant is to use the tested theoretical practices that have made the large companies profitable and to refrain from decisions that are based solely on intuition. Those who choose the route of franchising as a means of self-employment can easily follow the established training programs, regulations, requirements, and so on of the franchisor. It is all so clear-cut that little need be adapted from big business, because the success of the franchise is based on tried and proven methodology.

For the self-employed hopeful, it is quite another story. This individual can learn from two specific groups of sources to make a retail operation as profitable as possible. The first source would be the prospectuses and guidelines published by the franchisors, which often present a blow-by-blow description of location analysis, accounting procedures, employee management, selection of personnel, and so forth. By availing oneself of these packets of information (and many are available for the asking), the prospective small store owner can educate himself or herself with tried practices. The second source is to study the methods of operations employed by the giants of the industry. By carefully examining such trade publications as the National Retail Merchants Association's *Stores Magazine*, adaptation of what is being explored and practiced by the "big boys" can be attempted.

The remaining chapters provide specific, pertinent information that is relevant to small store success.

CAREER OPPORTUNITIES

While for a majority of people the American dream has been self-employment, the climate of the country indicates one should tread with caution before making the jump. It is certainly evident that numbers of Americans successfully begin retail operations each year, and many will continue to do so in the future, but success is not guaranteed. An examination of important statistics, relevant to business failure, shows that approximately 90 percent of the failures are attributed to insufficient capital and inexperience. Coupling these startling facts with the job opportunities afforded by the major retailers to the great numbers of individuals wanting to enter the field, it seems to make self-ownership less than fulfilling. With all of this negativism, there is some room for those who still feel the pot of gold at the end of the rainbow is within their reach. Cautious optimism is, perhaps, an appropriate outlook.

Having discussed the pitfalls of establishing one's own retail outlet, let's consider the areas for potential success. In franchising, where for an outlay of capital, individuals can open their "own" retail operations and have the benefit of large company recognition, training, advice, and the basic necessities to gain success, some are finding self-employment. After weighing the advantages and disadvantages of this type of ownership, many feel that franchising is the safest route to one's own business.

"Starting from scratch" is another route. With the enormous competitive edge enjoyed by the large retailers across the United States, it should be understood that this is risky business. Having weighed the costs and time commitment involved, it is wisest to establish an operation that capitalizes on a degree of expertise "owned" by the prospective retailer and the inability of the giants in the field to compete. For example, the small retailer wishing to operate a boutique stocked with "custom" designs of the owner will probably achieve more success than the one that carries a merchandise line available at many stores. Similarly, if a small merchant can establish a clientele based on discount prices, and operate in a less costly location than other retailers, success might be achieved. Flea markets are offering individuals the opportunity to own their own retail outlets. This might not be the "dream" operation, but it *is* self-employment.

It is unlikely that individuals will be able to begin their own operation at any location in which a major retailer wants to open. For example, examination of any mall immediately indicates that 95 percent of the stores are part of large chain organizations. Why would a realtor want to rent to the small independent retailer, if the giants of the industry, with greater capital and expertise, are better risks? The giant retailer is the dominant force in the retail industry.

KEY POINTS IN THE CHAPTER

1. The success of small stores is due to a number of reasons. Included among them are the growth of large shopping centers, which provides "runoff" from the larger stores, and specialization of operation.

2. The primary reason for small store failure is poor management due to the owner's lack of experience.

3. Inadequate financing often results in a store's failure before it actually opens for business.

4. Selecting the proper location is significant to success. Location analysis involving selection of the right general area, choosing the appropriate shopping district, and picking the best specific site is a must for success.

5. Franchising offers a safer alternative to opening an independent small store. The reason for the franchise's success is that it strengthens the very areas of weakness that cause new business failure.

6. Most franchises are of the conventional nature, namely, operating and territorial franchises.

7. In situations where very large capital outlay is needed, franchisors use either the coownership or comanagement technique of franchising.

8. For those seeking franchising opportunities, the *Franchise Annual* and the *Franchise Opportunities Handbook* are excellent sources of information.

9. Proponents of franchising believe that success is due to the skills and expertise of the franchisor and that franchising eliminates the pitfalls of individuals who lack the experience necessary for successful ownership.

10. Opponents of franchising cite high costs, disinterested franchisors, and complicated contracts as disadvantages of the franchise form of retailing.

Worksheet 2

COMPLETE THE FOLLOWING STATEMENTS

1. Careful planning is necessary before opening a small store. Reports by the

   Small Business Administration indicate that _____ percent of small businesses fail within the first five years.

2. A logical approach to store location is to begin by selecting the

   _____.

3. A _____ franchise gives the holder the privilege of enjoying an "override" on all sales within his or her area.

4. An _____ franchise is held by an independent operator within a given territory who runs his or her own business within the allotted area.

5. The U.S. Department of Commerce publishes the _____ *Handbook*, which helps prospective franchisees find franchisors.

TRUE OR FALSE

_____ 1. Small stores in malls benefit from the traffic generated by the anchor stores in the mall.

_____ 2. The Sears organization began with an initial investment of 5 percent.

_____ 3. Besides population considerations, it is necessary to check area characteristics when choosing a location.

_____ 4. A territorial franchise is held by an independent contractor who operates his or her own business.

_____ 5. Products are always involved in franchise operations.

_____ 6. Franchising contracts are straightforward, and legal advice is rarely necessary.

_____ 7. Franchising provides an opportunity to begin a business with no previous experience.

_____ 8. Franchising results in excess of $500 billion annually and represents about 10 percent of American business.

MULTIPLE CHOICE

_____ 1. Small store success is based on
   (a) the growth of shopping centers
   (b) greater specialization

        (c) the ability to interact directly with customers

        (d) all of the above

_____ **2.** Failure of small stores is usually attributed to

        (a) lack of experience

        (b) poor location

        (c) inadequate financing

        (d) all of the above

_____ **3.** Franchising is

        (a) a way of getting into business with guaranteed profits

        (b) a relatively new idea

        (c) a relatively simple way for an individual to get into business

        (d) all of the above

_____ **4.** Before signing a contract, the franchisee should

        (a) have a lawyer read it

        (b) select a location

        (c) get some business experience

        (d) all of the above

_____ **5.** Franchisors usually insist on the right to

        (a) approve the site selected

        (b) provide the product to the franchisee

        (c) supervise operational procedures

        (d) all of the above

DISCUSSION QUESTIONS

1. Discuss the reasons for the success of small businesses.

2. Poor management is usually the blame for small business failure. What are the causes of poor management?

3. What are the three major steps in location analysis?

4. Define the term "franchise contract."

5. Differentiate between coownership and comanagement.

6. How does the U.S. Department of Commerce help potential franchisees evaluate franchises?

7. Describe the two types of conventional franchises.

8. In addition to merchandise- or product-oriented franchises, what other type of franchise can one become involved with?

9. Discuss the assistance available from the *Franchise Opportunities Handbook* published by the U.S. Department of Commerce.

10. List three advantages and disadvantages of franchising.

CASE PROBLEM 1

A small but rapidly expanding franchisor has twelve locations within the state and is actively recruiting franchisees in neighboring states. The outlets are retail men's clothing stores. Every location is doing better than had been anticipated. The small number of franchisees, and their similarity of interest, have resulted in a very close franchisor-franchisee relationship.

The franchise contract contains a clause requiring that a 10 percent commission on annual sales be sent to the home office for advertising purposes. It has come to the attention of the franchisees that the advertising commission has been used to recruit prospective franchisees for new out-of-state locations. The franchisees are upset, since they feel that recruitment advertising should be a home office expense and that their advertising commission should be used for advertising that will increase their sales. The home office holds that, as the number of locations increases, the amount of advertising funds, as well as other home office assistance, will increase, and that, in the long run, recruitment benefits the franchisee.

1. Discuss the situation from the point of view of the franchisor.
2. Discuss from the point of view of the franchisee.
3. Would an increase in the number of outlets benefit the individual franchisee?
4. How would you resolve the problem?

CASE PROBLEM 2

Tom Watson has worked behind the counter in an ice-cream parlor for several years and feels that he knows the business thoroughly. He is interested in going into business for himself and is wondering whether to accept a franchised location or build his own place. After careful consideration, he is leaning toward his own business. He reasons this way:

1. Construction costs would be cheaper if he built his own place. Although this would take more initial cash than a franchised location, he feels he can just about manage it.

2. He would be able to serve the same menu as the franchisor offers, of the same quality, and at the same price, and earn a higher profit.

3. Not being under franchisor control would give him more flexibility and would ultimately lead to higher profits, a better chance of expansion, and less complications.

1. Discuss Tom's decision.
2. Are there any factors that should be taken into account that he has ignored?

CASE PROBLEM 3

Suburban Furniture, Inc., is located on a heavily traveled suburban highway. It is a freestanding store with ample parking and has grown along with the surrounding area. The competition in the area is practically nonexistent. As a result, selling prices are high, and its annual business of $500,000 yields an excellent profit.

Recently, a real estate developer has begun work on a thirty-acre shopping center about a half mile away. Among the tenants scheduled to move into the new shopping center is a branch of a large, highly successful, traditionally priced, urban department store. The inventory of the furniture department of the new store will undoubtedly be much larger than that carried by Suburban Furniture.

The real estate developer has offered to rent a well-located store within the shopping center to Suburban at a slightly higher rent than the store is presently paying. In addition, the builder will agree that no other furniture or appliance store will be allowed to rent space in the new area.

1. Should Suburban stay or move?
2. Should Suburban's price policy be changed in either event?

PROJECT 1

Contact a franchisee in your area and interview the person to determine the answers to the questions below.

1. Did any costs turn up in setting up the franchise that the company did not warn him or her about? List these.
2. Do the profits of the business live up to the franchisee's projections? If not, why not?
3. Does the franchisee resent the fees, commission, and so on, that he or she must give to the franchisor? Why?

4. Is the continuing help from the home office worthwhile? Why?
5. If she or he had it to do over again, would the franchisee take a franchise? Why?

PROJECT 2

Visit two competing franchises, such as Carvel and Dairy Queen or Kentucky Fried Chicken and Chicken Delight, and compare their deals in the following areas:

1. Initial investment
2. Franchise fee and commission
3. Extent of the training period
4. Use of franchisor's equipment, products, and supplies
5. Location analysis
6. Termination clauses
7. Available financing
8. Estimated profit

PROJECT 3

You are interested in opening a sporting goods shop in the area of a school. Select the best site within a half mile of the school. Support the location you select with comments on the following factors:

1. Population
   (a) age
   (b) size
   (c) income level
2. Traffic
   (a) local
   (b) out-of-area
   (c) amount of traffic
3. Future of the area
4. Competition

You are not required to make a scientific survey of the area. Use your judgment and be able to support your selection over those of your classmates.

Organizing and Staffing the Store

PLAYING FOR A TEAM IS NOT LIMITED TO SPORTS

Retailers are witnessing a problem that, from all indications, promises to escalate even further. One need only look at any store window or examine the classified ads to discover the need for employees at the lower level. Retailers are facing the problems that are troubling the likes of Burger King and McDonald's. Nobody wants to work for minimum wages at hours that are unreasonable compared to those of other fields. The initial reaction is to raise the hourly wage. Most experts agree, however, that a modest raise would be meaningless and would only increase the operational expenses of a company.

J. C. Penney developed a plan that would reward higher pay for increased productivity. It is not an individual commission plan, which often brings a host of problems, but a team approach that rewards groups of employees hourly bonuses based on increased productivity. At Penney's, the store manager divides the store into "teams," with each team having as its "players" sales associates, merchandising assistants, and wrappers.

For four or five weeks, the teams' sales efforts are compared to identical periods of the previous year. A sliding scale bonus arrangement has been worked out where each employee of a team receives a prescribed hourly bonus in terms of surpassing last year's sales figures. Specifically, if the team's sales amount to a 30 percent increase, each member receives 65¢ bonus for each hour worked in the four- or five-week period. At this time the maximum hourly bonus is $1.05 per hour for a 40 percent increase and a minimum of 1¢ for a 1 percent change. Through this plan, certain advantages accrue to the store and the employees:

1. Individuals are rewarded based on the number of hours worked so that the rewards are directly in line with time on the job.
2. Since the bonus requires cooperation, it is conceivable that the less motivated worker will be pushed by others to be more aggressive.
3. Team efforts often result in raising the level of employee satisfaction.
4. Employees will be better paid, and the store will gain from increased productivity.

In order to stop personnel defection from retail careers, it is obvious that creativity must be exercised by management. With action such as Penney's, the help-wanted signs might come down and workers return to the field.

LEARNING OBJECTIVES

Upon completion of this chapter, the student should be able to

1. Prepare a variety of organization charts, beginning with that of a small department store.

2. Describe the Mazur Plan and discuss its four-function structure.
3. Discuss the pros and cons of the separation of buying and selling.
4. List the three methods of organizing branch merchandising functions.
5. Describe the six functions of a personnel department.
6. Determine how retailers find new personnel for the various levels of employment.
7. Discuss the five requirements of a compensation plan.
8. Summarize the role of the personnel department in labor relations.

INTRODUCTION

Any effort that involves more than one person will be accomplished more effectively if it is organized. If all the individuals have a clear idea of their duties and responsibilities, there will be less chance of duplication of work or of tasks being omitted. A small sandwich shop run by a husband and wife must have organization. If there is no clear understanding of who is responsible for making the egg salad, there will be days in which twice the amount of required egg salad is made and other days in which none is made. Of course, a very small enterprise needs no formal organization. Where there are few people involved, each person's tasks and responsibilities are quickly and easily understood. An enterprise involving thousands of employees is another matter.

The organization of a retail store is accomplished by identifying and separating all of the similar functions (activities) of the enterprise and assigning responsibility for the performance of these functions to specific groups of individuals. The lines of authority and control must be clearly established and thoroughly understood by every worker in the organization. In other words, all individual workers in the organization must know what their jobs are, the people they supervise, and to whom they are responsible.

One of the most difficult problems facing management is that which is faced by the personnel department. A major portion of the success of the retail store depends on the quality of its personnel. The responsibility for the recruitment, training, evaluation, and compensation of the employees rests with the personnel department. In addition, labor relations, union negotiation, and employee benefits and services are all under the personnel manager's jurisdiction. Because buying, selling, and promoting merchandise are so emphatically stressed, the functions of the personnel department are often ignored. This is a serious mistake because an efficiently run personnel department is an important element of retailing success.

ORGANIZATION CHARTS

Many complicated problems can be more easily understood by the use of diagrams. The use of a map in a geography lesson gives a much clearer picture of relative positions than could possibly be given by words. The use of an organization chart to describe the functions of a retail establishment and the responsibilities of its personnel greatly simplifies the understanding of the position of each individual in the establishment. Naturally, since the chart is brief and concise, it must be backed up by descriptions, duties, and responsibilities of each job or job classification. All employees, by glancing at the organization chart, can understand the relationship of their jobs to the overall picture and the lines of authority above and below their positions.

Unfortunately, organization charts do not take into account the personal relationships that exist between employees as a result of the team-work and cooperation that is the keynote of a successful retailing operation. While the organization chart gives a brief sketch of how an institution operates, it is doubtful if any retailer follows the minor details of the chart to the letter.

Another disadvantage of organization charts is that they always seem to be out of date. No two retailers are apt to have exactly the same organization chart. Even an individual retailer, considering the speed at which retailing constantly changes, is not apt to use the same organization chart for a long period of time. It has even been said that organization charts are generally obsolete on the very day that they are published. While day-to-day changes are generally of a minor nature, the charts must be constantly revised if they are to be used effectively.

Given the disadvantages of organization charts, they are still necessary as a basis on which the retail operation functions. What follows are the various levels of organizational structures, many of which are used either in their entirety or as the foundations from which retailers have expanded to better suit their needs.

SMALL DEPARTMENT STORE ORGANIZATION

The principal difference between the operational plans of a small retailer and of a small department store is that the increased sales volume and the necessary additional personnel of the small department store permits more specialization of workers. The organization chart of the typical small department store is pictured in Figure 3–1.

The organization chart of the small department store recognizes two functions—that is, two vertical lines of responsibility of equal authority. Neither the director of merchandising nor the director of store operations has authority over the other. Dividing the store into two major functions has the effect of freeing all the merchandise personnel from the chores listed under the operations functions. In other words, although the small department store has too few employees for full specialization, there has been a grouping of functions into two major classifications.

FIGURE 3–1   Organization Chart for a Small Department Store

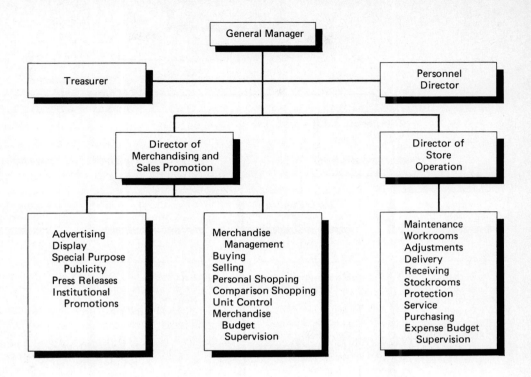

An organization chart is a graphic representation of a store's operation. As such, it is the result of a great deal of study and debate. For example, many stores include the personnel function under the responsibilities of the director of store operations. This would have the effect of giving that director a great deal of power in hiring the personnel required by the merchandising function. Note also that the manager of publicity is as important as the merchandising manager. By this arrangement, neither person has the final say on publicity. They must cooperate on decisions or appeal to the director of merchandising for decisions that they cannot work out between themselves. Note that the treasurer is a staff function, reporting directly to the general manager. Since the financial control of both major functions is the responsibility of the treasurer, to place this position under either of the other two departments might put the treasurer in the impossible position of complaining to the boss of the boss's incompetence.

As a store grows in size and increases in the amount of specialization, a third function may be added to the two-function plan. For example, a store in which credit sales are an important consideration may be operated under the three-function organization plan pictured in Figure 3–2. In this medium-sized department store, the office of the treasurer has been elevated to an equal standing with the merchandising and operations departments. Many stores of this size that are heavily involved in publicity might break the publicity department away from the director of merchandising and set it up as a separate function.

FIGURE 3–2 Organization Chart for a Medium-Sized Department Store

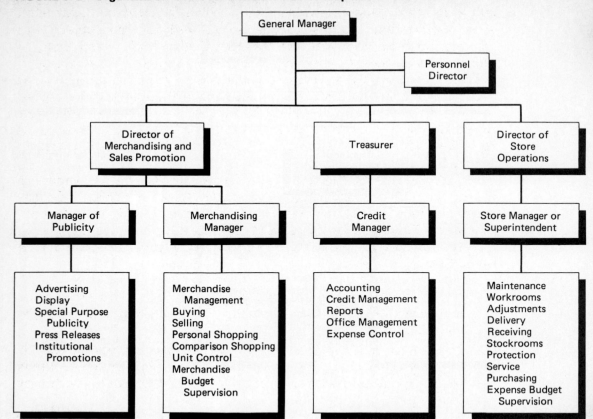

In comparing the two-function organization chart of the small department store with the three-function chart of a medium-sized department store, note the increase in the number of management and middle management positions that become necessary as a store grows. The director of merchandising and sales promotion of the small store cannot solely fulfill that responsibility in the larger store. The medium-sized store requires a manager of publicity and a merchandising manager to work with the director of merchandising and sales promotion to get the job done.

LARGE DEPARTMENT STORE ORGANIZATION

The large department store with its great number of employees has no trouble achieving a high degree of specialization. The very size of a large department store complicates its operation and makes operations planning extremely important.

Following the business recession of 1921–23, the National Retail Dry Goods Association (now known as the National Retail Merchants Association) formed a committee to study the operational plans of a group of successful stores and determine a sound plan for effective department store organization. Paul M. Mazur, an authority on the subject, was commissioned to work with the committee. After eighteen months, in which thirteen stores of varying sizes were studied, the Mazur Plan evolved. The Mazur Plan had a considerable effect on department store organization from the time of its publication. Although there have been many variations of the plan since its inception, it still forms the basis of most large department store operations. The organization chart for a large department store based on the Mazur Plan is depicted in Figure 3–3.

As is indicated in the organization chart, the Mazur Plan proposes a four-function operation, with the lines of authority grouped under the controller, merchandise manager, publicity manager, and store manager. The Mazur Plan offers several advantages that were unique at the time of its inception and have since been gradually accepted as basic to retailing operations:

1. It divided the store into four highly specialized divisions of store operations—control, merchandising, publicity, and store management.
2. The plan indicates the position of each employee group in relation to every other employee group in the store. All employees know their responsibilities and the lines of authority through which they must operate.
3. The board of managers, consisting of the heads of each of the four functions, provides a meeting place in which the heads of each specialty can get a perspective of the store as a total unit. This promotes cooperation among the various functions.

The most serious criticism of the Mazur Plan is that it fails to recognize the prime importance of the merchandising division. While the merchandising division is responsible for selling merchandise, it has no control over the publicity department, which has equal status. Similarly, the merchandising division is charged with selling but has no direct voice in the training of personnel, which falls under the responsibility of the store manager. Many large stores operate under adaptations of the Mazur Plan in which the merchandising, personnel, and publicity departments are responsible to the merchandise manager. Other stores have separated the personnel department from the responsibility of the store manager and elevated it to a major function. Operating under a five-function system, these stores leave it up to the general manager and board of managers to maintain the necessary cooperation among functions.

It is doubtful if any stores can be found that operate exactly as the Mazur Plan suggests. On the other hand, it would be difficult to find a store whose organizational setup is not in some way based on it.

FIGURE 3–3   Mazur's Four-Function Organization Plan

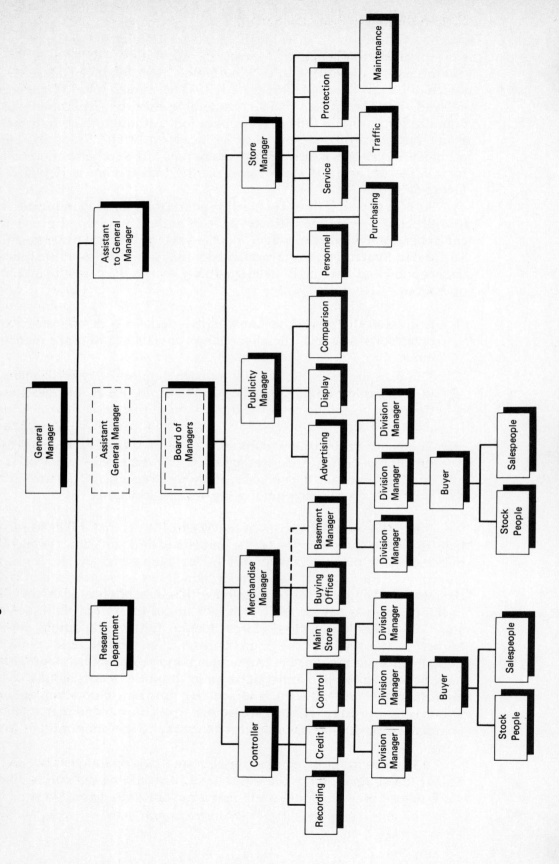

Separation of Buying and Selling

In many department stores the responsibility for both buying and selling rests with the buyer. The effectiveness of this procedure has resulted in an ongoing debate. Those who feel that the two responsibilities should be split between two individuals offer the following arguments:

1. In today's complex buying market, there is simply too much time spent buying to permit a buyer to do an adequate job as a supervisor of the sales force. As a result, buyers who are forced to spend part of their time on the selling floor cannot perform either their buying or their selling duties with maximum effectiveness. Often, it is the important selling function that suffers more.

2. The characteristics required of a good buyer are quite different from those required of a competent director of sales personnel. The skills, personality, and training of a buyer should be directed toward a knowledge of the wholesale market, current style trends, and the ability to negotiate with manufacturers. On the other hand, good sales managers must understand the consumer market and consumer personality. They should be interested in people, speak fluently, and be persuasive and imaginative. Because it is difficult to find both sets of characteristics in one person, the functions should be separated and the responsibilities of buying and selling split between two people.

3. Although it is true that a buyer cannot operate effectively without a finger on the customer's "pulse," computerized inventory reports make available to the buyer a much more scientific analysis of consumer demand than can be obtained by spending a few hours each week on the selling floor.

Despite these arguments, some stores favor a combination of the buying and selling responsibilities in a single person. They offer these arguments for such a combination:

1. It is not vital for a buyer to spend a great deal of time on the selling floor. Therefore, the buyer need not be a great salesperson. If buying requires long periods of time off the floor, the buyer's assistant should be available.

2. Computerized reports give scientific sales analyses, but they do not indicate other vital information. For example, while the data processing department may indicate that blue is the best-selling color for blouses actually sold, it will not reveal the number of requests that were made for red blouses that the department does not carry in stock.

3. Probably the most important argument against splitting the buying and selling responsibilities is that managerial control suffers from such a separation. When one person is charged with both areas, that person is also responsible for the department's profit. A department

with falling profits that is operated under the joint responsibilities of a buyer and a sales manager is frequently the focal point for friction, conflicts of interest, and "passing the buck."

The majority of experts seem to favor the division of the buying and selling areas. They feel that a system of standards can be set up to measure the effectiveness of each of the areas and that the division of the responsibilities allows both areas the benefits of specialization. In most stores, however, the buyer is also responsible for the department's selling.

Those stores that separate the buying and selling areas do so by removing the selling responsibilities from the merchandise function and placing them under the responsibility of a manager of personal selling, who, in turn, reports to the director of sales promotion.

Separation of the buying and selling areas is discussed later in this chapter in relation to branch and chain store organization, where the problem is somewhat different.

BRANCH STORE ORGANIZATION

Since World War II, masses of urban populations have moved to the suburbs of the large metropolitan areas. These people were generally of the economic class that provided the downtown department store giants with an important segment of their customers. To offset the resulting sales loss, many large stores followed their customers and located branch stores in prime suburban areas.

The branch store is usually one of several such units operating under a parent store and, in many cases, accounting for more than 50 percent of the total volume. In addition to increasing the sales volume, the typical branch operates more inexpensively than the main store. This savings is due in part to the branch store's use of many of the facilities of the parent, such as the data processing department. Similarly, many of the branch store's office functions and much of its advertising are directed by the parent with a relatively small increase in overall expenses.

The organization of branch stores depends in large part on the size of the branch, the distance between the branch and the parent store, and the policy of top management concerning the separation of buying and selling. It is likely that every branch store handles its own physical operations under an independent store manager. The personnel function of the branch is also generally under the independent control of the branch unless the distance from the parent is so small that the parent can take over personnel responsibilities more efficiently. The control function of the branch is generally split between the branch and the parent, with the branch performing the operating details and the parent doing the analyses and report making.

How the merchandising function is handled requires more discussion, since the success or failure of the branch depends on effective merchandising. The method of organizing the merchandising function of the branch varies considerably from store to store. Among the problems that must be faced are the following:

1. Is each department within the branch large enough to warrant a full-time buyer?
2. If each department is of sufficient size to require an independent buyer, can one be found in the area in which the branch is located?
3. If the departments are too small to support an independent buyer, shall groupings be made that will result in one buyer in charge of several departments?
4. Can parent store buyers, who may not be completely aware of the branch's customer demand, effectively service the branch?
5. What is the top management attitude toward splitting the buying and selling functions? It is unlikely that the parent store buyer can spend time on the selling floor of each branch.
6. Can effective communications be maintained between the branch and the home office, or will something be lost when managerial directives are transmitted to the branch?

There are three methods of organizing branch merchandising functions.

The Dependent Branch

Where the branch stores are few in number, located near the parent, and much smaller than the parent, parent store buyers generally take over the merchandising function of the branch. This can work quite effectively where the distance between stores is so small that the clientele is roughly the same for both units and the amount of extra work that must be done by the buyer is not burdensome. It must be borne in mind that as the time the buyer spends in the wholesale market increases, his or her time spent on the selling floor decreases. The resulting lack of supervision becomes magnified as the number of branch selling floors increases. In situations in which parent buyers take on the responsibility for branch buying, it is generally necessary to separate the buying and selling functions. Under such a plan, the branch salespeople are responsible to a branch department sales supervisor.

The Independent Branch

As the number of branches and the sales volume of the branches increase, it becomes obvious that sometimes the parent buyers cannot handle the increased workload. In such situations, separate buyers are employed by each branch. These stores believe that the clientele at every store is different and that only by employing independent buyers will each store be able to offer merchandise that meets its particular customers' demands. Part of the success of such an operation is due to the fact that each new unit is large enough to support independent buyers. Not every department store has been successful with this type of branch independence. Marshall Field, for example, opened its Milwaukee branch with independent buyers but was forced to withdraw them.

Equal Stores

Many stores, particularly those with many branches or large successful branches, have adopted chain store merchandising principles. This does not mean that they get no feedback from the selling floors. Quite the contrary, to be successful, the central buying headquarters must receive a constant stream of information from the selling floors. As branch sales volume and the number of branch units increase, it is likely that the equal store concept will become more common.

Successful stores such as Burdine's of Miami operate with considerable success with centralized buying, and others maintain successful operations with an exactly opposite point of view. Perhaps the organizational plan is less important than the personnel who make it work.*

CHAIN STORE ORGANIZATION

Chain store organizations use the most economical methods of retail distribution; the enormous volume that they do in similar types of merchandise permits the use of scientifically determined economical methods of performing many retailing functions. We have already discussed the independent store, in which each function is performed individually, and the branch store in which some of the functions of groups of stores can be economically grouped at one location. The chain store is a further extension of the movement toward retailing centralization. Some of the characteristics of chain store organizations are

1. Centralization and control of most of the operating functions are administered in central or regional offices.
2. The operation is generally broken into a greater number of functions than is generally done in department stores. Chain store operation requires such additional functions as real estate, warehousing, traffic, and transportation.
3. The relative importance of the personnel function increases.
4. Detailed reports must be filed frequently with the home office to permit adequate control of the various chain units.

The most important decision that must be made in chain store

*This discussion of department store branches should not be confused with ownership groups of stores such as the Federated Department Stores. These are groups of stores whose ownership is the same but whose operations are almost completely individual.

organization is the amount of independence that should be granted to the managers of the individual chain outlets.

Centralization

The argument favoring a highly centralized operation, in which most of the decisions are made at the home office, is that the home office provides highly trained specialists for decision making who are certain to be more competent than the individual managers. For this reason, having a weak store manager need not necessarily result in a poorly run store. The most serious disadvantage of centralization is that the home office, often a great distance from a specific outlet, cannot understand the local problems involved. Conditions vary considerably from store to store, particularly with fashion merchandise, and only the store manager is able to make decisions concerning the unique requirements of the store's particular clientele. Those favoring centralization argue that the home office experts are available for advice and that the close control of the home office tends to minimize errors.

Decentralization

As more responsibility and authority are delegated to the store managers, each store can better meet the requirements of its specific clientele. Moreover, managers, as their degree of control increases, have more incentive to improve their stores' profitability. True, a weak manager cannot be carried by a decentralized system, but the detailed system of control used by most chain store organizations permits the rapid identification of weak managers and quick corrective action.

An objection to decentralization is that it frequently leads to duplication of buying and other functions. The degree of decentralization depends in large part on the type of product handled. The buying function of a food chain, for example, is apt to be more highly centralized than the buying function of a fashion merchandise chain.

Regional decentralization is found in almost all nationally organized chains. Under a regional plan, the units in the chain are organized into semi-independent groups according to geographic location. Frequently the company itself is divided into geographic areas, each of which operates as a distinct entity, carrying out all the functions within its territory, including buying.

Organizational structures and charts serve as guides to how a company proposes to operate. Indeed, such procedures are necessary for any organization to function properly, but it is the people who fill the positions who make or break the operation. Employees at all levels are charged with a variety of responsibilities that are supposed to produce positive results for the store. Thus, it is of extreme importance that the people who fill the various job titles are capable of making the company a profitable one.

The personnel department of the retail organization is charged with a multitude of responsibilities that range from recruitment to involvement in labor negotiations. It is this department that plays the vital role of directly hiring lower level employees and screening candidates for management level positions. Most retailers agree that an efficient personnel department contributes considerably to the profitability of a company.

THE PERSONNEL FUNCTION

The overall function of the personnel department is to provide the store with capable workers. This is done by performing duties in the following areas:

1. Recruitment
2. Training
3. Evaluation
4. Compensation
5. Employee services and benefits
6. Labor relations

Recruitment

Before any steps can be taken to hire people, the personnel department must have a clear and exact understanding of the job to be filled. An analysis of every job in the store must be made to ensure that the characteristics of the person hired to do the job match the requirements of the job. Recruitment and training, to be effective, must be tailored to a specific set of job requirements. Those duties required for the job are called job specifications. The requirements of the individual are called worker specifications.

Job Analysis

Scientific analysis of each job in the store must be cooperatively accomplished by the personnel department and the supervisors of each department. Then a job description should be formally printed and available to the recruiting staff of the personnel department (see Fig. 3–4).

Based on the job analysis, the personnel department is able to formulate training programs and develop interview techniques and recruiting practices for each job. Furthermore, the job analysis focuses management's attention on working conditions and gives the prospective employee a clear picture of the job's responsibilities and chances for job improvement.

Sources of Personnel Supply

One of the most serious personnel problems in a large retail operation is the high rate of employee turnover. This is due, in large part, to

FIGURE 3–4 Job Description—Fashion Coordinator

LITT'S DEPARTMENT STORE

Job Description

DIVISION: Merchandising   **TITLE:** Fashion Coordinator

IMMEDIATE SUPERVISOR: Fashion Director

DUTIES:

Selects merchandise to be used in fashion shows, prepares commentary, hires models, selects music, and makes all other arrangements for shows.

Forecasts fashion trends based on market visits, resident buying office contacts, advisory bureau interaction, etc.

Coordinates styles, colors, fabrics, price lines of fashion departments to make certain that a unified image is achieved.

Accompanies buyers and merchandising managers to market for assistance in formulation of model stocks.

Performs personal shopping service for customers.

Works closely with display department in the formulation of fashion display promotions.

Visits branch stores periodically to advise staff on fashion direction.

---

relatively low wages, many young employees, a large number of part-timers, and the effect of the seasonal nature of retailing on personnel needs. Whatever the cause of turnover, it is a constant problem that can be met by establishing sources of supply that will provide workers when they are needed.

In-store sources. The high rate of retail personnel turnover is not restricted to sales personnel. Top and middle management jobs are constantly becoming available through turnover or expansion. Most stores prefer to fill such jobs by promotion. Moving people up builds morale by indicating that a person who has been in the store for a while will not be passed over for promotion by an outsider. Because managerial training programs are expensive, it is important that a store select managers who are not likely to leave.

The in-service promotion of one person opens a chain of promotions to the work force. For example, the promotion of a buyer to the position of assistant merchandising manager may be followed by the promotion of an assistant buyer to buyer, a department manager to assistant buyer, and a salesperson to department manager. In each case the new job-holder is a person whose personality, skill, and ability are well known to management. The most sophisticated personnel department cannot learn as much about an outside job applicant as the information it has in the personnel records of an in-service applicant. The chance for a happy marriage between worker and job improves as the information about the worker improves.

Stores depending on promotions from within to fill vacancies have relatively simple recruitment problems, since they need only worry about hiring for the lowest level jobs. Although the requirements of low-level jobs are modest, care must be taken that some entry jobs are filled by people of high qualification who will become the raw material for later in-service promotions.

Another advantage of in-service promotions is the ability of a store to attract highly qualified people for low-level jobs. A store with a reputation for having a good promotion policy will get more high-quality applicants than an organization in which promotions are rarely given. Stores such as the Edison Brothers chain of shoe stores mention in-service promotions in the brochures printed to attract job applicants.

Although it is generally agreed that a policy of in-store promotion has great merit, it should be understood that a policy strictly based 100 percent on promotion from within can actually act as a deterrent for new ideas. Very often this "inbreeding" results in a reaffirming of old-hat ideas. It is desirable for the growth and vitality of the organization to recruit managerial talent from other retail orientations; these people can often introduce needed fresh ideas into the company. A blending of applicants from within the organization and from outside sources is most beneficial.

Outside sources. Among the outside sources of personnel are advertisements, employment agencies (both private and governmental), schools and colleges, and transient applicants (persons coming directly to the store for work). Since retailing is highly seasonal, the personnel departments should know exactly which outside sources to use for the kind of personnel required.

1. *Want ads.* Advertising in the local newspaper is probably the most effective method of attracting large numbers of job applicants. The disadvantage of this source is that there is no preliminary screening for qualifications. Frequently, a deluge of applicants answer an ad, many of whom lack necessary qualifications. Thus, want ads are most useful when large numbers of relatively unqualified workers are needed.

2. *Employment agencies.* Private and government-sponsored employment agencies are another source. Employment agencies do not produce as great a number of applicants as advertising. However, the agency matches the applicant's qualifications with the job's

requirements and thus saves a considerable amount of the personnel department's time in interviewing.

3. *School and colleges.* Student recruiting generally begins at the high school level. Most high schools and colleges maintain a job placement office to help find part-time employment for interested students. It is important for the personnel department to keep in close contact with the neighboring educational institutions, even in times of slow recruitment.

Many schools and colleges include cooperative work experience programs among their course offerings. Under this plan, retailing students are given the opportunity to spend part of their school days at the work for which they are being trained. This affords the students an opportunity to learn under actual business conditions, while helping the store fill needed positions. Perhaps the most important feature of the cooperative work experience program is that it gives the store the opportunity to work with the student before an actual hiring decision is made. After graduation, the store is able to employ those students who have been found to be satisfactory under actual working conditions.

Many of the large stores compete for college graduates. It is felt that these people will eventually fill the top and middle management positions. Personnel managers regularly attend college career days specifically for this purpose.

Miscellaneous sources. Additional means of recruiting qualified personnel include the following:

1. *Recommendations.* The use of current employees to help find new people is common. Posting job vacancies on the bulletin board or circulating the information by word of mouth generally results in job applications from friends and relatives of the working staff.
2. *Transient applicants.* Certainly the cheapest, and probably the most widely used, means by which jobs are filled are casual (transient) applicants. These are people who show up at the employment department, fill out an application, and either go through the employment procedure if there is work available, or have the information placed on file for later use.

Selection Procedures

A series of procedures must be undertaken by the personnel department to ensure a proper matchup of applicant and job. Not only must this process provide the right worker for the job to be performed, but it must also make certain that attention is paid to the prospect's integrity. With the continuing increase in internal pilferage, management must concern itself with careful screening procedures. Any number of devices are available to determine honesty. One is checking the applicant's references, which is discussed later. The use of the polygraph or lie detector test is also being used in the selection procedure as a deterrent to dishonesty. While it has been argued that polygraph use is an affront to prospective employees, it has nonetheless proved to be beneficial to its users. Whatever the process used for screening applicants, care must be exercised to avoid costly errors in employment. Only careful attention, without the pitfalls of hasty decisions, can provide satisfactory employees.

The typical steps in the selection procedures of most retail stores are (1) application blank, (2) preliminary interview, (3) reference checking, (4) testing, and (5) final interview.

Application blank. Some stores require that an application blank be filled in before an interview, some interview first, and others do both simultaneously. In any event, the application blank serves several purposes:

1. It obtains necessary information from the applicant.
2. It provides a basis on which the interview can be conducted.
3. If the applicant is hired, it becomes part of his or her permanent file for future reference when necessary.
4. If the applicant is not hired, it may be kept for future use when a worker is needed.

Preliminary interview. The preliminary interview, sometimes referred to as a "rail interview" (it is a short, standup interview that may be done over the railing of the personnel department), has the function of correcting the application and weeding out those applicants in whom the store is not interested. The preliminary interview should be conducted by an experienced person who is thoroughly acquainted with available positions and the requirements for such positions. Although the preliminary interview must be short, time should not be saved at the cost of efficiency.

Checking references. Checking the background information given on the application is time consuming and expensive and is often ignored in cases of applicants for low-level jobs. The references given are from friends of the prospective employee who have no experience with the applicant's work habits. It is unusual to get a bad response from a reference supplied by an applicant. Thus, retailers must exercise caution when checking references.

An applicant's background can be more accurately checked by contacting prior employers. Although this can be done by mail, a telephone call can be more informative. The information supplied from former employers on work habits, attitudes, and quantity and quality of a prospect's work can be much more important in the hiring decision than the knowledge gathered by the application blank or interview.

Testing. At best, the application form gives raw facts that cannot always be verified, and the results of the interview reflect little more than the personal opinion of the interviewer. In an effort to get more objective information about prospective workers, many large retailers are turning to various types of testing. Among those used are tests of ability, aptitude, intelligence, and personality.

1. *Ability testing.* For many jobs, ability testing has always been used to rate performance. For example, rarely is a secretary hired without some sort of a typing or stenography test.
2. *Aptitude testing.* Aptitude tests are generally written and are used to determine an applicant's capacity for a certain type of work. While most aptitude tests are designed for testing mechanical ability, work has been done on the design of aptitude tests for salespeople.
3. *Intelligence testing.* Some large department stores feel that intelligence testing is important to successful employment and require all applicants to take a written intelligence test. They believe that every job classification should be filled by a person having an IQ falling within a certain range.
4. *Personality testing.* There is little doubt that such personality characteristics as friendliness and sociability are advantageous to a salesperson. Few would argue the premise that knowledge of personality is important in personnel placing. However, there are also excellent arguments to the effect that personality tests have little or no validity.

Final interview. After the application, preliminary interview, reference checking, and testing have been completed, the final interview is held. This interview may be conducted by a senior interviewer or the head of the department for which the applicant is slated to work. It has the dual purpose of informing the applicant of the duties and responsibilities that will be required by the job and of permitting the interviewer to judge the applicant's knowledge and personality in relation to the specific job opening.

Training Employees

A new worker in a small store requires very little time in which to "fit in" to the organization. Soon after an employee is hired, the proprietor introduces the worker to the rest of the personnel. After a few days the worker learns the details of the job's responsibilities and working conditions. In a large store, the orientation of new employees is done in a more formal manner. New employees may be given guided tours of the store, lectures on store regulations, and literature on the history of the store. A new employee's learning about the store helps him or her to "feel at home" and is part of the training program.

The training program itself can be informal, as in the case of a small store where a new employee is "broken in" by an experienced worker. It can be short, as it would be for a new unloader in the receiving department of a large store, who might merely have to be told where to put the cartons taken from the truck. In short, every new job requires a training period that is adapted to the specific job.

Training employees in a large store is generally the responsibility of the personnel department. It is an expensive procedure, both in terms of the time spent by personnel people and the nonproductive time spent by the employee during the training period. Since employees are fully paid during this nonproductive period, the expense of training employees is considerable.

Some of the advantages of training are

1. As a worker becomes more skilled, both the quantity and quality of work increase. A training program, by shortening the learning process, brings a worker to a high competence level much more quickly than could be done by informal learning.

2. As the productivity of individual workers increases, fewer employees are needed to handle any given volume of work.

3. There is a best way to perform every task. Employees cannot be expected to learn this way by themselves. An organization that has set up standardized procedures must be sure that all its employees are trained to follow these procedures.

4. A well-trained worker needs less supervision than a poorly trained person. The worker's knowledge and skill reduce dependence on supervisors. This permits a reduction in the amount of supervisory help needed and frees supervisors for other tasks.

5. The well-trained employee is confident and capable, feels secure at the job, and has good chances for advancement. A poorly trained employee, on the other hand, is nervous, lacks confidence, and as a result, frequently hates the work and is likely to quit.

6. Employees who have benefited from an expensive training program are made to feel that the store has a high regard for their potential. In addition, during the training period, the training personnel always show the store in its best light and attempt to improve morale.

Persons to Be Trained

Since the training program must be given to employees with a wide range of experience, the program must vary with the needs of the individual workers. Generally speaking, training groups may be broken down as follows:

Inexperienced sales personnel. The training of inexperienced sales personnel is usually done in two or three full days or spread over a few hours a day for several weeks. The program includes a full explanation of store policies concerning employees, such as dress regulations, employee discounts, and absenteeism. In addition, such store procedures as policy on returned merchandise, credit, filling out sales slips, and COD sales are explained at length. Product information is given by the buyer or department manager.

Many retail organizations believe that the training of sales personnel is the most important of all the training programs and provide handbooks that can be studied by the new employees at their leisure. The actual course work usually includes such up-to-date teaching procedures as role playing, slides and movies, and programmed instruction.

New, experienced personnel. Naturally, the training of experienced personnel will be of relatively short duration. These people have already learned the skills required by their jobs and need only be given instruction in the store's policies and procedures.

Follow-up training. Progressive retailers are becoming increasingly aware of the fact that job capability depends on educational growth. Brief introductory training rarely results in maximum job capability. New methods and questions are always coming up, and there must be an occasional meeting for discussion.

The training of regular personnel generally takes the form of individual conferences or small discussion seminars. At such small group meetings, the instructor does little more than guide discussion. The workers discuss their problems, suggest new approaches, and arrive at conclusions. When new methods or procedures are to be initiated, the instructor must take a more central position.

Follow-up training is eagerly sought by workers anxious for promotion. It provides them with an opportunity to improve the job skills on which their promotion will be based.

Part-time personnel. Training part-time help presents the store with a dilemma: Extras seldom work long enough to make an expensive training program worthwhile. On the other hand, it is impossible to put a poorly trained salesperson on the floor. Frequently, a compromise is made. The necessary training period is shortened, and the new employee is turned over to a sponsor as soon as possible.

Executive training. Since most large retailers fill many executive vacancies by promoting people from within the store, it is vital that well-trained persons are available. This can be achieved by means of an executive training program.

The training of executives generally includes conferences, sponsors, work-study arrangements with colleges, evening courses at colleges, rotation of trainees in various departments, correspondence courses, and lectures. The overall training period for executives may take several years. The individuals to be given executive training may be found among present employees or, more often, recruited from among college graduating classes. A college degree, earned either prior to or during executive training, if often mandatory.

Personnel Evaluation

If an organization is to maintain a high standard of employee performance, it must evaluate its personnel periodically. Some of the reasons for employee evaluation are as follows:

1. Nothing encourages workers more than rewards for good performance. Only by an evaluation of an employee's performance can

management make a fair decision on the rate of pay to which a person is entitled.

2. Constant employee evaluation earmarks those employees who are deserving of promotion and who would do well in an advanced job. Without proper evaluation, promotion tends to be haphazard. This can result in poor supervisory performance.

3. If employees are to improve their effectiveness, they must be informed of their areas of weakness. Such knowledge enables them to seek out means of improvement by training courses, self-help, or conferences with knowledgeable people.

4. All stores have on their payrolls people who have the necessary qualifications for the job, but lack the interest or capacity to meet the required standards of proficiency. Job evaluations are an aid in the process of weeding out such individuals.

Compensation

Probably the most important consideration of a person looking for a job is the amount of salary being offered. For persons on the job, a fair compensation plan is one of the important keys to high morale. It is likely that the principal cause of employee turnover is the worker's ability to find a better-paying job elsewhere. In short, a sound compensation policy is a vital responsibility of the personnel department.

Unlike the areas of recruitment and training, where the personnel department serves in a line or decision-making function, the responsibility of the personnel department in setting compensation policy is strictly staff or advisory. However, those who make compensation decisions rely heavily on the personnel department for advice and planning in this area.

Requirements of a Compensation System

To be effective, the compensation plan must be drawn up with the following factors in mind:

1. The level of earnings should be such that the employees can maintain a decent standard of living. Salaries must be equal or slightly better than the salaries offered by competitors if a high-quality work force is to be maintained.

2. An effective earnings plan must be easily understood by the employees so that they can predict their weekly earnings with accuracy.

3. Earnings must be keyed to productivity. The worker must be made to feel that increased effort will result in increased compensation.

4. Similar jobs should receive similar compensation, and the level of compensation should be fair. Of equal importance, employees must be made to believe that they are being fairly paid.

5. Since employee living expenses are stable from week to week, their salary requirements should be paid regularly. When salary rewards are offered as an incentive to better work, they must be paid promptly if they are to maintain their effectiveness.

Employee Services and Benefits

Both government statutes and union contracts provide other employee benefits than appear in a worker's paycheck. Employer payments for social security and unemployment insurance are required by statute. Many union contracts require employer contributions to union welfare and hospitalization plans. Most retail stores, to build employee goodwill, offer many other services and activities—profit sharing (Sears contributes more than $60 million per year for this), clubs, athletic facilities, savings and loan arrangements, life insurance and many other features.

While many of the benefits and services come as the result of government legislation or from the expertise of the union negotiator, these additional earnings are often the basis for the prospective employee to accept the job. It is certainly true that salary is the greatest motivational factor for employees, but often the salaries from one company to another are similar for particular job titles. This is particularly true at the lower levels, where wages may be set by unions whose involvement may transcend many retail organizations.

For these reasons, jobs are often refused or accepted because of the available benefit or service package. Very often it is the benefit plan that entices an employee who has served a company well to move to another operation. A salary cannot be the only consideration for employment. The extras are often as valuable as the actual take-home pay and are a significant part of the reasons for joining a particular retail organization.

Medical and Health Services

It is not unusual to find a doctor or nurse in continuous attendance at a large store for the benefit of employees. In addition, visiting nurses are made available to assist employees confined to their homes. Retailers that are not large enough to afford a full-time medical staff may offer this service on a part-time basis.

Hospitalization, dental, and life insurance are often arranged by the store in order to offer employees a low group rate. The cost of such plans may be borne by the store, the employee, or both.

Social, Educational, and Athletic Activities

Many large retail establishments provide facilities for employee clubs and equipment for a wide variety of employee activities for baseball teams to dance bands. Generally, these activities are conceived and sponsored by groups of employees, who find management more than willing to encourage any activity that might promote loyalty and enhance employee morale. Many retailers offer in-store classes given by local colleges or pay a portion of the tuition for courses taken by employees at colleges and universities.

Savings Plans

Typical of an employee savings plan is the one operated by Montgomery Ward. That retailing giant contributes some $2 million per year to a plan in which it deposits 25 to 50 percent of the amount its employees deposit in a savings account (the employees may deposit up to 3 percent of their annual earnings). Many such savings plans permit low-cost employee loans, to be paid back by payroll reduction.

Labor Relations

The growth of the labor movement in retailing has added a new dimension to the responsibility of the personnel department. Retail workers have generally lagged behind the rest of the labor force in union membership, but the growth has been real, if slow, and union contract negotiation has become an area of considerable importance. The personnel department continues to play a growing role in dealing with the labor unions. Perhaps more than any other part of management, the personnel specialists make certain that the employees deliver services for which they were hired.

While there frequently seem to be management-employee problems, a company can be successful only if the needs of its customers are served. Unhappy workers lead to a decrease in productivity, with profits often affected. Although personnel directors are a part of management, their role is seen as buffers between management and labor. How to satisfy employee demands without giving the store away perhaps best sums up personnel's most difficult function.

Prior to contract negotiations, the personnel department's team is often charged with the responsibility of examining employee demands and recommending avenues that would provide the best productivity for the store. In areas such as employee compensation methods and benefits, personnel provides insights on which top management can base negotiations.

Once a contract has been settled, the personnel department is usually called to participate in contractual disputes with employees and their unions. Although a contract is in evidence, the translation of legally worded passages is almost always an ongoing practice. Compromises between management and labor must be reached in the contract.

The work of personnel management is delicate. Only through tact and diplomacy can both sides of a labor dispute be satisfied. Personnel managers who appear to be too management-oriented can lower employee morale, while too much employee appeasement can hurt the company's role in managing the organization. A delicate balance must be struck.

Obviously, the small retailer will have neither the need nor the funds necessary for such specialists as personnel director, general merchandise manager, and chair of the board. It must be understood, however, that a poorly run organization, no matter how small, can cause financial disaster.

While organization charts and extensive job descriptions need not be required in a small firm; it is absolutely essential for each individual to understand his or her duties and responsibilities. With specialization of tasks generally out of the question, each employee must understand the lines of authority (to whom he or she reports and for whom he or she is responsible) and the jobs to be done. Duplication of effort must be avoided and attention paid to make certain that every chore, no matter how insignificant, be performed.

Recruitment of employees certainly cannot be the task of an employment specialist because there simply is not one on staff. The owner of the small store is generally responsible for hiring, and must do so keeping in mind individuals who would be able to perform a variety of duties. The best source of personnel for the small store is the placement of a help-wanted sign in the window to attract transient applicants. Not only does this source generally turn up those who are usually self-motivated but it is also cost-free. Since the employees function in a small area, performance can be scrutinized by the employer and corrections and suggestions can be easily accomplished. Similarly, on-the-job-training for new employees, under the watchful eye of an experienced employee, incurs no extra cost to the employer. An excellent method for motivating employees in small stores is offering merchandise discounts greater than those given by the large stores. Since the number of employees is relatively small, it will not be a complicated or costly benefit, but one that could easily make up for the small retailer's inability to offer the costly benefits of the giant companies.

By providing an atmosphere that is close to "family-centered," the small store can often encourage a more dedicated attitude on the part of the employees. Without incurring additional expense, the workers, if properly motivated, can be more productive.

CAREER OPPORTUNITIES

In any retail organization, the primary functions are divided between the merchandising division and the one that is classified as store management. The former concerns itself primarily with the buying functions; the latter is chiefly responsible for staffing, management of individual departments, and other responsibilities that are neither publicity- nor control-oriented.

With the enormous expansion in retailing today and the bright outlook in the field, those wishing to pursue management careers will find the doors wide open. In buying and merchandising, where most large companies are centrally organized and merchandised, the vast number of positions are at the company's central headquarters. Not so with management positions. One need only go from one mall to the next to see the vast number of opportunities available. Relocation is not necessary. Individuals can generally drive within five to ten miles of their homes to discover retail centers abounding with career opportunities.

Assistant department managers, as the title indicates, help manage a specific department. Involvement in such duties as scheduling, handling complaints, selling on the floor, and rearranging stock are commonplace to the job. Most companies promote from within in the case of department managers. Those assistants who prove to be the best regarded are often promoted to the manager position. The manager usually runs the department and is responsible for management of the department's selling staff. Many stores treat department managers as individuals who are running their own businesses with incentive bonuses awarded for achievement.

Personnel departments have the responsibility of supplying stores with capable workers. Members of personnel departments often have educational backgrounds in psychology, testing, and management courses. Dealing on a regular basis with recruitment, training, evaluation, and so on, the personnel department constantly handles employer-employee relations. With the high rate of employee turnover in retailing, personnel is an area where people are needed.

For the very best middle management employees, the ultimate goal, of course, is branch manager, store manager, or personnel director. While it should be recognized that the careers at the upper end of the ladder are certainly less plentiful than at the lower end or middle, the opportunity to reach the top is there. If room is not available at one's own company, there is always another willing to bring someone aboard if a solid foundation has been demonstrated. Unlike some jobs that are often dead end, management is far from it.

KEY POINTS IN THE CHAPTER

1. Organization charts, given all of their shortcomings, are used by retailers as a basis on which the retail operation functions.

2. As the organization grows, more specialization is needed to function properly. The problem facing retailers is where to place the specialists and under whose control.

3. The basis of most large department store organizations is the Mazur Plan, a four-function plan dating back to the 1920s.

4. In many large stores the responsibility of buying and selling rests with the buyer. There is, however, a great deal of thought that the separation of these two tasks would be favorable.

5. Branch stores are generally dependent on their "parents," but some parent organizations subscribe to the philosophy of independent branches and equal stores.

6. Chain stores use one of the most economical methods of conducting retailing businesses. However, some chains have made a move toward decentralization, giving store managers more responsibility.

7. The personnel function is to provide the store with capable workers through proper recruitment, training, and evaluation of employees, compensation input, development of employee benefits and services, and participation in labor relations.

8. Stores use both promotion from within and outside sources to fill vacancies. Each store evaluates the sources used to determine those most appropriate for its specific operations.

9. Selecting new employees usually begins with the completion of an application and terminates with a final interview. Personnel then makes its recommendations on hiring to the manager who makes the ultimate decision.

10. If an organization is to maintain a high standard of employee performance, it must evaluate its personnel periodically.

11. To be effective, a good compensation plan must be easy to comprehend, keyed to productivity, and reward similar compensation to jobs.

12. Employee services and benefits are necessary to motivate the prospective employee to take a job. It is especially true where salaries from company to company are similar.

Worksheet 3

COMPLETE THE FOLLOWING STATEMENTS

1. The organization of a retail store is accomplished by the identification and

   _____ of all of the similar functions of the company.

2. A glance at an organization chart shows the relationship of one job to another

   and _____ of authority.

3. The major four-function organizational structure is known as the

   _____.

4. Branch stores are organized as dependent branches, independent branches, or

   _____.

5. Chains are most often organized under the philosophy of

   _____ management.

6. A _____ is a complete statement of what the
   job entails.

7. A "rail" or _____ interview has the function of weeding out unsuitable applicants.

8. Rating performance is usually accomplished through _____ testing.

9. The training of employees is usually the responsibility of the

   _____ department in large stores.

10. Compensation decisions are made by _____ man-
    agement.

TRUE OR FALSE

_____   1. Once constructed, organization charts rarely need to be changed.

_____   2. The greater number of employees, the less specialization.

_____   3. Small stores do not require organization.

_____   4. The merchandise manager is probably the most important
            executive in the store.

_____ 5. In a highly centralized chain store operation, store managers do not do their own buying.

_____ 6. In-service promotion decreases morale.

_____ 7. The use of current employees to help find new ones is common.

_____ 8. Personality tests lack validity.

_____ 9. Part-time employees are rarely adequately trained.

_____ 10. In an effective compensation plan, earnings should be keyed to productivity.

MULTIPLE CHOICE

_____ 1. An example of centralization is
   (a) the home office buying for a chain of stores
   (b) limiting the responsibility of an employee to one specific function
   (c) limiting the responsibilities of a group of employees to one specific function
   (d) all of the above

_____ 2. One of the advantages of chain store centralized buying is that
   (a) individual stores have the ultimate decision
   (b) highly trained specialized buyers are used
   (c) store managers have increased incentive
   (d) reporting is minimized

_____ 3. An organization chart
   (a) is always necessary
   (b) indicates personal relationships
   (c) indicates lines of authority
   (d) none of the above

_____ 4. Which of the following should not be included in a job analysis?
   (a) duties required by the job
   (b) how the job is done
   (c) why the job is done
   (d) mental ability required

_____ 5. The responsibilities of the personnel department include
   (a) recruitment and training
   (b) evaluation
   (c) compensation
   (d) all of the above

_____ 6. Which of the following is a test of an applicant's capacity for a certain type of work?
   (a) ability testing
   (b) intelligence testing
   (c) aptitude testing
   (d) personality testing

_____ 7. The purpose of evaluation is
   (a) to promote the deserving
   (b) to weed out incompetents
   (c) to find areas of weakness that require improvement
   (d) all of the above

DISCUSSION QUESTIONS

1. How is the word "function" used in retail organization planning?

2. Describe the advantages of the Mazur Plan.

3. Give the principal arguments favoring the separation of buying and selling.

4. Why does the organization of the branch depend on its size and distance from the main store?

5. Discuss the advantages of having separate branch buyers.

6. Under what conditions might it be advisable to have the branch's merchandising function performed by the main store's buyers?

7. What are the economies in chain store organizations?

8. Give arguments in favor of the centralization of decision making in chain store organizations.

9. List six major functions of the personnel department.

10. What are the advantages of an in-store promotion policy?

11. How does an in-service promotion policy affect the personnel department's recruitment function?

12. Describe the purposes of a "rail interview."

13. Discuss the purposes of the final interview. By whom is the final interview conducted?

14. List the purposes and advantages of a training program.

15. List the requirements of a sound compensation system.

CASE PROBLEM 1

The board of managers of a large department store consists of the general manager and the heads of the merchandising, store operations, personnel, publicity, and controller functions. The merchandise manager has expressed dissatisfaction with the methods used in training sales personnel. It is his opinion that, since the prime function of the personnel department is the recruitment and training of sales personnel, the store should be reorganized to place the personnel function under his supervision. He argues that, since his department knows far more about sales than the personnel department, the ultimate decisions in training sales personnel should be his. He believes that much of the training program, such as role playing and films, is a waste of time and that by taking over the responsibilities of training he could shorten the present training period.

The personnel manager agrees that his people do not know as much about selling as the people in the merchandising division. However, he points out that the most knowledgeable people are not necessarily the best teachers. Teaching should be done by specialists; those who don't believe this could destroy the training program.

1. Can you think of additional arguments to support the merchandise manager?
2. Can you think of additional arguments to support the personnel manager?
3. Which manager do you support? Why?

CASE PROBLEM 2

The chief accounting officer of a large retail chain has given notice that he is leaving because of ill health. He is a highly competent man who has held the job for twenty years. During that period the chain has grown considerably, and all of its financial systems have been either initiated or implemented under his control. The large department that he supervises is made up of happy, loyal workers.

One of the following men will replace him:

1. His assistant, a middle-aged man who thoroughly understands all of the financial problems and procedures. He is competent but not brilliant. His ability to handle people and his qualities of leadership are mediocre. This man expects to be moved up and might quit if he is not promoted.

2. One of the section chiefs in the department is twenty-five years old and has a short but brilliant record. His section, although the most critical in the store, is very well run. Even the older people in the department are very fond of him. Although he is unfamiliar with the total accounting picture, he could pick it up easily. In short, he is unquestionably destined for a high managerial position.

3. A man not presently working for the firm, with a national reputation for excellence in the field. He has held similar jobs in other firms and would unquestionably bring new ideas and procedures that would improve the financial operation. He is perfectly suited for the job.

1. List the advantages and disadvantages of each person.
2. Which man would you choose? Support your answer.
3. How would you reorganize the department and why?
4. Discuss the effect of your answer to question 3 on storewide employee morale.

PROJECT 1

Obtain the organization chart of a large department store. Compare it with the Mazur Plan (Fig. 3–3). Discuss the following questions. Indicate which plan you prefer and the reasons for your choice.

1. How important is the personnel function?
2. Is there separation of sales and buying?
3. Who is responsible for the control function?
4. What theory of comparison shopping does the store operate under?
5. Who is responsible for the publicity function?

PROJECT 2

Obtain application blanks from two large retailers in your area, by mail or in person. Make the following comparison:

1. List the information they have in common.
2. List the areas in which they differ.
3. For each area of difference explain why it is included and your opinion of its importance.
4. Which application do you prefer, and why?
5. Prepare an application form you believe to be superior to both.

PROJECT 3

Almost every large retailing organization maintains an executive training program. Obtain the details of two such programs and make the following comparisons:

1. What are the requirements for getting into each program? Which one is more liberal?
2. Which is the better program from the point of view of the executive trainee? In which one will he or she get the better education? Which one offers quicker advancement?
3. Which is the better program from the point of view of the retailer? Which one is cheaper? Which one will result in better executives?

Buying for Stores

WHAT'S IN A NAME

For many years, most buyers agreed that merchandise that carried nationally recognized names or designer labels would sell faster and in larger quantities than goods that were unfamiliar to the customer—and they were right. Shoppers crowded into departments with merchandise that bore the signatures of the likes of Calvin Klein, Ralph Lauren, and Pierre Cardin. To wear the Izod "alligator" was to achieve status unobtainable with other clothing.

Recent years have seen a number of circumstances that have led buyers and merchandisers to reconsider this "name" philosophy. The coveted labels began to appear at flea markets at lower prices (they were often counterfeits of the real thing); at off-price retail emporiums, which prided themselves on the fact that they sold the "names" for less; and at manufacturer-owned outlets, which also sold for less. Not that the customer no longer wanted the "names," but they were able to get them for less money at bargain-type stores like Marshall's, Hit or Miss, Loehmann's, Syms, and the Burlington Coat Factory—all national organizations boasting a total of more than 800 stores. These newer establishments offered competition that quickly cut the traditional stores' volume with this type of merchandise; furthermore, the maintained markup and profits were shaken. Once the most profit-oriented merchandise in the stores, their departments now had to fight to stay alive. Confronted with such a problem that showed no signs of relenting, retail buyers and resident buying offices had to meet the enormous challenge presented by the off-pricers.

In a survey of customers' attitudes on brands and store image, 58 percent of those questioned indicated that it made no difference to them whose brand is on the merchandise if the store is reliable. This and other meaningful research gave buyers the signal that quality merchandise that was identified with the store's own name and had no identifying designer logo would be accepted by the consumer. Private label merchandise, although not new to stores like Sears that had built their empires on it, seemed to be the answer. The challenge to the buyers was to assemble a merchandise mix of private label and brand merchandise that would improve the stores' average markup and profit picture.

Stores have taken different approaches to their private label programs. Some have developed names, such as Marshall Field, that are totally exclusive with the stores. Marshall Field created names such as Club Fellow for heavy volume goods, Field Standard for prestige and basic wear, New Traditions for trend-oriented goods, Field Sport for active sportswear, and Field Gear for rugged wear. Made up of both domestic and imported goods, the concept is working well. Marshall Field by engaging in this is returning a markup that is not directly price-competitive with the "names" selling at the off-pricers.

J.C. Penney's approach was different. Cashing in on a high-fashion label, Penney entered into a licensing arrangement with Halston. Halston, a name that has captured all of the outstanding awards for design, including the Coty, is synonymous with expensive high fashion. The arrangement provides Penney with the Halston signature on merchandise that is made exclusively for that retail giant but at prices significantly lower than those of the Halston couture line. This marriage offers a private label of sorts plus the highly recognized designer signature to be found only at J. C. Penney. Thus the markup is protected, and fear of unfair competition by off-pricers is eliminated.

From all indications, buyers are busy helping to "design" merchandise for their private labels. The signal coming from the retailer is that the customers will buy it, even if the name isn't a household word.

LEARNING OBJECTIVES

Upon completion of this chapter, the student should be able to

1. List five responsibilities of the buyer.
2. Explain the duties of an assistant buyer, indicating five areas of responsibility.
3. Write an essay on "What to Buy," including at least six sources of buyer information.
4. Differentiate, giving advantages and disadvantages, between buying from wholesalers and buying from manufacturers.
5. List six reasons for buying from foreign sources.

INTRODUCTION

Once the organization's goals have been defined, its organizational structures initiated, and personnel, at all levels, have been hired, it is time for the retailer to fill the shelves. This task varies from company to company. In large organizations, the charge is given to the merchandising division. In small, individual proprietorships, the responsibility, most often, is in the hands of a jack-of-all-trades who merchandises, sells, displays, handles complaints, and performs a host of other duties.

Specialization becomes a key element in most retail operations as their size increases. Once the buyer of a store was burdened with department management and selling, but now the trend is toward concentration on purchasing. That is not to say that all companies subscribe to this philosophy, but whatever the situation, buyers have as their primary function the responsibility for purchasing. Whether it is a department store structure with the buyer functioning from the parent store, the chain organization where the individual in charge of purchasing functions from central headquarters, or the small boutique or specialty store where buying might be accomplished by vendor visits right on the selling floor, retail buyers perform certain functions that cut across all of these operations.

In this chapter, discussion focuses on the role of the store buyer. The resident buyer, one who functions in a more advisory capacity to the retailer, is discussed in Chapter 10.

BUYER QUALIFICATIONS

For managerial positions in retailing, particularly buying careers, individuals must possess certain qualifications and characteristics. Following are some of those considered most important by many of the leading retailers who were interviewed:

1. A college degree, preferably in retail business management, is necessary. It is rare for a high school student to climb the ladder of success from stock clerk to manager. The sophistication of today's retailing demands a knowledgeable individual to step into positions of authority. The success stories of "self-educated" retailers are part of the history of retailing and not of its future.

2. An enthusiastic attitude is a must. Buyers (unless the responsibility is not theirs, as in central purchasing for chain stores) are usually responsible for the sale of merchandise in their departments. Enthusiasm is one of the most effective methods for motivating employees to sell goods. The buyers' enthusiasm seems to transfer to their subordinates. Many stores will overlook some of an individual's shortcomings, but few, if asked, will choose an indifferent person for a buying position.

3. Product knowledge is extremely important for efficient buying. It is just about impossible to have complete knowledge of every item stocked by department stores. An understanding of style and textiles for the fashion buyer or a knowledge of grades of fruits and vegetables for the produce buyer is almost mandatory for success. Too many people deemphasize the importance of product knowledge, but the individual with the ability to examine goods knowledgeably and make discerning decisions will certainly be ahead in the buying game.

4. A simple working knowledge of retailing mathematics is a must for every buyer. The buyer must be able to determine quickly markup, markdown, open to buy, and other often-used computations.

5. Leadership ability is very important. The buyer not only is a purchasing agent but is responsible for subordinates as well. Assistant buyers and salespeople are as good as their leadership.

6. The ability to get along with people is an important quality for a buyer. In addition to the people in their departments, buyers continually meet with merchandise managers, vendors, and buying office representatives. Ability to get along with these different parties helps to guarantee a more efficient operation.

7. While retailing students agree that such characteristics as ability, knowledge, and leadership are important qualities that a buyer should possess, they often underestimate the importance of appearance. The buyer's appearance sets an example for the staff, makes a lasting impression on customers, and often sets the tone in relationships with vendors.

BUYER DUTIES AND RESPONSIBILITIES

Having learned that different kinds of organizations make different demands on their buyers, it is important to understand that the following discussion of duties and responsibilities is general. For example, the small store buyer usually performs a large number of tasks in addition to the actual purchasing. On the other hand, the department store buyer and the large specialty store buyer, who operate from a main store, perform fewer additional tasks; and the chain store buyer, who generally operates from central headquarters, is usually free of other responsibilities. Bearing this in mind, the following list is offered:

Buyer

1. The most important duty of a buyer is the actual purchasing of the goods. The buyer is faced with the perennial problems of what merchandise to choose, from which vendors, and in which quantity and the correct timing of delivery to meet customers' demands. Included in these tasks are negotiating the price, shipping terms, and extra dating (additional time in which to pay for merchandise). Since these are areas of great significance, an in-depth study of each is made later in the chapter.

2. After buying arrangements have been worked out, the buyer must price the merchandise to conform with the policies of the store and the markup to be achieved by the particular department. Included in this area are the pricing of the individual items and the repricing of goods that have moved slowly, in the hope the lower price will move them faster. New merchandise can then be put on the selling floor in place of the slow-moving goods.

3. After goods are received, marked, and moved to the selling floor (ticketing of merchandise, checking of quantities against invoices, and the moving of goods are done at either a warehouse or a receiving department in large stores), the buyer usually determines their placement. Such decisions as whether to display folded merchandise on shelves or put them on racks are left to the buyer's discretion. The buyer, who usually knows more about this merchandise than anyone else in the store, knows how best to feature the merchandise in the department.

4. In some department stores, the buyer also manages the department. Buyers are involved in the final selection of employees for their departments, the supervision of selling, and the arranging of sales meetings.

5. The buyer often selects merchandise for promotion, merchandise that should be displayed, and merchandise that should be advertised; the buyer sometimes plans fashion shows and any other special events that might promote goods.

6. Selling on the floor during peak periods is sometimes another buyer responsibility. This provides buyers with actual customer contact, which enables them to determine customer wants firsthand. This is usually done in small stores.

Assistant Buyer

Most buyers in large stores have assistants to help with the many chores of buying for a store or a department. Some of the more typical duties and responsibilities an assistant performs are the following:

1. Most reorders of merchandise are placed by assistant buyers. This is the replenishment of fast-selling merchandise.
2. Assistants often follow up orders that have not been delivered. Often these are orders that were especially placed for individual customers and if not delivered on time will be canceled.
3. The purchase of some new merchandise is done by assistants. Occasionally when a department is large, the buyer will allow an assistant to purchase some lines. Generally, the purchase is limited to staple goods.
4. When the buyer is planning for a new season, the assistant is included in the decision-making group. This arrangement allows for another opinion plus excellent on-the-job training in preparation for a full buyer's job.
5. By selling merchandise in the department, the assistant buyer acts as liaison between the buyer and the customer. This contact with the customer provides the assistant with information concerning the customer's wants.

THE FUNDAMENTALS OF EFFECTIVE BUYING

The merchandise available today is more varied in terms of style and price and more plentiful than at any other time in the history of retailing. So, too, are the numbers of retail organizations. The buyer must be capable of selecting the appropriate items and must present them in a manner that will defy competition and motivate customers to return again and again for future purchases.

In order to contribute to the success of their companies, buyers must diligently carry out prescribed merchandising policies. These policies, in large part, are based on merchandise availability and the competition. The merchandising policies also include such factors as price lines, quality of merchandise, exclusivity of goods, variety, timing of the introduction of goods, assortment, and pricing. It should be noted that store buyers are not usually responsible for establishing merchandising policies but are called upon to carry them out through appropriate purchasing. Top management, specifically the general and divisional merchandise managers, has that responsibility, with the buyers often asked for their input.

Given a budgeted dollar figure for their departments, the buyers are usually required to develop a model stock or inventory that contains an appropriate assortment of sizes, colors, styles, and prices. This model stock is developed through the buyers' evaluation of the customers' needs and demands that have been reflected in both past sales and outside sources of information. Specifically, based on these sources, the buyers plan purchases in terms of what to buy, how much to buy, from whom to buy, and when to buy, collectively referred to as the elements of buying.

By carefully developing these elements, and changing them as dictated by their findings in past sales records and through outside sources, the buyers then plan for the new season. While many professionals agree that buying might be considered an art, more and more are convinced that a scientific approach that involves strict attention to sales records and other indicators will make the buyer a more productive member of the merchandising team.

What to Buy

The decision of which merchandise to select from all that is made available by vendors is not made by guessing. While some misinformed or uninformed individuals feel that buyers are lucky when they choose the right merchandise, those who are knowledgeable understand the great deal of care that is exercised in the planning of purchases.

A buyer tries to determine, before purchasing, the customers' wants and needs and attempts to satisfy those desires by purchasing the right merchandise. Sound marketing tells us that products should be designed and produced with the customer in mind. Good buyers, too, purchase with the customer in mind. In order to determine what the customer wants, the buyer gathers information from a number of sources. While not all buyers use all the sources available to them, they all study past sales records. An investigation of past sales reveals which price lines sold best, which sizes were most popular, which were the peak selling periods, which vendors had the fastest-moving merchandise, and other pertinent information.

The method used to record such information varies from store to store. The smaller the operation, the less sophisticated the system used. One system used by small stores is to hand-record all goods received in an inventory book and include any information that might be meaningful for future purchasing (Fig. 4–1). For example, included might be the vendor's name, style number of the item, cost price and selling price (to show markup), color, sizes, number of pieces, and when goods were received. At the end of each day, the sales receipts or merchandise tags (Fig. 4–2) (either of which should record any information kept in the inventory book) are used to check off the items sold. The buyer can immediately check the records to see how the merchandise is selling. In

FIGURE 4–1 Inventory Page (Small Store)

CARYN JOY SPORTSWEAR
306 Eddy Street
New York, NY 10101
212-874-8200

STYLE	PRICE	COLORS	SIZE BREAKDOWN							
5835	10.75	RED	8	10	12	12	14	14	16	18
	25.00	GREEN	10	12	14	16	18	20		
		YELLOW	10	12	14	16	18	20		
	JUNE 1									
2564	14.75	BLACK	8	8	10	10	12	12	12	14	14
	30.00		14	16	16	16	18	18	20		
	JUNE 23									

FIGURE 4–2 Merchandise Tag (Small Store)

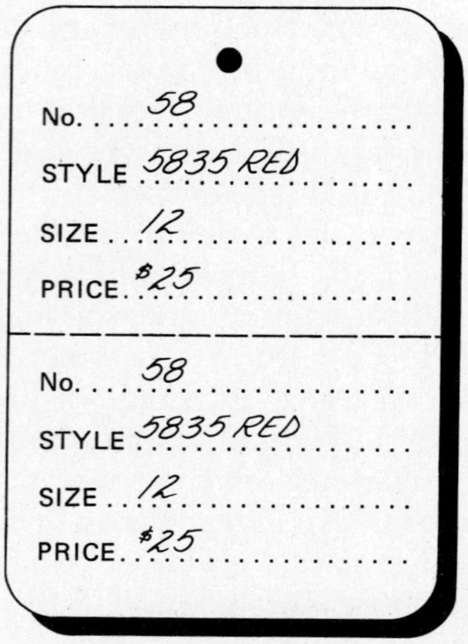

No. *58*
STYLE *5835 RED*
SIZE *12*
PRICE *$25*

No. *58*
STYLE *5835 RED*
SIZE *12*
PRICE *$25*

addition, this book serves as a perpetual inventory and shows what merchandise is still available for sale. This system is commonly known as a unit control system.

In large retail organizations, a more sophisticated system of recording sales is kept. The computer keeps the same records as those kept by hand, but does it more quickly and usually more efficiently. Buyers are given all sorts of past sales data by the computer, either daily, weekly, or monthly or at any interval necessary for the efficiency of the operation. Food store buyers, for example, often require daily sales information because their merchandise turns over so rapidly. Furniture store buyers, on the other hand, require less frequent information because of the nature of the goods. With the introduction of the point-of-purchase register, which is tied into the computer in many stores, past sales information is always available.

Various kinds of surveys are used by buyers to determine customers' wants. Stores often interview people to determine taste and buying habits, send out questionnaires to charge customers to inquire about merchandise that might interest them, hold consumer panels to discover likes and dislikes, and conduct fashion counts to discover what people are wearing. Through these techniques, buyers find out firsthand what their customers or potential customers desire.

Buyers constantly scan trade periodicals to keep up to date in their field. Supermarket buyers generally read *Chain Store Age*; fashion buyers faithfully scan *Women's Wear Daily* for women's fashions and *The Daily News Record* for men's clothing. Each segment of the retail store industry subscribes to the papers and magazines of its trade. These periodicals offer important information to buyers, such as new merchandise available for sale, information about consumers (from surveys taken), best-seller reports, trends in the market, and merchandise forecasting.

Market research is undertaken by some of the trade papers, as well as by newspapers and consumer magazines, and is reported on a weekly or monthly basis or in special editions. Fashion reports by such companies as the Fairchild organization offer significant statistics to buyers. Fairchild, publisher of *Women's Wear Daily*, has a worldwide staff to cover the latest news on fashion trends. Its reporters attend showings of fabric and garment manufacturers and of Parisian, Italian, Israeli, and other internationally known designers.

Among other widely read trade publications are *Home-Furnishings Daily*, which covers the home furnishings field, and *Footwear News*.

Consumer newspapers and magazines provide buyers with much information. By merely reading the daily newspapers, food buyers can learn the goods their competitors are promoting and at what prices. Fashion buyers learn about the styles that have been selected by the consumer magazines to be shown to their readers. Because many readers are influenced by magazines, the store certainly should know the merchandise to which their customers are being exposed.

Salespeople provide buyers with information. Since they are actually the ones who speak to customers, salespeople know the customers' demands. Such items as price information, styles desired, and qualities wanted are examples of the information salespeople can give their buyers.

Resident buying offices are extremely important aids to store buyers. Their role is great in some aspects of retailing, and chapter 10 describes how they help retail store organizations.

A very important factor for all buyers in making their selections is the store's image. It may be one of fashion innovation, such as in the case of Saks Fifth Avenue, conservative styling for the discriminating male, as is the Brooks Brothers image, or high fashion at rock-bottom prices, as in

Filene's Basement Store in Boston. Complete awareness of their store's image by all of its buyers will guarantee a unified impression to the customer. If buyers go off on their own and move in different directions, the entire operation will suffer.

How Much to Buy

While the ability to select the correct items from the many available is important in purchasing, the wrong quantities can still mean a loss for the department. Many retailing students are aware of the inherent dangers in overbuying, but few realize the dangers in not buying enough. There is nothing quite as aggravating to the buyer as having requests for certain merchandise but not enough pieces to suit the customers' demands.

Generally, the first step in determining how much to buy is to estimate the retail sales for the period of purchase. This is usually a job encompassing the entire organization and is the responsibility of top management. The buyer is interested in the sales estimate for his or her department and has important input in the planning stages. The estimate or forecast is for a designated period of time, the time varying according to the merchandise. For example, buyers of perishables might be concerned with daily requirements, whereas purchasers of staple goods might need only a semiannual picture. Although the purchase periods differ, the key items analyzed in forecasting retail sales are about the same for all retailers. Such factors as disposable income (what is available to be spent after taxes), unemployment, and shifts in population are of great importance to top management.

At the buyer level, estimating future sales is usually based on a comparison of how much is being sold this year with last year's sales. By determining the percentage of increase (or decrease) a buyer can add (or subtract) that percentage to last year's purchases for the same upcoming period. In many retail stores these figures are readily available through the computer. The buyer is also concerned with those factors that have a local effect. For example, a purchaser of men's workclothes, whose customers work principally for a large plant, must carefully watch that plant's progress. If it is apparent that the factory will lose certain contracts, layoffs will be inevitable. The small retailer is generally more concerned with local conditions than those of national importance.

Other factors that must be considered at the department level are expansion plans for the store (new branches or units), enlargement of the department's selling space, change in selling practices (service to self-service or the reverse), the size of the department's promotion budget (for display, advertising, special events), the possibility of a more diversified offering, and more specialization.

Although it would be easier for buyers to purchase only at the beginning of a new season, they must constantly add merchandise to their initial purchases throughout the period. Goods that were sold must be replaced and inventories kept at the designated levels.

Open to Buy

Buyers, in order to control their inventories effectively, must carefully plan the amount of merchandise they are going to add at a given time. Since inventory needs vary from month to month, depending on the season, sale periods, holidays, and so forth, the buyer must always adjust the amounts of merchandise needed. The amount of merchandise that can be ordered at any time during a period is the difference between the total purchases planned by the buyer and the commitments already made. The amount of this difference is called the open to buy, or the OTB. The formula used is

merchandise needed for period − merchandise available = open to buy

Illustrative Problem

The retail inventory for dresses in the budget department of Haring's Department Store figured at $42,000 on September 1, with a planned inventory of $36,000 for September 30. Planned sales, based on last year's figures, were $22,000 with markdowns of $2,000 for the entire month. The commitments for September were $6,000 at retail. What was the open to buy?

Solution

Merchandise needed (September 1–30)		
End-of-month inventory (planned)	$36,000	
Planned sales (September 1–30)	22,000	
Planned markdowns	2,000	
Total merchandise needed		$60,000
Merchandise available (September 1)		
Opening inventory	$42,000	
Commitments (on order)	6,000	
Total merchandise available		48,000
Open to buy (September 1)		$12,000

This problem indicates how a buyer can determine an OTB for a one-month period. Very often, buyers must determine their needs within the monthly period. By slightly adjusting the procedure to include the sales actually recorded and the goods actually marked down, the open to buy for any specific date may be obtained.

Illustrative Problem

On March 14, the blouse buyer for Kent's Specialty Shop decided to determine her open to buy. The following figures were available:

Present inventory at retail (March 14)	$12,000
Inventory commitments (March 14)	3,000

Planned end-of-month inventory (March 31)   15,000
Planned sales   6,000
Actual sales   3,000
Planned markdowns   500
Actual markdowns   200
What is the buyer's open to buy?

Solution

Merchandise needed		
(March 14–31)		
End-of-month inventory		
(planned)		$15,000
Planned sales	$ 6,000	
Less: actual sales	3,000	
Balance of planned sales		3,000
Planned markdowns	$ 500	
Less: actual markdowns	200	
Balance of planned		
markdowns		300
Total merchandise needed		$18,300
Merchandise available (March 14)		
Present inventory	$12,000	
Commitments	3,000	
Total merchandise available		15,000
Open to buy (March 14)		$ 3,300

From Whom to Buy

In most types of merchandise classifications, the number of sources from which to choose merchandise is practically limitless. The store buyers are not only faced with the problem of selecting particular sources, but must also decide whether to purchase directly from the manufacturer (or grower) or a middleperson, or sometimes perhaps even produce their own merchandise (if the retail business is very large).

The specific vendor from which to buy is determined by investigating the same information in the earlier discussion of what to buy. Other sources are the shopping of competing stores, trade directories, reporting services, and discussions with buyers of noncompeting stores (stores carrying the same type of goods but far enough away not to be a competitor).

Figures 4–3 and 4–4 are examples of forms used by buyers to record information about vendors from which they have purchased. The vendor information card gives the buyer a quick glimpse of the company in terms of sales representatives, factory location, terms, and discounts. The buyer's bible information card shows the buyer's past experience with the company's particular merchandise items. Both are important references for buyer use.

FIGURE 4–3 Vendor Information Card

LARGE CO. SMALL CO. PARTNERSHIP INDIVIDUAL	NATURE OF BUSINESS	CLASSIFI-CATION
NAME		DATE
ADDRESS		
CITY		ROOM NO.
TELEPHONE		
REPRESENTED BY		CODE NO.
FACTORY ADDRESS		
REMARKS		
TERMS	DISCOUNT	F. O. B.

FIGURE 4–4 Buyer's Bible

NAME			ADDRESS					
MERCHANDISE	STYLE NO.	COST	RETAIL	M.U.%	M.D.%	MNTD M.U.	RATING	

Simply stated, the main channels of distribution for consumer goods (those goods that are purchased for personal use) are

1. manufacturer ————→ consumer
2. manufacturer ——→ manufacturer's own stores ——→ consumer

3. manufacturer ———→ franchisee ———→ consumer
4. manufacturer ———→ retailer ———→ consumer
5. manufacturer ———→ wholesaler ———→ retailer ———→ consumer

In the first situation the manufacturer actually skips the most common type of retail selling, in a store, and sells directly to the consumer at the producer's factory or at the consumer's home. Examples of this distribution technique are the Fuller Brush Co. selling door to door and the suit manufacturer selling to the consumer at the factory—a method that is becoming more popular with producers throughout the United States.

The second channel presents a situation in which manufacturers, in addition to their production chores, also set up their own retail stores from which they sell their own merchandise. Examples of this method is in evidence all across the United States where manufacturers such as Ralph Lauren is retailing his Polo line, Hathaway is retailing its Chaps and Hathaway labels, Mikasa is selling its dinnerware and glassware, Bass is selling its shoes, Misty Harbor is selling rainwear, and Totes is retailing umbrellas and overshoes.

The third channel is one in which producers manufacture lines of merchandise and distribute them exclusively to franchisees of their company. Benetton is one of the most successful companies using this method of distribution.

The first three distribution methods do not involve store buyers. It is through the last two channels of distribution that most consumer goods flow. In one, the retailer buys directly from the producer; the other involves puchasing from a middleperson. The decision of whether to buy from the manufacturer or wholesaler is not always up to the buyer's discretion; some manufacturers, no matter how large the retail organization, sell only through middlepersons. When the manufacturer does distribute to both the wholesaler and the retailer, the decision is the buyer's.

Buying from Manufacturers

The purchase of merchandise directly from the manufacturer is generally restricted to large retailers, except for fashion merchandise, where even small retailers purchase directly. The very nature of fashion merchandise, with its constant changes due to consumer demand and the seasonality of the goods, necessitates this route. These goods must reach the retailer quickly, and the use of the wholesaler would slow down the process. The direct purchase of merchandise usually affords the buyer lower prices (than at the wholesaler) and a chance to make suggestions about changes in the manufacturer's design.

Buying from Wholesalers

Outside the fashion world, purchasing from wholesalers is important. Some factors that persuade the buyer to purchase from middlepersons are

1. *Quick delivery.* One of the main duties the wholesaler performs for the retailer is the storage of merchandise. With the wholesaler's warehouse stocked with goods, the retailer can expect prompt delivery, sometimes even same-day service.
2. *Small orders.* Most manufacturers require minimum orders that are too large for the smaller retailer. Wholesalers sell in smaller quantities than do manufacturers.
3. *Wide assortment.* While manufacturers sell only their own products, the wholesaler carries the offerings of many manufacturers. This affords the retailer a comparison of goods and also saves the time it would take to shop many manufacturers' lines.
4. *Easy credit terms.* Generally wholesalers offer more liberal credit terms than do manufacturers.

The wholesaler is really a service organization. It manufactures nothing. When a buyer feels that the services the wholesaler offers is more important than price, he or she will purchase from that wholesaler even though it may mean paying more for the goods. Even the largest retailers, able to buy directly, use wholesalers when they need immediate delivery and the manufacturer cannot accommodate them. In other cases, where, although their overall volume is large, some items are sold infrequently or do not move rapidly, they turn to wholesalers for small quantities.

When to Buy

When to purchase goods can vary from every day to semiannually, depending on the type of goods and/or the size of the retailer. In any case, timing is of utmost importance. Buyers must buy sufficiently early to allow enough time for the goods to reach the selling floor. Purchasing from wholesalers allows buying merchandise very close to the time the consumer will purchase the goods. It is the purchase from manufacturers, coupled with such elements as seasons, weather, and perishability, that poses problems for buyers.

The buyer of seasonal merchandise, such as swimsuits, almost always bought from manufacturers, purchases well in advance of the season. This is necessary because production takes a couple of months and the store wants the goods early enough to whet the customer's appetite. In the case of seasonal merchandise, manufacturers, as an inducement to retailers, often "date" the purchase orders. That is, they extend the period for payment of the invoices. The buyer of seasonal goods who purchases too late might not get delivery. Also, if the customers don't have enough advance exposure to the merchandise, they might be tempted to buy elsewhere.

Weather poses a special problem. Abundant snowfalls will sell snowblowers, just as long periods of extreme heat will sell air conditioners. While it's difficult to determine weather, it is an important factor to buyers.

Perishability also plays havoc with buyers. Perishable goods must be purchased as frequently as possible and in carefully determined quantities. There is nothing as unsalable as sour milk or wilted roses.

The efficiency of the buyer is extremely important to the store's success. We have discussed how important it is for this person to receive as much help as is available in order to do an effective job. There is, particularly in the fashion field, an aid without whose help many retailers would fail. This is the resident buying office, discussed in detail in Chapter 10.

Negotiating the Purchase

After preparing a purchasing plan that carefully considers all of the elements of buying, the buyer's next step is to seek out the appropriate vendors to negotiate an order.

Negotiating price requires an understanding of a piece of legislation known as the Robinson-Patman Act. This was enacted to limit price discrimination and to protect the small business owner from the industrial giants that could get lower prices. Basically, under the law, all buyers must pay the same price except in instances where

- The price reduction is made to meet competition.
- The price is lowered because cost savings result from sales to particular customers.
- The merchandise is obsolete or part of a "job lot."

Once these guidelines are understood, it is the buyer's knowledge of the market and product that enables attainment of a satisfactory price.

Negotiating with the vendor involves a number of purchasing decisions that require a knowledge of the particular market, product information, discounts, transportation arrangements, and so forth.

A variety of discounts enter into a purchase negotiation. Cash discounts for prompt payment, quantity discounts, seasonal discounts, advertising discounts, and promotional discounts must all be explored to gain the best possible deal.

An important aspect of the negotiation lies with transportation costs. An astute negotiator can often convince the vendor to assume costs of shipping and can thereby actually reduce the cost of the merchandise.

Other negotiating considerations include cooperative purchasing, where individual orders can be combined for better prices, and consignment buying, which permits payment of goods only when they are sold to the consumer.

Negotiation involves a great deal of expertise and understanding of psychology. Buyers must establish limits for goods they expect to purchase, justify the reasons for the price offered, be willing to split the difference in price when an impasse is reached, and develop relationships that would ensure the best possible future deals.

CURRENT TRENDS AFFECTING THE BUYER

As recently as ten years ago, retailers instructed their buyers to purchase the most appealing merchandise, mark it up "traditionally," provide service, and offer the right atmosphere to motivate the customer to return again and again. Retailing today is more complex. Not only are more and more goods available from all over the world to make the buyer's job more complicated, but off-price merchants continue to flourish and make inroads into the once "guaranteed" customer market of the traditional retail organizations. With these and other circumstances, the buyer's role has taken on new challenges.

Private Label Development

One need only carefully examine the inventories of most major retailers to find that, although the stock is still laden with labels of national and international recognition, the racks and shelves also contain goods that don't immediately call to mind their identification. In order to cope with the off-pricers merchants have taken the route of producing their own goods or having manufacturers produce goods for them on an exclusive basis. The result is merchandise that brings a healthy markup without fear of "unfair" competition.

Taking an idea from Sears, which has been merchandising private brands for years, the major retailers have called on their buying teams to develop private label programs. Most stores got their feet wet with small amounts of these goods, and have found, generally, significant customer acceptance and higher maintained markups. Buyers working for the likes of Bloomingdale's, Macy's, Saks Fifth Avenue, Dayton's and Marshall Field are well into such merchandising, with each season surpassing the last in terms of increased private label programs.

The buyers' problem is to determine the appropriate mix of private label and manufacturers' brands for their clientele. Will Izod's alligator become extinct and will the Polo pony stop galloping in favor of a logo that will be the exclusive right of a particular merchant? It will be interesting to see how buyers cope with the difficulty of determining a profitable balance.

Foreign Merchandise Purchasing

At one time merchandise whose labels had the word "imported" meant superior, high priced, and fashionable, and was reserved for the limited numbers who could purchase such goods. Today it is virtually impossible to venture into a store that does not stock items from such places as

Hong Kong, Taiwan, Japan, France, Italy, Great Britain, and other distant shores.

The reasons for purchasing goods from foreign sources are many. Besides prestige, others include the following:

1. In general, goods of comparable value cost less in foreign countries. By purchasing abroad, retailers can offer better value to their customers while at the same time achieving higher markups. One ready-to-wear buyer for a well-known department store revealed that a markup of 70 percent was realized on his foreign purchases. This is well above the usual markup for American-made clothing of equal quality.
2. Some merchandise is not available at home. For example, the label-conscious "jet set" spends enormous sums for original designs. Such names as St. Laurent, Givenchy, and Ungaro command prices that other (American) designers do not. Such merchandise is only available abroad.
3. For purposes of copying designs, stores spend great sums in foreign countries. Rather than sell the originals, stores visit the foreign fashion houses to purchase styles for the express purpose of copying them. This arrangement permits the average American to purchase copies at a fraction of the originals' cost. This market has become increasingly important in fashion retailing.

A retailer must weigh the advantages against the disadvantages before embarking on a program of purchasing imported goods. Some of the disadvantages cited by retailers that oppose buying from foreign sources are

1. The expense incurred from a buying trip abroad may be too costly to reap profits from the merchandise purchased.
2. The delivery period is generally uncertain, owing to the distance involved and the limited shipping facilities.
3. The outlay of cash necessary at the time of shipment might be extensive. Since the shipping period is so long, capital is tied up without having the goods for sale.
4. Owing to the time lag, purchases must be made far in advance of the selling period, when such considerations as color and size may not be made with knowledgeable certainty.
5. Sometimes the initial duty assessment is inaccurate owing to change. This may result in higher tariffs.
6. Reorders are generally impossible on imported goods, particularly in fashion, since the time it takes for delivery may be long.
7. Goods bought according to specification may fall short of what is expected. Since the distance between the vendor and the purchaser is great, return of imperfect goods is often impossible.
8. Damaged goods are costly to return to the foreign manufacturer.

Once the pros and cons are evaluated, the buyer must, as has been discussed in the case of private labels, determine the proper mix of imports and domestically available goods. When the quantitative considerations have been worked out, the buyer must develop a plan for acquiring foreign-made products. Some of the techniques used for foreign merchandise are.

1. *Periodic trips by store buyers.* In the case of large users, it is common practice for a buyer to visit the foreign markets in person. These trips are made frequently. Buyers of fashion merchandise go even more frequently. This method demands careful preplanning, since the time abroad is limited. Hotel reservations, transportation arrangements, and buying appointments must be planned in advance. Buyers, particularly of merchandise manufactured by the foreign haute couture houses, plan their trips to coincide with the couturiers' openings. In order to make certain that the leading fashion houses can be visited in the short time spent in Paris, the Chambre de la Syndicale regulates the times of the showings in France.
2. *"Commissionaires," or foreign resident offices.* This representation is similar to resident buying offices in the United States.
3. *Import wholesalers.* These are middlepersons who carry samples of merchandise available from foreign countries. The smaller retailer wishing to avoid the expense of visits to foreign countries can make purchases from the importers. The cost is a little more than if purchased directly, but because the purchasing power of the small retailer is limited, this arrangement is satisfactory.
4. *Privately owned foreign offices.* Organizations such as the American Merchandising Corp. maintain offices in foreign markets. This allows for maximum time to be spent in these markets in which to seek out the best goods, by professional buyers, at the best prices. Naturally, only the giant retail organizations can avail themselves of this arrangement.

SMALL STORE ADAPTATION

Although small retail operations do not usually have the services of fashion coordinators, sophisticated computerized reports, and merchandise managers, all is not lost for the buyer in a small company.

Many owners of small retail specialty stores and boutiques also perform the buying function. It is often the taste and creativity of these persons that account for the success of the store. In addition to being in the marketplace to find new sources and discover hot items, the small store buyer is generally found, regularly, on the selling floor. Whether selling or just being available to elicit customer wants and needs, the small store buyer has an edge over the large store counterpart whose decision making is based on computer printouts.

If the "customer is king or queen" philosophy is really believed, it is the small store purchasing agent who enjoys enormous customer contact on a daily basis. While the large store buyer must often "pass through the proper channels" to initiate a buying change, the small store purchaser can react immediately to change without petitioning a higher-up. Being visible on the sales floor not only can give the customer the feeling that someone is listening, but it can provide the information often needed for good buying decisions.

CAREER OPPORTUNITIES

Few would argue with the statement that the buyer is the lifeblood of the retail organization. Couple this with a projection from the U.S. Labor Department's Bureau of Labor Statistics that buyer positions will increase through the 1980s by 44.3 percent, and a buying career is an excellent bet for anyone who is moving in that direction. Buyers, or purchasing agents, as they are often referred to, work for stores or resident buying offices. The buyer's career explored in this chapter is the one directly involved in employment at the retail level. Resident buyer opportunities are discussed in Chapter 10.

It should be understood that rarely do graduates enter retailing at the buyer level to the goal for purchasing-oriented individuals. Most people must first prove themselves as executive trainees or assistant buyers. It is in these positions that merchandising managers (the buyers' supervisors) can best evaluate the potential of the store's employees. Through close scrutiny of the work of the assistant buyer in merchandise selection (usually limited to staples), following up of orders, vendor relationships, product knowledge, and so on, decisions on promotion to buyer can be made.

Store buyers' salaries and responsibilities vary according to the nature of the merchandise classification for which they purchase, the merchandising structure of the company, the volume of the department, and the variety of buyer-related responsibilities performed. For example, some companies still hold the buyer responsible for the department's sales force.

A significant fact that should be emphasized is the virtual freedom from discrimination in retail buying. Few fields can boast the number of women in executive positions. Many retailers, in fact, report that there are more women buyers in their organization than men. Another plus that motivates people to become professional purchasers is the time necessary to achieve the level of buyer—on average, four to seven years. What other career could boast such a short period to reach an executive-level position and at a salary that is often better than in most fields?

KEY POINTS IN THE CHAPTER

1. In addition to purchasing, the buyer's most important duty, there are the responsibilities of pricing, selecting merchandise for promotion, and, sometimes, selling in the department.

2. Assistant buyers reorder merchandise, follow up orders, help the buyer with the new season's plans, and sell in the department.

3. Buyers develop model stocks, which are inventories that contain appropriate assortments of sizes, colors, styles, and prices.

4. The elements of buying are what to buy, how much to buy, from whom to buy, and when to buy.

5. A unit control system is a perpetual inventory that indicates sold merchandise and merchandise still available for sale.

6. The best source for determining what to buy, and in which quantities, is past sales records. Other sources are trade publications, research studies, resident buying offices, and sales personnel.

7. Open to buy is the difference between the merchandise needed for a period and the merchandise available.

8. Merchandise may be purchased from manufacturers and wholesalers. The decision of from whom to buy is based on such factors as the size of the purchase, delivery requirements, credit terms, and assortments offered.

9. Negotiating price must be done within the framework of the Robinson-Patman Act, a law that prohibits price discrimination.

10. Foreign-made goods are important to most retailers and are available through many sources.

Worksheet 4

COMPLETE THE FOLLOWING STATEMENTS

1. In most traditionally structured department store organizations, the management of the department is the responsibility of

   the _____.

2. The inventory that contains an appropriate assortment of merchandise is

   called a _____.

3. The most important task performed by the buyer is _____.

4. The recording of inventory and its adjustment each time a sale is made is

   called a _____ system.

5. _____ is the difference between the merchandise needed for a period and the merchandise available.

6. Easy credit terms, quick delivery, and wide assortment of goods are characteristic of purchasing from _____.

7. Buyers are somewhat able to compete with the off-price retailers by developing _____ programs.

8. The regulation of fashion showings in Paris is controlled by the

   _____.

9. Foreign resident buying offices are known as _____.

10. Negotiating price requires an understanding of legislation known as the

    _____.

TRUE OR FALSE

_____ 1. Generally in department and large specialty stores, the buyer selects the merchandise to be promoted, displayed, and advertised.

_____ 2. Buyers, because they are constantly involved in purchasing, do not sell on the floor.

3. With the introduction of the computer, buyers no longer need a working knowledge of retailing mathematics.

4. The elements of buying are model stock development and pricing of merchandise.

5. An important factor in the selection of merchandise is the store's image.

6. Generally, the first step in determining how much to buy is to estimate the retail sales for the period of purchase.

7. Open to buy can be determined at any time in the month.

8. The purchase of merchandise from manufacturers is generally restricted to fashion items.

9. Wholesalers are actually service organizations.

10. Buyers need not leave the United States to purchase foreign-made merchandise.

11. A model stock is developed by exclusively paying attention to the demands of store management.

12. One of the earliest retailing innovators with private labels and private brands was Sears.

MULTIPLE CHOICE

1. Buyers
   (a) price merchandise
   (b) select merchandise for displays
   (c) sell on the floor
   (d) all of the above

2. In chain organizations, buyers
   (a) purchase from the main store
   (b) operate from central headquarters
   (c) rarely buy the merchandise
   (d) leave purchasing to the merchandise managers

3. In determining what to purchase, buyers
   (a) carefully study past sales records
   (b) discuss problems with sales personnel
   (c) scan consumer newspapers and magazines
   (d) all of the above

4. In determining how much to purchase, buyers
   (a) must consider the store's expansion plans
   (b) consider changes in selling practices
   (c) look at past sales figures
   (d) all of the above

5. Open to buy is determined
   (a) at the beginning of the month
   (b) at the middle of the month
   (c) at the end of the month
   (d) any time

6. Fashion merchandise is most often purchased from
   (a) wholesalers
   (b) manufacturers
   (c) rack jobbers
   (d) all of the above

7. Minimum order requirements and limited assortment are characteristic of buying from
   (a) manufacturers
   (b) wholesalers
   (c) rack jobbers
   (d) all of the above

8. Buyers keep source records on
   (a) vendor information cards
   (b) buyer's bible forms
   (c) both a and b
   (d) neither a nor b

9. Goods are purchased from abroad because of
   (a) lower prices
   (b) unavailability in the United States
   (c) prestige
   (d) all of the above

10. Basically, under the Robinson-Patman Act, all buyers must pay the same price except
    (a) when merchandise is irregular
    (b) when price is reduced to meet competition
    (c) when goods are obsolete
    (d) all of the above

DISCUSSION QUESTIONS

1. What are the important elements of buying?

2. Discuss the department store buyer's responsibilities for the promotion of merchandise.

3. Describe a reorder. Who is generally responsible for reordering in large stores?

4. Why is enthusiasm considered a good characteristic for store buyers?

5. Why do buyers read trade papers and magazines?

6. Is the salesperson an important source of information for buyers? Why?

7. What is meant by store image? Why is it important?

8. In planning how much to buy, what is the first step to consider? Describe the procedure.

9. What is the open-to-buy formula? Can the OTB be determined at any time? How?

10. Which channels of distribution are most common in retailing?

11. Why do small stores usually purchase from wholesalers?

12. Explain why large stores sometimes buy from wholesalers, even though they can go directly to the manufacturer.

CASE PROBLEM 1

The Henderson Co. is a large department store located in the downtown shopping area of a New England community. At present, it has three branch stores within a radius of 100 miles of the main store. Its clientele is made up largely of people in the $18,000 to $30,000 income bracket. A very small percentage of its customers is more affluent. Buying is done by the main store buyers, who purchase for the central store and the branch operations.

Henderson's board of directors recently decided to expand the present operation by opening another branch in an area different from those in which it currently operates. The new area is inhabited by families whose average income is $45,000. The branch would carry the full complement of hard goods and soft goods, but in some merchandise lines the price range would naturally differ from present prices.

Discussion is presently centering around merchandising the new branch. These unanswered questions have arisen thus far:

1. Should the present arrangement for buying be continued?

2. If the new store should have its own buyers, must it be for every merchandise category? Which merchandise classifications must it be for?

CASE PROBLEM 2

Value-Wise Supermarkets has thirty units in the southeastern United States. The chain has decided to expand its efforts, and after numerous top management meetings, has developed a ten-year master plan. This plan calls for opening five new units each year, fifty more in all, for a grand total of eighty-five after ten years. The expansion will take place on the eastern seaboard up to and including the Middle Atlantic states.

The main problem confronting the expansion is that all the competitors in the new areas offer trading stamps, which Value-Wise does not do. Its policy has been to offer the lowest prices through excellence in purchasing. The buyers contend that if they compete with trading stamps, prices will rise in all the units and their customers might shop elsewhere. At this time, top management is ready to use trading stamps, but the buyers insist that they continue to offer lower prices without the stamps.

1. With which side do you agree? Why?
2. Discuss the advantages and disadvantages of trading stamps.

PROJECT 1

The Benton Co., a retailer of hardware, has been purchasing its goods from six different wholesalers during the past few years. It has not purchased enough from any one wholesaler to be considered a meaningful account, although collectively its purchases amount to $200,000 annually. In order to become a more important account (which probably would result in better service), Benton is now trying to determine from which one or two wholesalers it should purchase.

1. Should Benton limit its purchases to one or two wholesalers, assuming their merchandise offerings are similar? Discuss.
2. Prepare a list of those items that would be important in considering the selection of a particular source.

PROJECT 2

These figures were available from the suit buyer for Eric's Men's Shop on February 16:

Present inventory at retail (February 16)	$125,000
Inventory commitments (February 16)	11,500
Planned markdowns	1,200
Actual markdowns	600

Planned end-of-month inventory (February 28)   150,000
Planned sales   65,000
Actual sales   35,500
Determine the buyer's open to buy.

PROJECT 3

Interview two buyers or assistant buyers from two different kinds of retail stores. After selecting two, record the information obtained in the interviews. By comparing two distinct buying jobs, you will be better able to select the type that most meets your needs and desires.

1. Select and check the types of buyers you have interviewed.

   _____ Small independent store

   _____ Department store

   _____ Large specialty store

   _____ Chain organization

   _____ Off-price store

   _____ Other (indicate type) _____

2. Complete the comparison form.

Comparison of Buyers (or Assistants)

	Buyer 1	Buyer 2
	(Indicate type)	(Indicate type)
Size of store		
Merchandise purchased by the buyer		
Merchandise price range		
Duties and responsibilities		
Personal qualities needed for job (as indicated by buyer)		

Other pertinent comments

1. After comparing both positions, which do you feel provides the better future?
2. What are your reasons?

CHAPTER 5

Merchandising

Opening Vignette
Learning Objectives
Introduction
Merchandising Philosophies
Merchandising Mathematics
Markup
Based on Retail
Based on Cost
Hand-Held Calculators
Factors Affecting Pricing
Buyer's Judgment of Appeal of Goods
Competition
Private Brands
Exclusive Offers
Characteristics of Goods
High-Risk Merchandise
Tradition
High Overhead Merchandise
Merchandise Turnover
Promotional Activities
Leaders and Loss Leaders
Store Image
Discounting
Alterations
Easily Soiled or Damaged Goods

Pilferage
Setting Price Lines
Markdowns
Reasons for Markdowns
Buying Errors
Selling Errors
Nonerror Markdowns
High Opening Prices
Weather
Poor Assortment
Timing Markdowns
Markdown or Carryover
Early versus Late Markdowns
Automatic Markdowns
How Much to Mark Down
Calculating the Percentage of Markdown
Small Store Adaptation
Career Opportunities
Key Points in the Chapter
Complete the Following Statements
True or False Questions
Multiple-Choice Questions
Discussion Questions
Case Problems
Projects

COLLECTIONS ARE NOT LIMITED TO ARTWORK

Until a few years ago, manufacturers and retailers were totally committed to merchandising by classification. That is, most merchandisers hired separate buyers for suits, pants, sweaters, shirts, and so on, and each category of items was arranged on the selling floor according to the specific classification into which it fell. Pants, regardless of manufacturer, were grouped together, as were sweaters, suits, and so forth.

A departure from this format was initiated by such designers as Calvin Klein and Yves St. Laurent, who sold some innovative retailers on the idea of merchandising their lines as a total concept, or collection, instead of mingling their offerings with other vendors' goods. The new concept required a number of changes that were previously considered inappropriate. Management, in general, wasn't sure that customers would be able to adjust to the new merchandising technique. Under the then-current classification arrangement, the shopper was given an assortment of sweaters that would generally satisfy his or her needs. He or she could choose from many labels, all displayed in one area.

Merchandising a collection provides the shopper with a total look. All of the merchandise has a connecting theme—color, fabric, style, and so forth. Once the customer is satisfied with a collection, chances are that he or she will purchase more than one item. For example, if the pants and sweaters are already coordinated, it is likely that both items will be bought.

The collections approach has become an important part of most major retail operations, but at first it presented problems. It took some stores two years to be convinced of the necessity for one collections buyer, rather than have several responsible for a particular category in the line. Space was also a problem. Retailers had to reorganize and reallocate their selling space to accommodate the collections concept. The visual merchandisers were given the challenge to create displays that would appeal to the customers and motivate them to buy. Finally, the customer had to be reeducated to understand the collections concept.

Today, every progressive retailer has jumped on the collections bandwagon. The likes of Perry Ellis, Liz Claiborne, Henry Grethel, Evan Picone, and Ralph Lauren are found in specific areas. These and other names designate areas that are set aside to house all of one manufacturer's offerings, enabling the shopper to find goods that go together. No longer need the customer who buys a sweater in the sweater department go to the skirt department to "make a match."

A further extension of the collections philosophy of merchandising is the concept of "crossover" or "androgynous dressing," where a manufacturer's offerings of both mens- and womenswear are housed in one area. Robinson's, the California-based company, presents men's and women's clothing in the Red Bag Sportswear Department. Robinson's has discovered that men and women feel comfortable shopping in the same department. What was considered taboo a couple of years ago is becoming an acceptable, and successful, method of merchandising.

At this time, the collections concept is well-entrenched. Stores are constantly shifting their spaces to accommodate the new philosophy. And the arrangement is no longer restricted to designer names, but to companies such as Jag, Esprit, Willi Wear, Guess, and Generra, all of which are being presented as collections.

LEARNING OBJECTIVES

Upon completion of this chapter, the student should be able to

1. List eight factors that affect pricing.
2. Explain the advantages and limitations of merchandise inventory turnover.
3. Define price lines, listing four advantages of their use.
4. List and discuss five reasons for markdowns.
5. Discuss the timing of markdowns, including automatic markdowns.

INTRODUCTION

The term merchandising is not simple to define. Some consider it a word that describes a retail organization's pricing strategy; others consider it a word that encompasses the activities involved in the buying and selling cycle; and still others use it as an overall definitive retailing term that signifies all of a store's concepts, including, but not limited to, pricing, display, promotion, and purchasing. One need only consult any large retailer's organization structure and job description of a merchandiser to find there is rarely any uniformity of definition from one company to another.

In the context of this chapter, all of the above-mentioned factors are considered. Because much of the material on such subjects as promotion and display is more fully explored in other parts of the book, most attention here is on the pricing aspect of merchandising. Too few novices appreciate or comprehend the mathematics and considerations of a store's pricing policy and why specific merchandise pricing considerations are carefully planned.

MERCHANDISING PHILOSOPHIES

From the outside, looking in, the customer should at once recognize what the store's message, image, or philosophy is. When one looks into any of The Limited's more than 500 units, the immediate impact is a current color story, a promotional sale, or a specific type of a designer that is The Limited's alone. Display is the key to The Limited's merchandising philosophy. Large posters at the entrance and throughout the store tell the shopper what's currently hot. For example, Kenzo, the designer of international fame, may have the spotlight for his exclusive collection for The Limited. Another merchandising policy for this organization deals with "preseason" sales. Recognizing the fact that customers are willing to spend before the season if the price is right, The Limited offers discounts much the same as others do for after-season goods. At a particular date, merchandise is readjusted to the regular price.

Syms, the off-price retailer, has another merchandising philosophy. In its women's department, the company combines the concept of off-price with that of automatic markdown. Each piece of merchandise not only ensures the customer a bargain price, but an even lower price, premarked according to specific dates, the longer the merchandise remains in stock. Through Sym's television advertising, the shopper is alerted to the store's merchandising policy and motivated to return again and again for prices that promise to fall.

Some philosophies are traditional and commonplace in retail, with others reaching for uniqueness. With branches on Rodeo Drive in Beverly Hills, California, and on Fifth Avenue in New York City, Bijan, a men's specialty store, provides exclusivity and snob appeal for would-be purchasers. Its philosophy is based on "appointments only." Passersby cannot simply enter the store to browse or purchase. The "no open door policy" seems to be working for this store, which features, among other items, $2,000 suits.

Whether its merchandising policy revolves around service, discounts, fashion innovation, unique pricing, or imaginative promotions, a store must pay attention first to the bottom line, or profit potential. Thus, it is essential for those interested in this aspect of retailing to have a keen understanding of the mathematics used to reach the desired goals and the various factors that affect merchandise pricing.

Whatever the pricing policy is for a retail organization, it rarely changes. Customers expect certain prices at certain stores. Once these are set in the minds of customers, a change is unlikely unless the entire organization is to undergo change.

MERCHANDISING MATHEMATICS

Computers afford the merchandiser endless analytical information, but it is still vital that the basic mathematical computations be understood. One area of merchandising math that provides the retailer with invaluable figures is markup.

Markup

Markup is the difference between the amount paid for goods and the price for which the goods are sold. In retailing, where profits are only made through selling, the markup must be high enough to provide for all of the expenses of operating the store plus a profit. For example, a store with merchandise on hand that cost $100,000 and operating expenses of $25,000 must sell the goods for $125,000 to break even. The store's profit thus depends on the amount in excess of $125,000 for which the goods can be sold.

Whatever the selling price, the markup is the difference between cost of the goods and its selling price:

$$\text{selling price} - \text{cost} = \text{markup}$$

A dress purchased for $25 and offered for sale at $40 would have a markup of $15:

$$\text{selling price } \$40 - \text{cost } \$25 = \text{markup } \$15$$

The determination of the cost of the goods frequently requires calculation.

Illustrative Problem

A store purchases 100 sweaters at $10 each. It must pay incoming freight on the order of $12, and it is entitled to a quantity discount of 10% and a cash discount of 2%. What is the cost per sweater?

Solution

Cost of goods purchased 100 × 10 =	$1,000.00
Less quantity discount 10%	100.00
	$ 900.00
Less cash discount 2%	18.00
	$ 882.00
Add freight costs	12.00
Actual cost of 100 sweaters	$ 894.00
÷ 100 = actual cost per sweater	$ 8.94

Note that the cash discount is taken before freight is added on and after the quantity discount has been taken. The reason for this is that the cash discount is given for prompt payment of the amount of cash due on the merchandise, and vendors do not allow discounts on freight. The rule in determining costs is to adjust the price by all additional costs and reductions.

Although it is important to know the dollar markup, buyers and merchandisers whose responsibility it is to set markup are more concerned with markup percentage. The markup percentage can be based on either retail (selling price) or cost. Markup expressed as a percentage of retail is used primarily by department stores and fashion merchandisers. Retailers of perishables and hardware lines usually figure markup as a percentage of cost.

Based on Retail

Formerly, markup was always based on cost. However, thanks to the efforts of the National Merchants Association, retail research bureaus, and many universities, department stores and other alert retailers are now using a system of markup based on sales. These are the advantages:

1. Since sales information is much more easily determined than costs, a markup based on sales greatly facilitates the calculation of estimated profits.
2. Inventory taking requires the calculation of the cost of merchandise on hand. The retail inventory method used by most retailers is based on markup at retail and provides a shortcut for determining inventory at cost.
3. Most retailers calculate markup based on retail. This provides inter-store comparisons of such vital information as gross profit and net profit.
4. To the consumer, the smaller the percentage of markup, the more reasonably priced the store. Markup based on retail provides a smaller percentage.
5. Salespersons' commissions, officers' bonuses, rents, and other vital operating information are based on sales. It is reasonable to base markup on sales as well.

To find the markup percentage based on retail, the dollar markup—the difference between the cost and the retail price—is divided by the retail price.

Illustrative Problem

A shirt that cost $13 retails for $20. Find the markup percentage based on retail.

Solution

To find the dollar markup:

$$\begin{aligned} \text{markup} &= \text{retail} - \text{cost} \\ &= \$20 - \$13 \\ &= \$7 \end{aligned}$$

To find the markup percentage based on retail:

$$\frac{\text{markup}}{\text{retail}} = \text{markup \% on retail}$$

$$\frac{\$7}{\$20} = 35\% \text{ markup on retail}$$

Illustrative Problem

A retail store buyer purchases a jacket for $35 and sells it for $42. What is the dollar markup? What is the markup percentage based on retail?

Solution

To find the dollar markup:

$$\text{markup} = \text{retail} - \text{cost}$$
$$= \$42 - \$35$$
$$= \$7$$

To find the markup percentage based on retail:

$$\frac{\text{markup}}{\text{retail}} = \text{markup \% on retail}$$

$$\frac{\$7}{\$42} = 16 \ 2/3\% \text{ markup on retail}$$

Comparing the markups in both problems, we find they have the same dollar markup. By computing and comparing the percentages, we see the importance of markup percentage to the retailer. The first markup percentage, 35%, is certainly better than the second, 16 2/3%.

Based on Cost

Although basing markup on retail has become common, some retailers still use a markup system based on cost. This is frequently the result of inertia and resistance to change, but some establishments are better served by calculating markup on cost. Typical is a dealer in produce whose costs of fruits and vegetables vary from day to day, according to the supply and demand at the wholesale produce markets. Under such conditions, where the cost of inventories is unimportant (they completely sell out every few days), and the profit and loss figures can be easily determined, markup based on cost is preferable.

To find the markup percentage based on cost, the dollar markup is divided by the cost.

Illustrative Problem

A camera cost the retailer $33 and sells for $44. Find the markup percentage based on cost.

Solution

To find the dollar markup:

$$\text{markup} = \text{retail} - \text{cost}$$
$$= \$44 - \$33$$
$$= \$11$$

To find the markup percentage based on cost:

$$\frac{markup}{cost} = markup\ \%\ on\ cost$$

$$\frac{\$11}{\$33} = 33\ 1/3\%\ markup\ on\ cost$$

Hand-Held Calculators

When visiting the market to make purchases, the buyer often finds it necessary to determine the individual markup on an item, markup percentage, unit price, average markup, cumulative markup, markdown, and so forth. The best tool to come along to perform these calculations is the hand-held calculator. For as little as $10 (sometimes even less), this type of calculator can be purchased to perform these arithmetic chores quickly and easily.

FACTORS AFFECTING PRICING

As we have seen, the selling price of an item consists of its cost plus a markup that will be sufficient to yield a profit after covering operating expenses. The prime function of management is to maximize profits, and the pricing policy is the key to profit determination. This does not mean that the higher the prices, the greater the profit. It does mean, however, that management must choose a pricing policy that will result in the greatest profitability. Pricing schemes may range from that of a discounter that feels that the additional business brought into the store by low prices will more than offset a smaller profit margin to that of a high-fashion store that offers many services and a prestigious label in return for a higher price. Before a pricing policy can be selected, however, many factors must be considered.

Buyer's Judgment of Appeal of Goods

It is unusual to find a store that uses a uniform percentage of markup for all of its goods. Even within a department, the percentage may vary from style to style. A good merchant should have a feel for pricing. This person should know what customers are willing to pay for an item, and mark up accordingly. In fact, there is sometimes little relationship between the actual cost of an item and its customer appeal. Within certain established minimums and maximums, a buyer should set prices at what he or she thinks the goods should bring in. Bearing the competition in mind, the retailer can frequently improve the overall markup of a department by pricing certain styles in excess of the average markup. The department's average markup, rather than individual markup, is most important to the store.

If all buying decisions were automatic, it would not be necessary for retail operations to employ buyers. Most professionals, however, agree that buyers and their judgment provide in great part for the success or failure of a store. If buyers' skills were rated, their ability to judge the appeal of goods would be at the top of the list.

To retail an item at a fraction lower than is possible is a potential threat to profit, whereas marking merchandise too high could result not only in lower sales but also in later markdowns. It is the ability of the keenly aware buyer that sets the proper price for the greatest sales potential.

Competition

One consideration to bear in mind when setting prices is the pricing policies of competing stores. Decisions must be made as whether to set prices above, at, or below those of a competitor. If the services, conveniences of location, and other factors are such that consumers will pay a higher price for goods from our store than from a competitor's, perhaps we should use a high pricing policy. On the other hand, a high pricing policy would certainly drive some business away. How much? Does it pay to set high prices? These are the sort of problems management must face, and they fall into an area for market research specialists.

Whatever the pricing policy selected, it is vital that a store know the prices and quality of goods being offered by its competitors. For this purpose, stores employ comparison shoppers—people who spend their working hours studying the competition and reporting on prices, hot items, services, and other vital information.

To emphasize the importance of competition in pricing, it should be pointed out that some retailers advertise that they will meet all prices of competition. Some go as far as to refund the difference if it can be shown that merchandise purchased at their store could have been purchased cheaper elsewhere. (This is usually checked by the comparison shopper.)

To have customers find that they can buy the exact item at a lower price in a competitor's store is damaging to a retailer's image. The customers' impression is that not only were they overcharged on the item in question but that overpricing may be the general policy of the store. To overcome this situation, retailers are forced to find, in addition to their regular goods, items they can mark up liberally with no fear of being undersold by a competitor—the principle of exclusivity. This merchandise is made available as private brand items and exclusively offered goods.

Private Brands

One way to minimize competition is to sell an exclusive item, and thus one that cannot be compared in another store. It is only when a customer can find the same item, exact in every detail and carrying the same label, in two stores that prices can be compared. If the items are dissimilar, the store can always claim that the higher priced item is of better quality and worth more. It is for this reason that the use of private brands is becoming increasingly important.

There are virtually no large retailers that have not plunged into the private brand market. Mitchell Paige, a manufacturing consultant, has worked successfully for such major retailers as Bamberger's, Marshall Field, Garfinckel's and Sakowitz in the creation of specifically designed merchandise bearing their own private labels and thus defying competition. Dayton's, Minneapolis, has moved full speed ahead in private brands and reports great success.

Smaller stores, unable to go into private brands and labels on their own because of limited purchasing power, do so through their resident buying offices. Frederick Atkins, a resident office, has private label merchandise for its member stores.

Exclusive Offers

Another method of limiting price competition by the principle of exclusivity is by agreement with the manufacturer. For example, a dress shop in a small town gets an agreement from the manufacturer that the manufacturer will not sell to any of the shop's competitors in that town. A customer is then unable to compare prices between stores. Agreements with manufacturers are not limited to small users. In large cities with many competing department stores, often only one particular style is available in one store.

Characteristics of Goods

The amount of profit that various classifications of merchandise must bring in depends in large part on the specific characteristics of the goods. For example, staple goods, which are not subject to style or seasonal losses, may be sold at a smaller markup than goods that are seasonal or perishable. Similarly, some goods are bulky and require large amounts of floor space, whereas others require expensive selling personnel. In large part, it is the nature of the goods that dictates pricing policy.

High-Risk Merchandise

High-risk merchandise is items that, because of their perishability, seasonable nature, or high styling, are almost certain to suffer some markdown before being sold. The markup on such goods must be sufficient to cover such eventuality. This merchandise can be best described as fashion, seasonal, or perishable goods.

Fashion goods. When we speak of fashion goods, high-styled womenswear comes to mind. The characteristics of this merchandise can be explained by example. The buyer of the women's dress department has a hot style. Ten of the initial order of fourteen dresses were sold in two days. Since then, the buyer has brought 200 pieces into the store, of which 180 have been sold. Sales of the dress are beginning to slow down, and some markdowns must be taken. Thus, the markup will have to be high enough to cover both this style and other less successful numbers.

Contrast this with sales in the hardware department, where staples are sold and markdowns are negligible. It is obvious that high-risk fashion goods are subject to markdowns and that to be successful, their selling price must be sufficient to cover these losses.

Seasonal goods.   Another type of high-risk goods for which the selling price must be high enough to cover future losses is seasonal goods, such as swimsuits, furs, and toys. Characteristic of such goods is the fact that once the season is over, the retailer is faced with the choice either of cutting the price drastically or holding the goods until next year. Holding merchandise until the following season ties up capital that should be used for salable merchandise throughout the year. Moreover, heldover merchandise must eventually compete with newer styled goods; further, it has been handled, and customers may remember it from the previous year. Also, the merchandise may no longer be desirable. When retailers of swimsuits walk around with a worried expression on their faces during an unusually rainy spring, there is good reason for it. Many stores charge high prices at the beginning of the season, under the assumption that customers who shop early are willing to pay more. This provides a cushion for the markdowns that will come later in the season.

Perishable goods.   Consider florists. They run businesses without markdowns. Once a rose is withered, it is unsalable. Florists can't sell out to the last piece, since they do not want to lose trade by not having goods always available. Here, again, we find retailers with built-in inventory losses that must price their goods at a level that will cover such losses.

A produce market where fruits and vegetables are sold faces a similar problem. These retailers, too, cannot be in business without taking inventory losses. Every day a certain percentage of produce must be drastically reduced in price or actually thrown away. This must be taken into account when prices are set.

Tradition

Traditionally, some goods command a higher markup and selling price than others. This is true despite the fact that they may be less risky, perishable, or seasonal. Men's shoes, although they are much more of a staple item, usually afford a better markup than the much riskier women's shoes. Apparently, people are accustomed to paying certain prices for certain articles, and the retailer is able to set a price accordingly.

High Overhead Merchandise

By their nature, certain classifications of goods require an unusual amount of overhead. In pricing such goods, provision must be made for any unusually high overhead costs so that a normal profit will remain after the additional expense is paid. Merchandise of extreme bulk or high value is part of this group.

Bulky merchandise.   Such merchandise as furniture and carpeting, because of its size, requires an unusually large amount of floor space and, consequently, rent expense. In marking up such goods, the selling price must be high enough to cover the excessive rent charges. As a result, traditional furniture stores usually double their costs to arrive at the selling price (50 percent on retail). Failure to set a high enough selling price would result in losses.

Precious jewelry. The additional expenses required to carry a line of precious jewelry are considerable: A vault must be installed to store the goods. Highly paid salespersons are necessary, since the items are expensive and a knowledge of the subject matter is required. However, some of the additional overhead is counteracted by the fact that less rental area is required for a jewelry store or department than for displaying many other goods.

Merchandise Turnover

Of great importance to the pricing policy of a store is the effect that lower prices will have on sales. In a competitive economy, as selling prices decline, sales rise. Suppose store A does $100,000 per year at a 40% markup on sales. The cost of operation is $20,000. This is its income statement for 1984:

Sales	$100,000
Cost of goods sold	60,000
Gross margin (40%)	$ 40,000
Less: operating expenses	20,000
Net profit	$ 20,000

In 1985 the pricing policy is changed, reducing the markup to 33 1/3% of sales. The 1985 income statement follows:

Sales	$150,000
Cost of goods sold	100,000
Gross margin (33 1/3%)	$ 50,000
Less: operating expenses	25,000
Net profit	$ 25,000

A comparison of the two statements indicates that the decrease in markup resulted in an increase in sales. The larger sales required a relatively small increase in operating expenses because the rent, heat and light, advertising, and many other costs do not vary directly with sales.

Certain merchandise is slower moving than others. Retailers describe this by saying the stock turns over fewer times per year. A produce market sells (turns over) its stock every few days, whereas a furniture store's turnover is rarely more than a few times per year. A store with a quick turnover can afford a small markup and low prices because it will receive that markup many times during the year. This is another reason for the variation of pricing policies among various classifications of merchandise.

Promotional Activities

Another factor affecting retail pricing policies is the amount of promoting and advertising a store does. Promotional activities are expensive, and the cost of getting the customer into the store must be included in the selling price of the goods. This does not mean that stores with the highest advertising budgets are those with the highest markup. Quite the reverse. Frequently, the biggest promoters are those stores that depend on small markups to increase their turnover and in this way pay for their promotional activities. The point is that whatever the pricing policy of the store, the markup must be sufficient to cover the advertising budget.

Should each individual department's pricing policies be sufficient to cover its individual advertising budget? This becomes slightly more difficult, since a store might be willing to break even on a department (such departments are called leaders) or even sell below cost (loss leader department) as a promotional means of getting people into the store. It is felt that a customer who is brought into the store by a leader or loss leader is likely to buy other items from more profitable departments.

Leaders and Loss Leaders

Several fundamental requirements of a good leader follow:

1. It must be an item that would interest a large number of customers. Since the purpose of the leader is to bring customers into the store, to be successful the item must appeal to a large segment of the buying public.
2. It must not be an item used as a leader by a competitor, since this would reduce the number of customers brought to the store.
3. The price cut must be important enough to bring the customers to the store in quantity.

There are disadvantages to the use of leaders. For one thing, the shopper may not buy anything but the leader, resulting in a loss. Some stores featuring leaders in their promotional schemes advise their salespeople to try to sell the customer regular goods. This frequently leads to customer resentment. Leader merchandising is unfair to competitors that charge a legitimate price for the same item. This last aspect is so important that many states have laws making it illegal to sell goods below cost.

Store Image

It is wrong to assume that all purchasers are price-conscious. Many stores, particularly in the higher price ranges, are able to attract customers despite a higher than normal markup. The store's "name," for example, is more important to some customers than the prices it charges. Many shoppers willingly pay a premium to have a Lord & Taylor, Saks Fifth Avenue, or Brooks Brothers label on their garments. Other customers are willing to pay more to these prestige stores for the extra services offered, or because they like the wide assortment of merchandise, the way it is displayed, and so forth.

Prestige stores, although they benefit from their higher than normal markup, are not necessarily more successful than their opposite number, the discounters. The prestige factor often requires a very high cost of operations. Improved sales service means more and higher priced sales help. The store's furnishings, fixtures, displays, and so on are more expensive, as are many of its other operating expenses. Since massive clearance sales would be detrimental to their image, prestige stores have serious problems in disposing of their slow-moving goods. Consequently, although they have, to some degree, taken themselves out of the rat race of price competition, it is only at the cost of a new set of problems.

Discounting

While prestige stores and neighborhood stores fight price competition by offering "label appeal" and special services, the discounters are squarely in the center of the price battle—and that is exactly where they want to be. They reason this way: The one most important element in selling is price. The great majority of customers are not interested in frills. When the price is right, they'll buy. Moreover, they'll buy so much, and the merchandise will be turned over so quickly, that small profits per sale will be more than offset by the increased number of sales. In the typical discount operation, one finds bare walls and a minimum of customer services. The operation is designed such that all expenses are held to a minimum with the exception of advertising. Since one of the functions of markup is to cover the operating expenses, less markup is required, and the goods may be sold less expensively.

Not all of a discounter's merchandise is sold at a low markup. Like the more conventional retailers, the discounter sells many high-profit items. These items, of course, must be off-brands that cannot be comparison-shopped elsewhere.

Alterations

Once pricing policy has been set, the question of whether or not the customer is to be charged for alterations has been answered. That is, stores that have decided on an above-normal markup in return for additional services generally consider the cost of alterations as one of the services that is offered to their customers. On the other hand, a discount store that has curtailed services so that it can employ a less than normal markup would be unlikely to offer "free" alterations. There is room for compromise in this area. For example, a menswear department may not charge for shortening sleeves or cuffing trousers. However, it may refuse to do major alterations or charge extra. In the event that alterations are free to customers, the selling price must be adjusted to reflect this additional expense.

Easily Soiled or Damaged Goods

Toys, white gloves, and a host of other merchandise classifications become shopworn in a short time. They frequently require special handling on the shelves and special care from the sales personnel. Markup, by definition, must be sufficient to cover the costs of the item and provide a profit. If no such provision is made in the markup, the profit on fragile goods will be below the amount expected.

Pilferage

In recent years losses through pilferage have increased at an alarming rate. This has occurred despite a substantial increase in the cost of security maintenance. It is unfortunate that honest shoppers are forced to pay for the losses incurred through dishonest people. If a store is to be successful, however, its markup policy must be one that will cover the high cost of security, as well as the merchandise losses that result from shoplifting.

SETTING PRICE LINES

It is impossible to find a retailer, no matter how large the organization, that offers merchandise in every possible price category. When Macy's decided to alter its merchandising structure a few years ago and "traded up" to carry merchandise at the highest price levels, it did so at the expense of its "lower end" goods. The reasons for limiting merchandise to within a certain range or line are many.

Space limitations necessitate narrowing the merchandise assortment offered. If every conceivable price were made available, there wouldn't be sufficient selling space to offer the customers the necessary breadth and depth of each item to make a choice.

Different priced merchandise warrants different customer services. The higher the price, the more attention each shopper is generally given. Thus, a $1,500 dress would require the finest in personal attention, whereas the $35 garment might be merchandised on a self-selection basis. Which would the store lean to if all of the price lines were stocked?

Store image would be hard to protect. Most people entering a store know what to expect from the decor, displays, promotions, and so on. An enormously wide price line wouldn't lend itself to easy image association. Customers, on entering a store, know how much they will be expected to spend. This awareness rids the store of disinterested browsers and motivates people to enter who can or will buy.

There are no real trends in price lines today. There is, however, a tendency for stores to be at the lower or upper end in regard to price, with middle of the road philosophies becoming less popular.

Even with the best planning marking merchandise doesn't totally work out. To get rid of goods, often prices must be reduced. To understand the nature of markdowns—reductions in selling price—one must start with the concept that the original price is nothing more than a temporary estimate of what the customer is willing to spend.

Reasons for Markdowns

Markdowns may be caused by faulty sales price, buying errors, selling and merchandise-handling errors, and other reasons not related to human mistakes. When the original selling price is set at too high a level, or at a level above competitors' prices, markdowns inevitably result. Generally these price reductions are such that the final selling price is lower than the amount that the goods could have been sold for if they were properly marked originally.

Buying Errors

Many markdowns are the result of buying misjudgments. Overbuying is probably the principal cause of markdowns. It may come about through large initial orders instead of small lot ordering to test consumer appeal. Overoptimistic sales planning is another common cause of over-buying.

The inability to forecast perfectly the buying habits of a store's clientele frequently leads to markdowns. Often, goods that would be readily salable in the proper colors and sizes cannot be sold because of these errors. This, of course, results in markdowns.

Markdowns are frequently the result of ordering goods too late in the season. Goods bought too late often cannot be sold because the customer is no longer interested.

Selling Errors

Faulty sales practices result in markdowns. Merchandise that could have been sold with proper display or salesmanship or departmental neatness is sometimes marked down—thus decreasing profits. Lazy sales personnel who take the line of least resistance by selling the fast-moving numbers instead of taking the time to sell the slower movers also cause markdowns. Furthermore, overeager salespersons whose high-pressure tactics end up in returns late in the season are a cause of markdowns.

Nonerror Markdowns

Not all markdowns are the result of errors. Some are beyond human ingenuity; others are actually planned. Occasionally, new products reach the market that make the older goods obsolete. In such cases the entire stock of obsolete merchandise must be marked down drastically and quickly.

No matter how competent a buyer is or how talented the salespeople, there will always be odd sizes and styles and shopworn merchandise that cannot be sold without markdowns.

High Opening Prices

Reasoning that a person willing to purchase early in the season will be willing to pay a premium for their purchases, some buyers set higher than normal opening prices on their goods. This both helps to make up for future losses and gets a good price from those shoppers who wait for markdowns before making their purchase.

Weather

Seasonable goods depend on the weather. A store stocks a certain amount of merchandise in anticipation of certain weather conditions. If the weather is not as expected, the goods are not sold and customers must be lured in by markdown prices. In New York City, spring is short and uncertain. After a particularly rainy spring, markdowns follow as certainly as summer.

Poor Assortment

It is bad policy for a store to offer a limited assortment of goods at any time during a season. Future sales depend on a customer's confidence in being able always to find an abundance of goods to choose from. Many merchandisers will protect the store's image by buying goods, to provide a rich assortment, late in the season. They do this knowing full well that many of the goods are destined for eventual markdown.

Timing Markdowns

Markdown or Carryover

When the markdown required to sell merchandise becomes excessive, a merchant has to decide whether to carry the goods over to the same season of the following year. Frequently, the goods will bring a higher price at the beginning of the season in the following year than at the end of the current season. This fact must be weighed against the following disadvantages of carrying over:

1. The money tied up in the carried-over inventory will not be available for new styles for a full year. This will have the effect of reducing the assortment of new styles until these old goods are sold.
2. It is expensive to carry over in terms of warehousing costs, insurance, warehouse labor, and interest on money borrowed to carry additional inventories.
3. Carried-over goods tend to become shopworn or broken.
4. The store's image will be damaged in the eyes of those shoppers who remember the goods from the previous year.

Generally, well-managed stores limit their carryovers to those staple goods that are packaged in such a fashion that they will retain their fresh look in the following year. Fashion merchandise should never be carried over.

Early versus Late Markdowns

Of principal importance in the timing of markdowns is whether to reduce prices early in the season on an individual basis or to hold the prices firm until late in the season and then have a storewide sale. There is considerable difference of opinion among retailers on the issue of when to mark down. The arguments favoring early markdowns are

1. Goods that are reduced early in the season while the customers are still in a buying mood can generally bring in more money than they would at the end of the season. Thus, the amount of markdown will be less.
2. The money brought in by early markdowns can be used for newer and better styles that may be turned over many times.
3. End-of-season sales frequently require additional sales personnel and therefore raise the cost of operations.

Arguments favoring late markdowns are

1. Customers become aware of a store's early markdown policies and will wait to make their purchase, knowing they can buy reduced merchandise early in the season.
2. Some goods that do not sell well early in the season suddenly take off and do very well. If these goods are marked down early, they will not bring in as much money as they should.
3. Prestige stores prefer not to have bargain hunters in their stores until they need them. A policy of limiting markdowns to season-end sales accomplishes this.

Many stores compromise between early and late markdowns. When the sales of an item slow down, and the quantity on hand is excessive, the item will be reduced for quick sale. At the end of the season, a clearance sale will be used to clear out all of the unsold goods.

Automatic Markdowns

The policy of automatic markdowns is best illustrated by the basement store of Filene's of Boston. Filene's marks down all goods that have been in the store for a specific number of days, by a specific percentage. Goods that fail to sell after two weeks are marked down 25 percent and are reduced an additional 25 percent each successive week. At the end of five weeks all unsold goods are given to charity.

How Much to Mark Down

Because the purpose of markdowns is to move goods, the amount of price reduction must be enough to satisfy customers. A $19.75 item marked down to $18.75 will probably not increase its sales appeal; shoppers willing to pay $18.75 would probably pay $19.75 as well. To sell the goods, a reduction to $16.75 would probably be necessary. When markdowns are taken early in the season, there is frequently time for a second markdown before the season ends. Consequently, early markdowns are usually smaller than late-season reductions. Markdowns are usually taken on an individual basis, depending on quantity, original price, and time of markdown.

Calculating the Percentage of Markdown

An important aspect of markdown is the markdown percentage based on actual sales. The markdown percentage may be calculated when the markdown from the original retail (selling price) is known.

Illustrative Problem

A retail store buyer decides to reduce the price of her entire inventory 15%. The inventory is $5,000 at retail. What is the markdown percentage based on sales, assuming she sells the entire inventory?

Solution

1. Determine the dollar markdown:

original retail × reduction percentage = markdown
$5,000 × 0.15 = $750

2. Determine the actual sales:

original retail − reduction = sales (new retail)
$5,000 − $750 = $4,250

3. Determine the markdown percentage on sales:

$$\text{markdown \%} = \frac{\text{markdown}}{\text{sales}}$$

$$= \frac{750}{4,250}$$

$$= 17.6\%$$

SMALL STORE ADAPTATION

Merchandising in a large retail operation involves an enormous number of line and staff personnel who help create the store's image and merchandising philosophy. As we have discussed, merchandising encompasses all of the buying and selling activities and the advisory functions, such as fashion coordination, comparison shopping, and so forth. Of paramount importance is the entire area of merchandise pricing and the ramifications of satisfactory markups and timely markdowns.

The concept of merchandising in a small store often lies in the hands of the owner or, at best, in the hands of a very small team. This individual, or team, must constantly examine the competition's offerings through window display investigation, comparison of advertisements, and other store activities to see if their own operation is current and timely. Not one of these activities requires substantial cost, the worry of every small store.

In pricing, attention must be paid to two specific factors, markup and markdown. It is wisest never to mark up higher than the large store does (its prices are regularly seen in advertisements) and to take markdowns as soon as the indicators require it. It has long been the practice of many small stores to maintain the original price too long, only to find that when the price has finally been reduced, there are no takers. Customers have already been satisfied by the large companies that know the value of stock turnover. Failing to mark down early often leaves merchandise that some small merchants choose to carry over to the next season. If the small retailer follows no other rule, the one to adhere to religiously is never, never, never store merchandise for sale next year. With constant style changes and new fashion direction, as well as the "tired" look of the past season's merchandise, it usually becomes dead inventory.

When attention is paid to those simple principles, the small retailer can surely compete with the knowledgeable giants.

CAREER OPPORTUNITIES

The ultimate goal for most buyers is to reach the level of merchandise manager. Examination of the organization chart of any large retail organization shows two levels of merchandisers. The top position is that of the general merchandise manager with the divisional merchandise managers directly under the supervision and authority of this individual. Since the actual number of a store's merchandisers is few by comparison with the buyers and assistant buyers, the likelihood of rising to this position is limited to few. To reach the level of divisional merchandise manager (DMM) usually demands a great number of years as a buyer, and attainment of the general merchandise manager (GMM) position, several years as a buyer and divisional manager.

The career of the top merchandise manager, the GMM, is most demanding. The position is one of policymaker as well as operating officer. The GMM is a member of the store's top management team and is directly responsible for meeting management's objectives in merchandising and enforcing the company's policies. He or she is directly involved in policy matters concerning price lines, image, quality levels, and style emphasis. Serving as the only link between the buyers and divisional merchandise managers, the position is one of the most powerful in the store.

Directly under the general merchandise manager are the DMMs. Each is responsible for a separate merchandise classification and for the number of buyers in the specific division. For example, the DMM for menswear might be responsible for individual buyers who purchase for such departments as clothing, furnishings, sportswear, shoes, and so forth. The role includes coordinating the efforts of the buyers, evaluating and informing buyers of particular merchandising trends concerning color, fabric, style, and so on, overseeing unit control systems, keeping track of open to buys, planning major purchases with the buyers, recommending promotional ideas, and overseeing the entire division. Whereas the GMM's role is one of overall merchandising management, the DMM operates specifically within his or her division, always bearing in mind the policies established by the senior merchandiser, the GMM.

Where retailing once gave the opportunity for reaching the level of merchandiser to anyone in the organization who showed merit, the career of merchandising manager today is generally restricted to those with advanced formal education as well as store experience. With the analytical know-how necessary to perform the rigors required of these top-level managers, it is unlikely that anyone less prepared could capably meet the challenges of the positions.

KEY POINTS IN THE CHAPTER

1. A store must project a merchandising philosophy so that the consumer will quickly understand what the store is trying to sell. These philosophies include off-price, high fashion, service, sale by appointment only, and many others.

2. Markup is the difference between cost and selling price. It is important that markup reflect a price to cover expenses and return a profit to the store.

3. Prices are based on a number of factors, including competition, appeal of the merchandise, perishability, overhead and image.

4. Merchandise turnover is how often the average inventory sells, and is a key factor in how a store prices its goods.

5. Stores establish price lines that indicate to the consumer the range of prices offered for sale from the lowest to the highest.

6. The best planning cannot sell every piece of merchandise at the price initially marked. Markdowns are taken because of buying and selling errors and such situations as poor weather, poor assortment, and high opening prices.

7. Unsold merchandise should not be carried over because it ties up capital, might go out of fashion, or is shopworn and unsalable the next season.

8. Automatic markdowns are used by retailers such as Filene's Basement of Boston and Syms. Customers are made aware of reductions on the sales tag for various selling periods.

Worksheet 5

COMPLETE THE FOLLOWING STATEMENTS

1. _____ is the key to The Limited's merchandising philosophy, with considerable attention paid to color.

2. Markup is the difference between _____ and

   _____.

3. Most retailers figure their markup percentage based on _____.

4. _____ are reductions in selling price.

5. The policy of _____ markdown is best illustrated by

   Filene's basement operation in Boston.

6. To determine markdown percentage one must divide _____ by

   _____.

7. Merchandise that is carried exclusively and bears the store's name is

   _____ merchandise.

8. Merchants restrict the goods they offer for sale to a particular dollar spread

   known as a _____.

TRUE OR FALSE

_____ 1. When the cost of inventories is unimportant because the merchandise sells out completely in a few days, merchants use the markup system based on cost.

_____ 2. Competition is a key factor in price determination.

_____ 3. Private branding enables the retailer to sell for less while at the same time increasing profits.

_____ 4. Tradition sometimes influences a particular markup.

_____ 5. There are disadvantages to the loss leader type of promotion.

_____ 6. Large department stores, because of their size, pay little attention to price line restriction.

_____ 7. Some markdowns are considered to be nonerror markdowns.

_____ 8. Most merchants agree it is better to carry all merchandise to the next season than to reduce it below cost.

_____ 9. The rate of turnover is a tool for judging managerial effectiveness.

MULTIPLE CHOICE

_____ 1. Markup percentage is based on
   (a) cost
   (b) retail
   (c) a and b
   (d) neither a nor b

_____ 2. If a shirt costs $20 and it sells for $40 its markup percentage is
   (a) 100
   (b) 50
   (c) a or b
   (d) neither a nor b

_____ 3. High-risk goods are best described by
   (a) women's dresses
   (b) toys
   (c) fresh flowers
   (d) all of the above

_____ 4. Buyers determine prices through
   (a) judgment or goods' appeal
   (b) store image
   (c) cost
   (d) all of the above

_____ 5. Markdowns are caused by
   (a) buyer error
   (b) nonbuyer errors
   (c) neither a nor b
   (d) a and b

DISCUSSION QUESTIONS

1. The success of a retail store depends in large part on its pricing policy. Why is this so?

2. Describe some of the merchandising philosophies of today's retailers.

3. Discuss the objections to a department store's policy of letting each buyer set his or her own pricing policy.

4. What are the difficulties involved in changing a store's basic pricing policies from pricing above competitors' prices to pricing below the competition?

5. A store's profits depend on the amount of its markup. Which factors must the markup be large enough to cover?

6. An item that cost $72 per dozen is sold for $8.75 each. Calculate the dollar markup per piece.

7. How much must be paid to settle an invoice of $740 that includes $14.50 for freight if it is subject to a quantity discount of 3% and a cash discount of 8%?

8. A belt costs $8 and retails for $12. What is the markup percentage on retail?

9. What markup percentage on retail will the buyer derive from a sweater costing $30 and retailing for $50?

10. Discuss the advantages of private brands.

11. Are high-risk goods marked up in the same manner as other goods? Discuss.

12. Why is the pricing policy of high overhead goods different from that of other goods?

13. Price lines are restrictive, that is, they limit the type of merchandise a store may carry. Why, then, are they extensively used?

14. Compare the stock turnover in a discount store with that of a traditional store. Does high turnover in itself indicate a successful operation?

15. Discuss five types of unavoidable markdowns.

CASE PROBLEM 1

Kings is a large, moderately priced department store located in the downtown shopping area of a large city. The store is profitable, well established, and popular. Its pricing policy is mostly traditional, but buyers frequently obtain closeouts and odd lots that they are able to offer at substantial savings. As a result, the store has the reputation of a place where bargains may be found.

The dress buyer, after carefully studying the operation of his high-image competitor, believes that a line of high-priced women's dresses would be very successful at Kings. He reasons that he could offer merchandise similar to that in the competitor's store. By pricing such goods at a traditional markup, a customer would be offered a considerable savings. The buyer understands that his store has a different clientele but argues that many well-to-do people are price-conscious and would come to Kings if the merchandise were available. In addition, he feels that many of Kings' customers frequently buy high-priced goods. Some customers are moderate-price buyers for certain goods and high-price buyers for other goods.

    1. Discuss fully why you agree or disagree with the dress buyer.

CASE PROBLEM 2

The Youth Shop, a partnership, has been in business for ten years. It is a small, popular-priced women's sportswear shop located in the downtown commercial area of a large midwestern town. The store has been successful despite vigorous competition, thanks to the partners' careful buying and excellent styling. The many years of profitable operation have put the store on a sound financial basis.

The Youth Shop's clientele consists chiefly of office help from the neighborhood. The busiest time of day is lunch hour. Since the weather during June was wet and cold, the sale of bathing suits was very poor. By July 4, 60 percent of the swimwear remained unsold.

One partner is in favor of carrying the goods over until next year. He argues that most of the customers have not shopped for swimwear and will not recognize the goods next year. In addition, there is no doubt that the price the suits will sell for next year will be more than the closeout price this year.

The other partner believes that a closeout sale as soon as possible is the wisest choice, since no money will be tied up for a year. Also, carried-over goods become shopworn, and the store's reputation for up-to-date styling might be hurt next year if new goods are limited to fill-ins.

1. Can you think of any other arguments to support either partner?
2. Is a compromise possible?

PROJECT 1

Find two items that are offered by different stores at different prices, and answer the following questions

1. Which store is more successful?
2. How can the high-price store survive if its goods are priced higher than those of its competitor?
3. What does the more expensive store offer to compensate for its higher prices?

PROJECT 2

Visit a large department store that carries private label merchandise. Select a private label item and compare it to a manufacturer's item. Complete the comparison chart.

Comparison Factors	Private Label	Manufacturer's Label
Price		
Packaging		
Special details		
Fiber content		
Size range		

Advertising and Sales Promotion

A GLOBAL ADVENTURE

Without question, the lion's share of a retailer's promotional budget is spent on advertising. One need only examine any major city's newspapers, especially on Sunday, to discover a wealth of store advertisement. The formats vary from store to store, as do the messages they convey. Each retail establishment hopes to capture the reader's attention and sufficiently motivate him or her to make a purchase.

It is every company's dream to be able to imaginatively motivate consumer spending. Directors of advertising and promotion are paid for their innovative and creative skills and ideas that will capture the minds and dollars of customers. Promotional dollars are not exclusively limited to advertising, however. Other concepts for promotions run the gamut from storewide sales to such institutionally oriented events as marathons for charity. Whatever the event, the bottom line must be profits for the organization.

Considered in the industry to be the height of promotional creativity has been the Bloomingdale's organization. It is evident from the extravagance of Bloomingdale's promotions and the enormous sums of dollars needed to carry off many of its events that management firmly believes that it is promotion that sets Bloomingdale's apart from the pack. While the company sponsors such events as artist demonstrations, fashion shows, charity galas, and so forth, none has gained as much publicity and profit for the store as its "Salutes to Nations." These undertakings are not merely cosmetic but involve a major effort by all of the store's divisions. In recent years, the nations "honored" have included Ireland, Israel, the United States, Portugal, China, and France. China, and "Fete de France," as the French promotion was called, were two "spectaculars" that involved considerable expenditures and enormous planning.

When Bloomingdale's promotes a country, it doesn't simply decorate the flagship store and its branches with display materials that bear the flavor of the country. Each merchandise classification is stocked with goods that originate from the country being promoted. This usually involves buyers and merchandisers traveling abroad to seek out merchandise that will fit the merchandising concept. Quantities must be carefully calculated to make certain that amounts are appropriate for the period of time in which the promotion is being staged. Both under- and overpurchasing can hamper the profit picture. Another problem associated with the purchase of foreign goods is the value of the American dollar. In the "Fete de France" event, the dollar was weak, and goods lost more than was anticipated.

Not every country's "salute" carries equal involvement. The most ambitious to date has been China. The extravaganza took years to assemble and was destined to be more successful than anticipated for its six-week stint. Adorned with flags, banners, artwork, craft demonstrations, ceremonial robes, food delicacies, and so on, the flagship store and all of its branches were transformed into a China adventure. Special shops created solely for this event, such as the Palace of Spring for lingerie, the Temple of Perfect Harmony for accessories, the Kingfisher Pagoda for jewelry, the Friendship store for collectibles, Marco Polo's Caravan for fabrics, and the Great Wall Gallery for Chinese artworks—all contributed to an Eastern atmosphere.

The most recent "salute" promoted by Bloomingdale's has been Ecco L'Italia, a promotion that featured a wide assortment of Italian-inspired and

-produced merchandise. The flagship store as well as the branches were transformed into sales floors that immediately presented the shopper with the feeling of the old as well as the contemporary Italy.

Such shopping experiences have given the Bloomingdale's customer more than just a place to shop. Bloomingdale's "salutes" have become regular events that have set the company apart from others in its class. Other retailers have gone the special-events route in promoting their stores, but few have approached it with such commitment.

LEARNING OBJECTIVES

Upon completion of this chapter, the student should be able to

1. List four organizations that offer advertising services to the small retailer.
2. List in sequence the steps required for a buyer in a large retail organization to place an advertisement.
3. Differentiate between promotional and institutional advertising.
4. Give the advantages and disadvantages of newspaper advertising.
5. Discuss magazine advertising, explaining the type of retail organizations that use this medium and why they do so.
6. Understand the legal aspects of advertising.
7. Write a brief essay on special events, including three examples.
8. Define publicity and give several examples of it.
9. Discuss the aspects involved in the multimedia concept.
10. Understand the purpose of storewide celebrations.

INTRODUCTION

Making certain that the store is stocked with merchandise that will motivate the customer to purchase is the task of the merchandising division. A company, no matter how enticing the merchandise mix, will not turn over its stock without consumers who are willing to buy. It is certainly agreed that a certain percentage of a store's customers shop with regularity without the store's constantly "going after them," but without a continuous appeal, the number of purchasers will certainly be likely to decline.

It is the primary function of the advertising and sales promotion division of any retail organization to get its message across to the consumer. It is inconceivable that even the smallest store can achieve success without some amount of advertising and promotion. Whether it is merely an informal direct-mail card telling customers about a private sale, as small retailers often do, or a full-blown multimedia campaign to herald a "salute," as Bloomingdale's regularly does, direct appeal to the customer or prospective customer is the lifeblood of retail organizations.

Stores develop their advertising and promotional campaigns in a number of ways, generally dictated by the size of the company and the promotional budget. In this chapter most of the discussion centers on the large store organizations, since they spend enormous sums in trying to get the customer's attention and use all of the various media to do so. Because display is such a large part of a sales promotion division, it is dealt with separately, in Chapter 7.

THE SALES PROMOTION DIVISION

In most large retail organizations there is a division that is separate from the others, with responsibility for creating the store's promotional activities. Figure 6–1 illustrates the typical departmental structure of the division. It is headed by an expert in promotion, whose task it is to manage all of the division's activities. Although each department is headed by its own manager, the promotion manager has responsibility for ultimate approval of advertising and displays and coordinates events that involve all of the areas of promotion. For example, in a storewide special event, it is the sales promotion director who must ensure that each aspect of the event complements the others. Only with cooperation among the various departments within the division will a successful campaign be realized. In contemporary retailing, where the multimedia concept is prevalent, a spirit of cooperation is necessary to convey the store's desired image.

FIGURE 6–1   Organization of a Sales Promotion Division

SALES PROMOTION DIVISION Sales Promotion Manager			
ADVERTISING Adv. Mgr.	DISPLAY Display Mgr.	SPECIAL EVENTS Spec. Evts. Mgr.	PUBLICITY Publicity Mgr.
Staff	Staff	Staff	Staff

ADVERTISING

As defined by the American Marketing Association, "advertising is any paid for form of nonpersonal presentation of the facts about goods, services, or ideas to a group." By comparing advertising with some other promotional techniques, we can more easily understand its concept: Publicity is free, whereas advertising is paid for; display actually shows the merchandise, but advertising merely tells about the goods through words and illustration.

Store-Operated Advertising Departments

The size of the advertising department in a store varies according to the size of the organization and the type of advertising it engages in. Figure 6–2 shows a typical advertising department in a large retail organization.

Whatever the organizational structure of the advertising department (and these examples are by no means the only ones in operation), the functions are the same. The advertising department is completely responsible for the planning and preparation of advertising. The preparation of the advertisement includes such areas as the following:

1. *Writing copy*. Copy is the written text found in the advertisement.
2. *Artwork*. This involves the creation of the illustrations, either by photographers or by artists who prepare sketches.
3. *Production*. After the creative aspects, such as the illustrations and copy, have been arranged and presented in a layout (the overall arrangement of the ad), the next step is to set it up for printing. The

FIGURE 6–2 Advertising Department of a Large Retail Operation

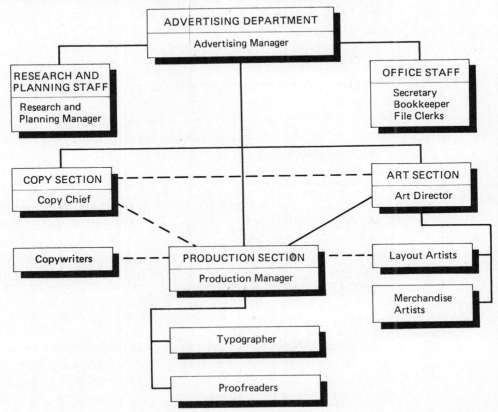

people involved in this procedure must have complete knowledge of the various printing processes. (Since retailing managers rarely become involved in production, its more formal aspects are not discussed here.)

The smaller advertising department depends on a limited number of persons to perform all of the advertising responsibilities. Therefore, each person must be proficient at more than one task. For example, one person might create the artwork and the accompanying copy. In the very large department, specialization is common.

Small Store Advertising Arrangements

It would be impossible for a small store to afford its own advertising department. Furthermore, such a department would be unnecessary because of the limited amount of advertising it would be required to generate. Several outside organizations offer advertising services to the small retailer.

Advertising Agencies

Advertising agencies offer complete services ranging from the execution of a single advertisement to an entire advertising campaign. Remuneration to the agency can be in the form of an allowance or a discount on the space the agency purchases for its customer from the various media (that is, it receives the difference between what the store would pay directly to a newspaper and the price it actually pays for the space), or it can be a flat fee.

Wholesalers and Manufacturers

The wholesaler and manufacturer, which are only as successful as the retailers to which they sell, sometimes offer advertising assistance. Most commonly, manufacturers offer advertising mats (paper composition printing plates) to their customers with complete layouts of artwork and copy, and space for the retailer to insert the store's name.

Free-Lancers

A free-lancer is an individual who prepares a complete advertisement. The free-lancer is generally experienced in one aspect of advertisement preparation, such as layout, and engages others to execute the artwork and copy, which the free-lancer then arranges in the ad. Free-lancers usually specialize in one type of merchandise, such as children's clothing or groceries.

Media Services

Generally the media, in addition to selling space or time, offer complete advertising service to their retail customers. Their services range from the planning stages to the actual preparation of the advertisements. The media are continuously involved in research in order to service better the needs of their clients. For example, research will offer such information to retailers as the characteristics of a newspaper's subscribers—invaluable to a store when selecting the proper newspaper in which to advertise.

Preparation of the Advertisement

In stores with advertising departments, the advertising specialists are responsible for the preparation of the advertisement. The buyer, though, determines which merchandise is to be advertised. In some large operations, the buyer works in conjunction with the merchandise manager in making the decision. Since advertising cannot sell merchandise that people don't want but can improve the sale of desirable goods, only the buyer, with more knowledge about the goods than anyone else in the store, should select the items to be promoted. Small, inexperienced retailers often waste promotional funds by advertising slow-moving merchandise in the hope that these goods will sell.

In the small store, the proprietor usually provides all the pertinent information about the merchandise to the outside agency—price, color, fabric, sizes, and anything else specific to the specific item. The rest of the advertising tasks are performed by the company charged with the creation of the ad; final approval rests with the proprietor.

In large stores, the procedure followed is along these lines:

- The buyer completes an advertising information sheet like the one used by Abraham & Straus (A&S) in Figure 6–3. Since the buyer is the most familiar with the goods and all of the details that should be highlighted, this individual starts the advertising process. Such information as the desired media, product features, branch quantities on hand, artwork specifications, pricing, and so on are indicated on the form and sent to the advertising department for execution into an advertisement. In cases where cancellations, changes, or additional advertising are to be ordered, a form similar to Figure 6–4 is used. Since this is an alteration from what was originally planned, it requires authorization from a divisional merchandise manager, merchandising vice president, and executive vice president, a system used to make certain that the change is warranted.

- The buyer sends the item to be advertised and the accompanying form to the advertising manager. The advertising manager checks the request form to see that all pertinent information has been provided. The advertising manager also verifies that the department has sufficient funds to produce and run the ad. Then staff members are notified of their roles in the construction of the impending advertisement. In a small company-run advertising department, the advertising manager might be responsible for copy and layout, and only the artwork would be executed by someone else. In very large departments, different specialists in layout, copy, and art work as

FIGURE 6–3 Advertising Information Sheet

AREAS IN RED MUST BE FILLED IN   PRESS HARD YOU ARE MAKING 4 COPIES   USE BALL POINT PEN

| A&S | ADVERTISING INFORMATION SHEET SHEET____OF____ | DATE SUBMITTED TO ADVERTISING | AD DATE(S). OR EVENT | AD SIZE | DEPT. NO. | ADVERTISING INFO. SHEET NO. 56799 |

| ☐ NEWSPAPER | ☐ INSERT | ☐ CATALOG | ☐ RADIO | ☐ TV |

ITEM DESCRIPTION(ONLY ONE ITEM PER FORM)

LIST IN ORDER OF IMPORTANCE

| ☐ FEATURE | ☐ SUBFEATURE | ☐ LINER | ☐ NOT SHOWN | SALE ENDS |

STYLE OR MODEL NO.	CLASS NO.	SELLING PRICE	COMPARATIVE	SIZES	COLOR	MATERIALS	TRADEMARKS, F.T.C. REQ.,ETC.

IF THERE IS A VENDOR OR FIBER CONTRACT CONNECTED WITH THIS AD, PLEASE ATTACH(FOUR COPIES)

VENDOR REQUIRED INFORMATION LIST BELOW ALL INFORMATION REQUIRED BY YOUR VENDOR(S), E.G. LOGO, COPYRIGHT, FABRIC NAME, ETC.

THIS INFORMATION IS NOW REQUIRED BY THE F.T.C. AND MUST BE INCLUDED ON THIS FORM

1. DOES THIS ITEM CARRY A WRITTEN MANUFACTURER'S OR A&S WARRANTY?   YES   NO   FULL   LIMITED

2. IF YOU WISH TO USE THE WARRANTY AS A SELLING PLUS, LIST BELOW OR ATTACH ALL CONDITIONS

AVAILABLE FOR MAIL & PHONE
YES   NO   DELIVERY HANDLING CHANGES

BROOKLYN SAMPLES ONLY	QTY	SUNRISE SAMPLES ONLY	QTY	GARDEN CITY SAMPLES ONLY	QTY	WOODBRIDGE SAMPLES ONLY	QTY	SHORT HILLS SAMPLES ONLY	QTY	CARLE PLACE SAMPLES ONLY	QTY
MANHASSET SAMPLES ONLY	QTY	HEMPSTEAD SAMPLES ONLY	QTY	SMITH HAVEN SAMPLES ONLY	QTY	MONMOUTH SAMPLES ONLY	QTY	K.of PRUSSIA SAMPLES ONLY	QTY	SECAUCUS SAMPLES ONLY	QTY
QUEENS SAMPLES ONLY	QTY	HUNTINGTON SAMPLES ONLY	QTY	WHITE PLAINS SAMPLES ONLY	QTY	PARAMUS SAMPLES ONLY	QTY	WILLOW GROVE SAMPLES ONLY	QTY		

PICK UP INFORMATION   ART ☐ COPY ☐

TYPE OF AD (CHECK ONE)

☐NEVER ADVERTISED   LAST ADVERTISED

☐REGULAR PRICE   SPECIAL PURCHASE

☐INSERT   DATE: /   /   PAGE

☐AT SALE PRICE   MFRS. CLOSEOUT

☐CATALOG: DATE: /   /   PAGE

☐CLEARANCE   ☐OTHER(SPECIFY)

☐NEWSPAPER   DATE: /   /   PAPER

☐B&W   ☐COLOR

☐ ATTACHED ART

AUTHORIZED COMPARATIVE WORDS:

1.☐ "REGULARLY" MEANS TEMPORARY REDUCTION, REFERS TO YOUR PRICE IMMEDIATELY BEFORE SALE AND PRICE TO WHICH MERCHANDISE WILL RETURN FOLLOWING SALE.

2.☐ "ORIGINALLY" YOUR FIRST PRICE DURING THE RECENT COURSE OF BUSINESS WHICH IS:
(1) CURRENT SELLING SEASON FOR SEASONAL MERCHANDISE SUCH AS APPAREL AND SPORTING GOODS, ETC.
(2) NOT MORE THAN 12 MONTHS FOR NON-SEASONAL MERCHANDISE SUCH AS FURNITURE, APPLIANCES, ETC.

3.☐ SPEC. VALUE

FOLD HERE   PICK UP ART INSTRUCTIONS

SPECIAL NEW ART INSTRUCTIONS:
(WHAT TO EMPHASIZE, ACCESSORIES, MODEL TYPES, ETC.)

AD. NO.	INFORMATION PREPARED BY: (PLEASE PRINT)
	NAME TITLE EXT. ADV 3/84

COPY

Courtesy of Abraham & Straus. Used with permission.

FIGURE 6–4 Advertising Department Supplemental Media Request

A&S	**ADVERTISING DEPARTMENT SUPPLEMENTAL MEDIA REQUEST**

☐ CANCELLATION ☐ ADDITION ☐ CHANGE

DMM/DIVISION:_____BUYER/DEPT._____DATE_____

MEDIA: ☐ NEWSPAPER ☐ BROADCAST ☐ DIRECT MAIL ☐ INSERT ☐ OTHER

FROM DATE:_____
AD NUMBER:_____
FROM: PAPERS   LINEAGE

☐ TV ☐10 SEC ☐30 SEC
☐ RADIO 30 SEC ☐60 SEC
EVENT:____
AIR DATES: ☐ ADDITION____
            ☐ REVISION____
SALE DATES:☐ ADDITION
            ☐ REVISION____
NOTES/EXPLANATION:____

DATE:_____
TITLE:_____

REQUEST:_____

DATE:_____
TITLE:_____

REQUEST:_____

MEDIA:_____

REQUEST:_____

TO DATE:_____
AD NUMBER:_____
TO: PAPERS   LINEAGE

NOTES/EXPLANATION:

NOTES/EXPLANATION:

NOTES/EXPLANATION:

NOTES/EXPLANATION:_____

VENDOR$_____   VENDOR$_____   VENDOR$_____   VENDOR$_____   VENDOR$_____

BUDGET$ BUDGET$ BUDGET$ BUDGET$ BUDGET$

DMM APPROVAL:_____   MVP APPROVAL:_____   EXECUTIVE VP APPROVAL:_____
MEDIA

Courtesy of Abraham & Straus. Used with permission.

teams to complete an advertisement. Whatever the situation, those responsible for the advertisement consult the request form for information and often discuss ideas with the buyers when additional assistance is needed.

- After the layout is completed and approved by the advertising manager and the buyer, it goes to the production department. The production manager is responsible for following the orders indicated on the layout, such as the selection of type that is to be used. It is the production manager who marks instructions on the layout and sends it to the newspaper or magazine. The instructions are indicated with specific advertising terminology. Figure 6–5 shows an example of an A&S proposed advertisement that is marked and "arrowed" to show instructions to the newspaper. Some of the terminology used follow:

Point. A unit of measurement describing the height of type is the point. One point is equal to 1/72 of an inch. Type that is 1 inch high is 72 points.

Pica. A unit of measurement describing the width of type is called a pica. One pica is equal to 1/6 of an inch in width, or 12 points. Two picas would be 1/3 of an inch, or 24 points.

FIGURE 6–5 Advertisement with Production Instructions

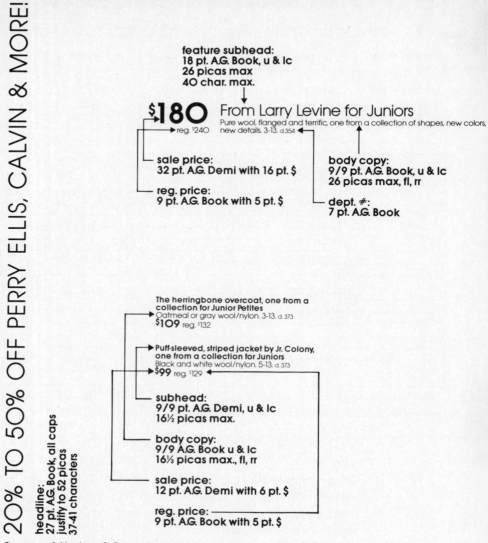

Courtesy of Abraham & Straus. Used with permission.

Typeface. Typeface refers to the style or shape of the specific type used. Different typefaces convey different moods. For example, Old English is very ornate and is similar to the lettering used in old manuscripts; Sans Serif offers a modern impression.

U & l.c. Uppercase (capital letters) and lowercase (small letters).

- The newspaper prepares a proof (a sample of the printed advertisement) and sends it to the store. All the interested parties examine the proof and make notes on it wherever changes are necessary. Proofreader's marks, which are easily understood by everyone in advertising, are used to note such changes. The corrected proof is then returned to the newspaper.

- After receiving the returned proof and making the corrections, the newspaper sends a final proof to the store for authorization. At this point, the store gives permission to run the ad. After the ad has been run, a "tear sheet" (actual copy taken from the publication) is sent to the store.

- It is at this time, if the advertisement is to be fruitful, that all the divisions of the store must work as a team. Stockpeople should be notified to replenish the advertised item's inventory, and salespeople should be made aware of the advertised merchandise through a meeting with the buyer or a copy of the ad on the employee bulletin board. Even elevator operators should be notified of the whereabouts of the advertised goods if unusual traffic is expected to be generated. The display department should be contacted to arrange an interior display of the item to make it more easily located and eye-catching. Any other interested departments should be alerted to guarantee a successful promotion.

- Advertisements should be evaluated after they have run. Some stores carefully compare an item's sales before it was advertised and while it was being advertised. This evaluation is important to future advertising and can be checked by using any number of research techniques.

Types of Retail Advertising

The type of advertising a store uses depends on the clientele served, the merchandise offered, and the image the store wishes to project. Basically there are two types of advertising, institutional and promotional. Institutional advertising, as defined here, is used to project an overall image rather than to sell a specific item. A store that advertises something other than merchandise or that promotes its numerous customer services is engaging in institutional advertising. The objective of promotional advertising is to promote particular items. It is promotional advertising that results in immediate business for the store. The effectiveness of institutional advertising is more difficult to measure. Figure 6–6 shows an example of a promotionally oriented advertisement.

Whichever method is used, and many organizations use both, it is important to bear in mind that neither type of advertising, if used very sparingly or irregularly, will be beneficial to the store. Advertising must be used on a continuous basis so that customers can become familiar with a store's ads and learn to recognize them quickly.

Advertising Media

The advertising media include newspapers, magazines, shopping publications, radio, television, direct mail, hand-distributed circulars, signs and billboards, car cards, and even skywriting. Some organizations make use of all these media listed (plus others), and some limit their use to one type.

FIGURE 6–6   Promotionally Oriented Advertisement

$100 OFF ON SHARP 19" COLOR REMOTE T.V.

Just in time for the new TV season! Gives you outstanding definition on every channel. Automatic fine tuning. 1-year in-home service. #19663. d. 718

$349 orig. $449
19" meas. diag.

$220 off: Panasonic VHS VCR with wireless remote
107-channel cable-ready tuner. 14-function wireless remote. 14-day/4-event programming capability. Stereo sound with Dolby® NR. #1430 d. 711
$799 orig. $1019

$130 off: Sharp 13" color portable with electronic tuning and remote control
Linytron Plus 1-gun in-line picture for clear, accurate color. Electronic tuning and lighted channel indicator. 1-year carry-in service. Only 500, all stores. #13663 d. 718
$249 13" meas. diag., orig. $379

$130 off: Sharp 19" cable-ready color portable with 1-year in-home service
Linytron Plus 1-gun in-line picture tube. Dependable Sigma 7000 chassis. 18-position electronic tuning, 105-channel cable-ready. LED channel display, automatic fine tuning. 1-year in-home service. #19633 (d. 718)
$239 19" meas. diag., orig. $369

$100 off: RCA 25" color with Super Accufilter picture, automatic color control
Single knob electronic tuning. Unitized extended life chassis for dependability. Delivers true-to-life color. 90-day in-home service #648 d. 717
$399 25" meas. diag., orig. $499

BROOKLYN   QUEENS   WHITE PLAINS   GARDEN CITY   HEMPSTEAD   MANHASSET   HUNTINGTON   SUNRISE   SMITH HAVEN   MONMOUTH   PARAMUS   WOODBRIDGE   SHORT HILLS   KING OF PRUSSIA   WILLOW GROVE

PHONE: A&S 9 A.M. - 6 P.M., 7 DAYS A WEEK. Call N.Y.C. (718) 625-6000; Nassau (516) 481-8600; Suffolk (516) 586-2200. Write Abraham & Straus, G.P.O. Box 41, Bklyn., N.Y. 11202. Add local sales tax. Orders filled on $10 or more. Add 3.50 delivery charge within delivery area, or specific charges as shown. No additional charge for multiple items delivered to the same address. Sorry, no C.O.D's. A&S open Sundays 12 to 6 p.m. 12 to 5 in Brooklyn and White Plains (Paramus and Garden City closed). All stores open late Mondays (except Brooklyn 'til 7 p.m.)

Courtesy of Abraham & Straus. Used with permission.

Newspapers

The medium that receives the greatest share of retail advertising is the newspaper. Stores run the gamut of advertising from such widely distributed papers as the *New York Times* to small local publications. Which newspapers are best suited to the needs of the store can be determined through independent research, or more commonly, by calling on advertising agencies or the newspapers themselves for advice. Both have considerable information on newspaper readership.

Some of the advantages of newspaper advertising are the following:

1. The newspaper's offerings are so diversified that it appeals to almost every member of the family. Even a child looking for the comic strips can be attracted by an advertisement.
2. The cost is low when the number of prospects reached is considered. The cost per consumer is lower than for any other medium.
3. The newspaper can be examined at one's leisure and therefore its life is greater than broadcast advertising. A moment away from the television set and the commercial won't be seen.
4. Newspapers enter into almost every home daily and therefore easily reach a large consumer market.

There are also some drawbacks to advertising in a newspaper:

1. Some of the readers are too far from the retail store for the advertisement to be meaningful. This problem has been lessened somewhat with the continued increase in telephone ordering.
2. The life of the message, although longer than radio or television, is still only for a short period of time. Sometimes it's for only part of the train ride home from the office.
3. The quality of the stock (paper) used often limits the attractiveness of the item being offered for sale. Color is rarely used because of this reason.

Cost and placement of newspaper advertisements. The cost of running an advertisement varies from newspaper to newspaper, depending on the size of the paper's circulation. Space is sold on the basis of the number of lines used for the ad. To determine the true value of the money spent on newspaper space, stores must figure the cost of the ad per reader. The cost per reader is determined on the basis of the "milline rate." The following formula is used to determine the milline rate:

$$\frac{\text{rate per line} \times 1{,}000{,}000}{\text{circulation}} = \text{milline rate}$$

If the rate per line is 90¢ and a paper's circulation is 900,000, the milline rate is

$$\frac{0.90 \times 1{,}000{,}000}{900{,}000} = \$1$$

By applying this formula to the various newspapers' rates and circulation, a store can determine whether a higher line rate might cost less per reader.

In addition to the cost per line in newspapers, costs vary according to placement, or position, of the ad. The least expensive method of advertising placement is called "ROP," or "run of press." This means that the advertisement will be placed at the discretion of the newspaper. "Regular position" guarantees that a store's advertisements will be placed in the same position all the time. Regular position is costlier than ROP, but readers eventually know where to find a store's advertisements. "Preferred position," the most expensive, locates the advertisement in the most desirable spot in the newspaper for that particular ad. The position may be adjacent to a pertinent newspaper column. For example, men's sporting goods advertisements would be more effective if placed next to a sportswriter's daily column. This positioning guarantees exposure to the appropriate readers.

Taking all of these factors into consideration, a retailer is often wise to run a smaller advertisement in a newspaper with a larger circulation positioned in the best location than a larger ad without these important features. After a careful examination of all of the variables, the actual rate per line might not be the most important consideration.

Magazines

The magazine is infrequently used by retail stores. Only those organizations operating such prestige outlets as Saks Fifth Avenue make some use of this medium. One of the principal reasons magazine advertising is limited is that the store's trading area is generally much smaller than the market reached by the magazine and thus the store is spending—and magazine advertising is very costly—a considerable amount to reach people who are unable to become customers. Some magazines, however, overcome the disadvantage of "reaching past the market." Through their regional editions, some magazines enable retailers to reach a narrower market and, thus, advertise at a lesser cost.

Another reason for limited magazine advertising is that most magazines take many weeks to prepare before their publication date. Most retail stores cannot plan to advertise particular items so far in advance. Such stores as I. Magnin, Bonwit Teller, and Lord & Taylor, which do use long-range magazine advertising, feel that magazine advertisements in such periodicals as *Harper's Bazaar* and *Vogue* lend prestige to their operations and do bring a certain return. Also, stores such as Sears, with sufficient outlets and catalog customers available across the country, advertise in magazines. This type of advertising is more institutional than promotional and therefore can be planned well in advance of the publication date.

Independent Shopping Publications

In many cities periodicals are published primarily for the purpose of retail advertisements. They are almost completely devoted to the advertising of local retail stores. Such periodicals are extremely attractive to this segment of retailing in that periodicals advertising is less expensive than regular newspaper or broadcast advertising and reaches a clearly defined market. These publications are either mailed to prospects in a particular area or are hand-delivered to homes free of charge. Their success can be evidenced by the increasing number of shopping publications now in print.

Radio and Television

By comparison with the other media, broadcast advertising is still sparingly used by retailers. There is much evidence, however, that the dollar amounts spent by retailers on radio and television have increased.

Radio is showing a spurt, particularly with local commercials. It is not unusual to hear local merchants advertise their goods as "spot" commercials on the airwaves. It should be understood that they do not sponsor complete programs but purchase commercial time throughout the day at the most appropriate time slots and on the most suitable programs for their products. For example, retailers of teen-oriented merchandise would generally choose as sponsors radio stations and programs that feature rock music.

One example of successful radio use is that of Innovation Luggage, a New Jersey-based chain of fifteen stores. Innovation Luggage couldn't compete with the major stores in newspaper advertising; its small ads were buried by the giants in the field. Thus, the company turned to radio, where there is little competition, and has had considerable success.

Television is, in two ways, being used considerably more than before. Retailers are paying for "spots," as in the case of radio. When such TV programs as the "David Letterman Show" or the "Tonight Show" pause for station identification or break for a commercial, it is often the retailer that purchases the spot. These spots are local and perfect for the retailer that can present merchandise to a preselected, limited audience.

The giant retailers are beginning to sponsor complete television shows. It is not unusual for Sears or J. C. Penney to sponsor entire television specials. Although such advertising is costly, it serves two purposes: First, it reaches the largest market possible in the shortest amount of time, and second, it provides the retailers with a medium to replace the dying magazine field. It should be noted that only retailers with national organizations invest in complete sponsor arrangements.

Direct Mail

One of the most effective methods to bring a particular advertisement to specific individuals is direct-mail advertising. Nationally, direct mail is the third largest of the advertising media. In some retail organizations, it is first. Using the mail, retailers are able to send, to both regular customers and prospective customers, a variety of direct-mail pieces, such as merchandise brochures, sales announcements, letters, catalogs, booklets, and circulars.

At the beginning of the Christmas selling season, most major retailers distribute sales booklets that rival the quality, size, and cost of many magazines. So successful are these pieces that many of them feature as many as 100 pages and well over 1,000 items. Not only are typical merchandise offerings made available through this advertising medium, but the unusual is also featured. The Neiman-Marcus Christmas book is a production that not only satisfies the needs of its affluent clientele, but also, with its unusually selected merchandise, delights other retailers and those studying retailing. In retailing circles, these publications are collected and as carefully saved as many regular magazines.

Many department stores are increasing the portion of their advertising budget designated for direct mail. This is the result of dissatisfaction with newspaper advertising, coupled with their computerized capability of both massive and narrow direct-mail pieces. Hochschild's of Baltimore spends 68 percent of its advertising budget on direct mail with great results. Merchandise that has wide appeal is mailed to the mass market. Goods that are of interest to only a select few of their customers are directed to that narrow group by a sophisticated data processing system.

A summary of the reasons for direct mail's popularity follows:

1. Direct-mail pieces may be enclosed with end-of-month statements to charge account customers without incurring additional mailing charges.
2. Direct mail permits the retailer to appeal to a particular group of people. Mailing lists can be compiled from names of satisfied customers or purchased from commercial list houses that categorize the population according to occupation, income, education, religious background, and so on. Stores can then mail their advertisement to the group that most closely identifies with what the store offers for sale.
3. In comparison with periodical advertising, direct mail affords the retailer the undivided attention of the reader. A newspaper reader is offered many advertisements that compete for attention.
4. Costs for direct mail can vary according to the budget allowance of the store, whereas the rate charges for newspaper space or television time remain constant. An announcement of a private sale to steady clientele need be nothing more expensive than a printed postcard.

Figure 6–7 shows a direct-mail advertising catalog, and Figure 6–8, a direct-mail order form used in these catalogs.

One of the pitfalls of direct mail is poor maintenance of mailing lists. If these lists are not continuously updated, a percentage of the mailing pieces will not be delivered. Customers who have moved are the main reason it is necessary to alter the list. If the postage is guaranteed, the post office will return all undelivered mail to the retailer. Thus, the retailer that makes use of this service can easily "clean up" the store's mailing lists. Often, in an attempt to solicit new customers, stores prepare a mailing addressed to "occupant." This directs mail to a particular address but no particular person. This system is employed, for example, when a new store wishes to announce its opening.

FIGURE 6–7 Direct-Mail Advertising Catalog

Courtesy of Abraham & Straus. Used with permission.

Direct mail response has improved with the use of the 800 telephone prefix. These special 800 numbers have the effect of transferring the cost of the phone call from the caller to the store. Customers are much more likely to order if the call if free. Naturally, this is even more apparent for long-distance calls.

Hand-Distributed Advertisements

Some of the forms used by the direct-mail medium may also be hand-delivered to a store's prospects. In particular, supermarkets make extensive use of this medium. Many supermarkets distribute circulars to announce their weekly specials. Since prices fluctuate rapidly in the food

FIGURE 6–8 Direct-Mail Order Form

Page and Item No.	Item	Size	Color 1st Choice	Color 2nd Choice	Quan.	Unit Price	Total

A&S order form: There are delivery charges on all items. Please read delivery information before ordering.

Check or money order ☐

A&S charge account number

☐☐☐ ☐☐ ☐☐☐ ☐ x ☐

PURCHASED BY:
NAME (PRINT) _____
ADDRESS _____
CITY _____ STATE _____ ZIP _____
HOME PHONE _____ BUSINESS PHONE _____

Merchandise Total _____
Tax _____
Del. Chg. Total _____
Total _____

Mail your order to: **Abraham and Straus** G.P.O. Box 731 Brooklyn, NY 11202

Mail and phone orders filled on $10 or more (6.50 on cosmetics), exclusive of tax. Within motor delivery area, where a specific delivery charge is shown, add the indicated amount for each item. Where no specific charge is shown, there is a 2.50 charge. There is no additional charge for multiple items delivered to the same address. Outside our motor delivery area there is a 3.50 charge for one piece, $5 for two or more pieces, and in cases where an item has a specific delivery charge, the higher charge will apply. Do not send cash. Add local sales tax for NY, NJ, PA, and CT deliveries. Sorry, no C.O.D's. Items ordered at the same time will not always be shipped together.

To order call seven days a week: 9 A.M.–6 PM.

In NYC (5 boroughs)	(718) 625-6000
In Nassau	(516) 481-8600
In Suffolk	(516) 586-2200
In Westchester	(914) 428-2800
In Northern NJ	(201) 967-1600
In Central NJ	(201) 494-1600
In Southern NJ	(201) 544-8866
In Short Hills NJ	(201) 467-9555
In Philadelphia PA	(215) 641-0777

Alternate Address: Please complete for shipments sent to an address other than your own.

Name _____
Address _____
City, State, Zip _____
Item No. _____

Name _____
Address _____
City, State, Zip _____
Item No. _____

Name _____
Address _____
City, State, Zip _____
Item No. _____

Courtesy of Abraham & Straus. Used with permission.

industry, it is important to notify the customer at what prices their key items are being sold during a particular period. Many shoppers carry these circulars to the supermarket as a guide to purchasing.

It should be noted that some communities have passed legislation that no longer allows hand-delivered advertisements. They consider them "eyesores." In these areas, merchants must distribute through the mails.

Billboards

Retailers make some use of billboard advertising. Billboards are either permanently painted or are covered with prepared advertisements that can be frequently changed. Billboard space is generally available on a rental basis, the cost depending on size and location of the billboard. While it is an inexpensive medium, as the cost per observer is little, the audiences attracted are usually moving quickly (in an automobile, for example) and are not selected on any scientific basis. Newspapers, for example, have particular audiences and a retailer can select the most appropriate one. The billboard medium does not allow for such precise selection. Since the reader is aware of the billboard for such a limited period, the message must also be brief. Thus, billboards are used by retailers more in an institutional manner than a promotional one.

Capitalizing on the fact that billboard advertising is seen by a huge daily audience, Hastings (a division of Hart, Schaffner & Marx), an apparel chain based in San Francisco, was able to dramatically increase its awareness factor overnight. The chain is an old, established retailer that had been losing out to its younger, more aggressive competitors. Hastings concentrated 149 billboard displays in the city's 12-square-mile downtown area. In a week, everybody in San Francisco was reminded of Hasting's, and at a relatively modest cost. As the vice president for advertising of Boston's Filene's put it, "If you buy both the *Boston Herald* and the *Boston Globe* on Sunday, you reach 60% of the households." Billboard advertising, for all of its shortcomings, reaches everyone, every day.

Car Cards

Car cards are advertisements that are displayed inside buses and trains. Since the number of people traveling the many public transportation systems across the country is enormous, and the time spent in these vehicles is extensive, the car card is of value to some retailers. The desired audience is easily reached by the cards being placed in the appropriate spots. For example, a high-fashion women's shop seeking the proper clientele would locate its car cards in a commuter train originating in an affluent community.

Car-card space is purchased in "runs"—full, half, quarter, and often double runs. A full run would place one card in every car, and so on. Messages are brief, printed in color, and lettered sufficiently large to be seen by most people in the car. Since passengers usually remain in one place for an entire trip, careful planning is necessary to guarantee a maximum amount of exposure.

Miscellaneous Media

Among the additional media used by retailers are skywriting or airplane banners used to advertise nearby restaurants to people on the beach, in-store loudspeaker systems to call attention to special merchandise, station posters, neon signs, and telegrams.

Whichever and to what extent the various media are used is a challenge faced by management. Most important is that extreme care should be exercised in making these decisions.

Cooperative Advertising

The cost of advertising is usually alarming to the newcomer to retailing. In spite of the bite it takes from the promotional budget, advertising is necessary if a company is to be successful. One of the avenues an organization has available for expanding its advertising dollar is cooperative advertising. By definition, cooperative advertising is an arrangement in which the retailer and supplier share the advertising expense. A cooperative advertisement is easy to recognize. Not only does the retailer's name appear in the ad, but the manufacturer's or wholesaler's name is also prominently displayed. Figure 6–9 shows an example of cooperative advertising between A&S and Timberland.

In practice, two parties generally share the expense for cooperative advertising. The amount usually made available by the manufacturer or wholesaler is a percentage of the retailer's purchases from that company. For example, retailer A buys $200,000 of goods from a manufacturer that offers a cooperative advertising allowance in the amount of 5% of total purchases. The allowance would be

$$\$200,000 \times 0.05 = \$10,000$$

Retailer A then would receive $10,000 in advertising allowances toward $20,000 of the store advertising, or 50% of the cost of the ad.

Not all suppliers offer advertising allowances. Those that do, however, under provisions of the Robinson-Patman Act, must make the same offer to all their customers.

The Law and Advertising

As are other industries, retailers are under the constant scrutiny of a number of governmental agencies that regulate advertising practices. Although many businesses choose to operate in the vein of caveat emptor—let the buyer beware—government at all levels has become the watchdog for the unsuspecting consumer. Through any number of practices retailers can color advertisements by subtly using words, or blatantly deceiving customers, with enticing offers. Whatever the reason and approach, governmental agencies regulate retail advertisements.

Bait and Switch

Probably the oldest ploy for luring customers into stores is to offer attractive merchandise at lower than expected prices. In this practice a store advertises a particular product at a very low price to "bait" customers and motivate them to come to the store. Once the customer arrives, high-pressure selling takes over, with the store hoping to "switch" the customer's original want to a higher priced product that brings in a larger profit.

Bait-and-switch advertising is illegal and carries penalties in the form of fines. Retailers that not only understand the legal ramifications of such deception but also understand that the frustration of the disgruntled customer can lead to a negative store image, are unwise to use bait-and-switch tactics. Not only will the penalty pose an immediate cost to the company; the customer unhappiness it causes could also spread through word of mouth.

FIGURE 6–9   A Cooperative Advertisement

25% off
TIMBERLAND BOOTS! MOUNTAINS OF SAVINGS!

Rough. Tough. Insulated to keep your feet warm even when the temperature goes below zero. And now, every Timberland® boot is on sale. We show just three. 7½-11, 12W. Not at Garden City. d 420

The waterproof 6" hiker
A. Carefully crafted in tan nubuck leather with glove soft leather lining, padded collar.
$67.50 reg. $90

The waterproof 8" mountaineer
B. Silicone impregnated leather with full cambrelle® lining, super ruberized lug-sole.
$60 reg. $80

The rugged chukka boot
C. Made to take it. Water repellent brown leather with Cambrelle® lining. Self-cleaning bottom.
$45 reg. $60

BROOKLYN   QUEENS   WHITE PLAINS   GARDEN CITY   HEMPSTEAD   MANHASSET   HUNTINGTON   SUNRISE   SMITH HAVEN   MONMOUTH   PARAMUS   WOODBRIDGE   SHORT HILLS   KING OF PRUSSIA   WILLOW GROVE

PHONE A&S 9 A.M. - 6 P.M., 7 DAYS A WEEK · Call N.Y.C. (718) 625-6000. Nassau (516) 481-8600. Suffolk: (516) 586-2200. Write Abraham & Straus, G.P.O. Box 41, Bklyn., N.Y. 11202. Add local sales tax. Orders filled on $10 or more. Add 3.50 delivery charge within delivery area, or specific charges as shown. No additional charge for multiple items delivered to the same address. Sorry, no C.O.D.'s. A&S open Sundays 12 to 6 p.m. 12 to 5 in Brooklyn and White Plains (Paramus and Garden City closed). All stores open late Mondays (except Brooklyn 'til 7 p.m.)

Courtesy of Abraham & Straus. Used with permission.

Deceptive Terminology

Key words or phrases are often part of advertisements that tend to mislead readers and listeners. Comparative terminology such as "regularly," "originally," or "comparable value" are extensively used, with customers being misled about their real definitions. Generally, the local governmental agency polices the use of these terms and serves notice on retailers that abuse their placement in ads. "Regularly" indicates only a temporary reduction in price, "originally" indicates the opening or first price of an item, and "comparable value" is an indicator of a product's value in relation to similar products. The last term is the one generally responsible for customer confusion, as it is incorrectly interpreted to imply the same meaning as "regularly" and "originally." As in the case of bait and switch, misuse of terms can result in fines and customer decline.

Media Regulation

Many newspapers, magazines, television, and radio networks regulate proposed advertisements before they are accepted for production. They do this not only to comply with government regulations but also to protect their subscribers from unscrupulous practices and to avoid any consumer backlash. Although the advertisement is the responsibility of the store, and the copy is its creation, any customer unhappiness may be attributed to the medium in which the ad appeared. Media managers are aware of the problems associated with unethical practices and generally choose to police themselves.

Whether it is the Federal Trade Commission, the local department of consumer affairs, or the local better business bureau (the latter without legal bite), retailers are wise to engage in self-regulation. With the enormous amount of direct competition each retailer faces, unethical practices can only turn customers into angry badwill ambassadors.

THE MULTIMEDIA CONCEPT

In advertising, professionals generally agree that the use of one particular medium exclusively is insufficient to reach all customers. Just as it is unwise to involve the store solely in newspaper advertising, it is also unwise to limit promotion to one tool. Sophisticated promotional campaigns require the blending of all worthy promotion techniques to reach the desired sales goals. A melding of advertising, through the various media, displays, and special events, will achieve better results.

Whereas advertising informs the customer of the promotion or event, display continues to whet the appetite as the customer enters the store. By rounding the package out with appropriate demonstrations and other activities, the flavor of the campaign will be constantly absorbed by the store's clientele. Relying on the multimedia or multipromotional concept, most retailers agree that increased sales will be achieved. An example of the concept is evident in the use of a special event coupled with newspaper advertising by The Broadway, a California-based retail organization.

The Broadway's San Diego branch featured two baseball players for a pre-Father's Day special event. It bought two exclusive commemorative plates of Steve Garvey and Reggie Jackson, to be sold at $60 per plate. They couldn't get Jackson, but Garvey was there, chatting and signing autographs. The event was advertised in the newspapers, and on the great day, it was a mad scene with more than 2,000 people in attendance. Sales of the plates were slightly disappointing, but sales in the gift department were excellent.

SPECIAL EVENTS

Whatever the type of retail organization, special events can be used to increase volume. Supermarkets, discount operations, traditional department stores, and specialty shops alike have avenues available to them for reaching their customers. The breadth and depth of these endeavors depend considerably on the available promotional dollar commitment as well as the experts employed to achieve the desired results.

Large companies employ sales promotion directors whose responsibility it is to coordinate and manage the various promotional departments. Without proper leadership to ensure a joint effort by all departments, the money set aside for promotion will not bring about the best results. In promotion, as in any other aspect of retailing, cooperation is essential to success. Special events are often major undertakings, with many planning months needed before the presentation. Sometimes outside agencies are called on to assist with the promotion if its magnitude is too much for the regular staff to handle, or if the staff's capacity is just sufficient to handle regular advertising and display.

As does merchandise, special events come in all sizes, shapes, colors, and prices. Typical as well as specific store promotions are explored here to give insight into how retailers of all sizes and classifications participate.

Grand Openings

The initial impression that the retailer makes on the consumer public is one that may last for years. In order to boost their images, stores must have a solid foundation on which to build. No time seems more appropriate for greater impact than when a retail organization is about to herald the opening of a new branch or unit. The approaches taken and the dollars budgeted for such special events vary from company to company. Some rely on such typical standard practices as "personality" guest appearances and special prices; others invest their budgets on the unique and unusual.

Macy's, in its opening of the Willowbrook store near Houston, Texas, spent significant sums on twenty-three days of special events.

Typical were fashion shows and product demonstrations. Musicians, magicians, and dancers provided a show business-like environment. A charity benefit provided donations to many charitable organizations, with Macy's matching the $50,000 generated by the event.

Jordan Marsh's opening promotion of its Connecticut store in New London's Crystal Mall followed the prestigious route. Since this was Jordan Marsh's first venture in the state, the store wanted to make certain that its name would reach as many consumers as possible. The fanfare began eight weeks prior to the official opening, with ads on construction progress, institutional advertising featuring names in the fashion world, notification to charities, and gala opening announcements. For the actual grand opening, there was television coverage, radio interviews with executives, and appearances by local and state dignitaries. The investment was made to ensure the company's goal of $200 per square foot for that store, much above its overall average of $126.

Sanger Harris, the Dallas-based store, opened its Albuquerque, New Mexico, branch with a "We're Enchanted" campaign that culminated with an "Enchanted Evening" benefit that raised $50,000 for the Albuquerque Community Foundation. Much mileage was gotten from the event, as was evidenced in the free publicity the store received in the next day's lead editorial of the *Albuquerque Tribune* thanking the store for its effort.

Foley's, the Houston-based store, presented a "Helping Hands" theme for the opening of its Post Oaks Mall branch. Six weeks before the store's opening, children were invited, through an advertisement, to place their hands in the clay of six-inch square tiles that would be worked into the store's wall design. The event met with such success that Foley's has decided to make it a regular event for future openings.

Fashion Shows

The display of fashions on live models has been a regular sales promotion device for both large and small retail stores. Although some executives feel that a fashion show is primarily for prestigious purposes, stores can achieve immediate business from them. One need only watch customers rise from their chairs to rush over to the racks of clothing right after an Ohrbach's showing of European fashions to realize the instant success of the event in terms of immediate sales. The partly emptied racks surely dispel the theory of prestige value exclusively. Even if a fashion show presentation doesn't result in immediate sales, it is valuable in that it exposes the store's fashion merchandise to potential buyers in a lively and exciting manner that is unobtainable in any other medium. If the production is properly conceived and executed, appetites are likely to be whetted for future patronage.

Types of Shows

Fashion shows are by no means limited to womenswear. At a rapidly increasing rate, the male model is becoming important in fashion shows. It is not unusual to see menswear take up about one-third of the merchandise shown at what was once a "women's" fashion show. Although it might be considered wasteful to include menswear, since fashion shows are almost exclusively attended by women, stores feel it is practical, because a large proportion of purchases are either directly made or influenced by women.

To be considered a fashion show, the presentation needn't be an extravaganza. Shows run the gamut from informal modeling to elaborate productions staged in imaginative settings.

Fashion parade.   The fashion parade is perhaps the easiest show to produce and also the least costly. This type of production simply presents a succession of models displaying their outfits on a runway in the store or on the floor of a restaurant, in and around the tables, while patrons are dining. This type of show doesn't make use of any particular theme but simply presents the store's most timely merchandise. The staging doesn't lend itself to complicated backgrounds or space for the models to do intricate turns. Music is generally limited to a pianist.

Formal fashion show productions.   A major production requires a great deal of preparation. This show is presented in an auditorium or theater and is truly theatrical. Generally, the fashion coordinator (the person responsible in most large retail operations for the show's production) selects a theme for the show—travel, back to school, the wedding. After the theme has been established, background sets are constructed, a script complete with commentary is written, and appropriate music is selected to be played by a band.

Parades

An institutional device used by a number of large retailers is a parade to mark some occasion. For example, an annual event costing thousands of dollars is Macy's Thanksgiving Day parade in New York City—the official opening of the Christmas season. The show provides entertainment for the public while reminding them that it is time to begin shopping for Christmas gifts. Similar parades are presented throughout the United States. Even in small towns, groups of independent retailers often collaborate on similar presentations, spreading the cost among the participating businesses.

Storewide Celebrations

Every so often, stores make a commitment to promote a special event that encompasses almost all of their selling departments. Not only does such an activity require the cooperation of each of the store's divisions but also an investment far more than the amount usually budgeted for the typical special event. Such a happening was Bloomingdale's undertaking to promote the treasures of China. With an investment of $10 million and an effort that took years to assemble, the extravaganza opened in the flagship store and its branches. Rarely, if ever, has a retail organization so fully transformed its selling floors into a combined cultural as well as shopping experience. Creativity is probably the hall-mark of the Bloomingdale's China adventure. The success, in Bloomingdale's own words, was bigger than ever anticipated for its six-week run.

Another storewide celebration was that mounted by Carson Pirie Scott. Annually, the store presents a major spring promotion. For a two-week period, the company presented "Futurescope," an event that took a look at how Americans' lifestyles would change during the 1980s. Planning took three months and involved a total consistent look throughout each of the store's floors and individual departments. Special shops, demonstrations, window displays, and advertisements were created to give a total picture. As with Bloomingdale's China event, the increased traffic and media coverage surpassed what had been expected.

Institutional Promotions

Stores throughout the country are finding that programs that promote their images are bringing positive results to their companies. One technique is to use areas of interest to their customers such as health and physical fitness. These are considered to be "institutional" in nature.

One such event that has had a far-reaching effect for its organization is Macy's Marathon, sponsored by Macy's, Kansas City. The race is a one-day affair that attracted 1,100 runners from twenty-four states its first time and has since become an annual event. Although the actual event is for only one day, the race, as indicated by Macy's management, has had tremendous influence in establishing Macy's as a community leader in the Kansas City area. The race has worked positively as a public relations tool for the entire year. While no merchandise is sold specifically because of this special event, its impact on the public is one that promotes community involvement. This type of event is similar to institutional advertising, which is intended to bolster the store's image, but sales increases cannot be immediately measured.

One-Day Sales

Abraham & Straus, a Brooklyn, New York, based department store, has found enormous success in one-day sales. The customer has a very limited time to take advantage of special price reductions that, on conclusion of the sale, revert back to the regular prices. Figure 6–10 shows an advertisement for a one-day sale. One need only witness the crowds to become aware of such an event's success.

Special Programs

To strengthen its "Stork Club" baby registry, Dayton's ran a four-day program called "The Magic Years." Seminars were held in the auditorium of the Minneapolis store on prenatal to preschool issues. Forty-

FIGURE 6–10   One-Day Sale Event

Misses' cotton shaker knit vest in white, black, 5 color brights, by FWM Workshop **25% off** reg. 19.99 (d 395)	Junior fleece basics: crew tops, pull-on pants, button-front V-neck vests **25% off** reg. 7.99-14.99 (d 355)	All handbags by Etienne Aigner: clutches, totes shoulder bags, carryalls, more **25% off** original prices (d 174)
Misses', petite, and half-size soft spring dresses: silks, crepes, cottons, and more! **20% off** regular prices (d 557 Not at Garden City)	Misses' great all-cotton shaker knit oversize sweaters **25% off** original prices (d 359,382,395)	Lowest price of the season for misses' & jr. wool, wool-blend coats & jackets **25% off** already-reduced prices (d 311,339,341,343,345, 354,373,386)
Selected junior denims from Calvin Klein, Gloria Vanderbilt, Bongo, Sasson **25% off** original prices (d 234,364,378)	Every dress in our stock for misses, juniors, petites, and half sizes **20% off** ticketed prices (d 026,333,335,340,348,361,362,365,366,368, 371,374,385,440,491)	All misses' and jr. spring shoes from 9 West, Mia, Etienne Aigner, Calico, Esprit **$10 off** regular prices (d 425,426,428,435)
Great selection of leather and vinyl handbags from B.H. Smith, and more **25% off** original prices (d 170)	All regular-priced shoes in our spring collection: Caressa, Bandolino, Gloria Vanderbilt **15% off** regular prices (d 421)	Every down coat and jacket for misses & juniors: now at our lowest prices **25% off** ticketed prices (d 314,339,343,345,380")
Misses' sportswear selections: Summit, Briggs, and more **20% off** original prices (d 000)	All fleece active separates for misses and juniors **25% off** original prices (d 230,357)	All misses' reduced and sale-prices belts, socks and legwarmers **50% off** ticketed prices (d 252,473)
All misses' cotton sundresses & caftans in our loungewear dept. **25% off** ticketed prices (d 483)	Misses' new spring career coordinates from PantHer **25% off** original prices (d 000)	Season's lowest prices on every fake fur coat and jacket **30% off** ticketed prices (d 342)
Misses' selected denims: basic, designer and fashion jeans **25% off** original prices (d 353,367,423)	Every peignoir set: Ms. Elaine, Valmode, Dreamway, and more **25% off** ticketed prices (d 431,480)	All boys' and girls' casual and dress shoes from Buster Brown **$5 off** ticketed prices (d 437)
Women's sportswear selections: jeans, sweaters and shirts **25% off** original prices (d 315,352,387,388,492)	All Playtex bras and girdles: 18 Hour, Cross Your Heart, more **30% off** original prices (d 101)	Warner's lace-trimmed nylon tricot bikinis, hipsters and briefs **3 for $7** reg. 3 for $10 (d 430)
All Totes® famous stick umbrellas: in prints and solid colors **25% off** regular prices (d 180)	Every casual & dress shoe from Calico and Lifestride **7.50 off** regular prices (d 428-433)	Our entire polyfill jacket collection or misses & juniors **25% off** ticketed prices (d 314,339,343)

BROOKLYN   QUEENS   WHITE PLAINS   GARDEN CITY   HEMPSTEAD   MANHASSET   HUNTINGTON   SUNRISE   SMITH HAVEN   MONMOUTH   PARAMUS   WOODBRIDGE   SHORT HILLS   KING OF PRUSSIA   WILLOW GROVE

39

Courtesy of Abraham & Straus. Used with permission.

two seminars were presented in all, given by nationally known physicians, educators, and neighborhood hospitals and child-care centers. Booths were set up with people from local hospitals, child-care centers, and vendors to answer specific questions. In-store day care was provided for people who brought their children. Attendance for the four-day symposium totaled about 5,000 people, most of whom targeted specific seminars. Many others took days off from work to attend all of the events. Needless to say, the pre-event promotion was excellent, including radio, newspaper, and handout advertising and a direct-mail piece to "Stork Club" registrants.

As a result of the special event, the "Stork Club" registry enjoyed a huge increase. The event coincided with one of the store's three annual sales. Sales in the children's department ran 25 percent above that of a similar sale in the previous year.

When a special event provides a program that is of genuine interest to the community, it can be of great benefit to the store in both immediate sales and as an image-builder for future sales.

SPECIAL DEMONSTRATIONS

In recent years there has been a resurgence in the use of live demonstrations in retail stores. Demonstrators showing how easy it is to manipulate wigs, apply cosmetics, clean rugs with miracle solutions, or prepare meals in a matter of minutes are often found in the high-traffic selling areas of medium and large stores. Some of these demonstrations last for a day and are confined to one counter. Others are major special events requiring a large space and a number of demonstrators.

An example of a major demonstration was that at a major department store to promote Corning Ware, pyroceram cooking utensils, manufactured by Corning Glass. Counters were equipped with demonstrators who prepared food in Corning Ware equipment for the shoppers to taste. They also showed the ease with which the objects can be transferred from extreme cold to extreme heat without breakage and displayed the simplicity of cleaning Corning Ware. Closed-circuit TV was employed to show Corning Ware's resistance to breakage, with a brief film of a bull in a china shop knocking over Corning Ware without damaging it.

In addition to the special demonstration of the product, complete success was guaranteed by the involvement of the entire sales promotion division. The advertising people brought customers to the store; the display people and sign shop brought the customer to the appropriate selling floor, where the demonstrators took over. Without the cooperation of all the promotional staff's departments, the selling of goods isn't likely to be successful.

A different type of demonstration is used by Jordan Marsh, Boston, in its computer department. There, the customer is urged to self-demonstrate with hands-on participation. The thoroughly trained salespeople are encouraged to sit prospects down at computers and balance checkbooks, coordinate income tax records, turn lights and appliances on and off while they are away from home, and so on. Computers are a high-ticket item, and two or three visits for an hour or so each are generally required before a sale can be made.

SAMPLING

A method of promoting sales that is very closely related to demonstrations is the use of samples. Sampling is similar to demonstrations in that it shows the customer how to actually use the merchandise. The major difference between the two methods is that, in a demonstration, the merchandise is used by a representative of the store; in sampling, the customer uses the product. The decision on whether to sell by demonstration or sample is based on the characteristics of the merchandise. Expensive merchandise that requires skill to operate is sold by demonstration. Products that can be inexpensively sampled, and the use of which requires no previous training, can be effectively sold by sampling. Where sample selling is used, it is not unusual to have the producer of the goods share in the retailer's sampling expense.

The important characteristic of the sample method is that it allows customers to "get their hands on" the product. Depending on the merchandise, sampling can effectively take place on the selling floor or in customers' home. Food products, stationery, candies, and yard goods are generally given out by salespeople in the selling departments. Soap powders, razor blades, and swatches of material for shirts, bed linens, and a variety of other uses are frequently mailed to customers' homes. As long as the cost of the sample is relatively low, sampling is an effective way for a store to sell merchandise and get publicity.

IN-STORE VIDEO

Many stores, such as A&S, Dayton-Hudson's, Lechmere, Macy's, and Maas Brothers, use in-store video as a promotional device. Sears has been doing it for the past eight years. Depending on the size of the store one to four 19-inch video sets and VCR units are placed a few feet from a heavily trafficked aisle. The store gets four new tapes each month, and these are changed throughout the day. the tapes are generally hard-sell and include a wide variety of products, from lingerie to tractors.

Neusteter's, Denver, won an industry award for its blending of in-store video and regular television and print promotion. The print portion consisted of a color brochure sent to all charge customers and a few selected areas. It announced an in-store video event "30 minutes of great music, spellbinding images, and fabulous clothes." Conventional television pictured more of the same, calling attention to the coming in-store video show. The costuming consisted of clothes available in the store. According to Neusteter's ad director, the response was beyond belief.

SCHOOLS AND CLASSES

Many stores carry the concept of demonstrations far beyond the selling floor. Certain products require consumer skills that cannot be taught in a simple demonstration period. For instruction in such products, classrooms and teachers are provided, with classes in many cases extending over a period of weeks. The Singer Sewing Machine Co. is a typical example. Since sewing machines are of value only to people who can operate them, Singer offers its customers courses in their use. Unquestionably, such classes are considerably helpful in selling machines.

Stores, frequently with the cooperation of utility companies and appliance manufacturers, offer courses in gourmet cooking. Classes are also offered in baby care, and beauty culture. That this sort of continuing instruction is also typical of small retailers is evidenced by the amount of teaching that takes place in knitting shops, hobby stores, and many other small retail establishments. Frequently, courses are given in churches and women's clubs as a convenience to customers.

The use of instructional classes promotes both sales and goodwill. The sales are made by requiring the students to purchase the materials at the store. In addition, bringing the people into the store to attend classes results in purchases that might not otherwise be made at the store.

PREMIUMS

Premiums—that is, giving special merchandise (products that are not regularly offered for sale by the retailer) as an inducement to buy goods—have become popular during recent years. The premiums may be of any type. Figure 6–11 shows an offering of an umbrella with the purchase of a product.

PUBLICITY

In this chapter, publicity refers to the promotion of the store without cost—in other words, free publicity. Free publicity is the result of a store's advertising, display, special events, and other promotions that are noteworthy enough for a publication or commentator to mention—without cost to the retailer. For example, a store might present a fashion show that is so outstanding that the local newspaper's fashion editor will review it in a column. A store's holiday parade might get attention on a television news broadcast. Large stores employ a public relations person who is charged with the responsibility of preparing releases about the store's activities that might attract media and, therefore, customer interest. The free publicity a store receives is not always kind, and could work adversely. For example, a recent newspaper exposure of incorrect weights on meat packages in some New York City supermarkets certainly hurt sales.

Free publicity can be in the form of favorable comments concerning the store's community activities, merchandise promotional activities, or standing in the business community. The purpose of free publicity, like all other sales promotional activity, is to create sales by presenting the firm's name in the most favorable light. An advantage of free publicity over conventional advertising (in addition to the cost savings) is that promotional material found in advertising is presumed to be biased and is not taken as seriously as the same material would be if it were found in the nonadvertising section of the newspaper.

FIGURE 6–11 Premium Promotion

THE RAIN MASCOT! YOURS WITH ANY $10 ARAMIS BUY!

Bright blue and black nylon coverage to bring a ray of sunshine to a stormy day. Get this spacious, duck handle protector with any purchase of $10 or more from the Aramis, Devin, Aramis 900 or J.H.L. collections.

A&S, Box 41, Brooklyn, N.Y. 11202

Send The Aramis Rain Mascot to me with my selections below.
Aramis Cologne: 4 oz. $21.50 □ 2 oz. $13 □
Aramis Moisturizing After Shave: 2 oz. $10 □
Devin Country After Shave: 4 oz. $15 □
Aramis 900 Herbal Cologne: 3.4 oz. $25 □
J.H.L. Custom Blend Cologne: 3.4 oz. $45 □ 1.7 oz. $30 □
d. 123

Name
Address
City
State   Zip
A&S Account No.
Check   M.O.
Offer good through April 8th.

BROOKLYN   QUEENS   WHITE PLAINS   GARDEN CITY   HEMPSTEAD   MANHASSET   HUNTINGTON   SUNRISE   SMITH HAVEN   MONMOUTH   PARAMUS   WOODBRIDGE   SHORT HILLS   KING OF PRUSSIA   WILLOW GROVE

PHONE A&S 9 A.M. - 6 P.M., 7 DAYS A WEEK. Call: N.Y.C. (718) 625-6000, Nassau (516) 481-8600, Suffolk (516) 586-2200. Write Abraham & Straus, G.P.O. Box 41, Bklyn, N.Y. 11202. Add local sales tax. Orders filled on $10 or more. Add 3.50 delivery charge within delivery area, or specific charges as shown. There is no additional charge for multiple items delivered to the same address. No C.O.D.'s. A&S store hours for Queens and Long Island Monday-Saturday 10 a.m.-9.30 p.m., Sundays 12 to 6 p.m. Garden City Monday and Thursday 10 a.m.-9 p.m. Tuesday, Wednesday, Friday and Saturday 10 a.m.-6 p.m. Sunday closed

Courtesy of Abraham & Straus. Used with permission.

The term "free publicity" is somewhat misleading. In fact, large firms spend a considerable amount of money on publicity. Large stores frequently assign the responsibility for publicity to one or more members of their sales promotion department to spend their full time in reporting newsworthy information to the local media. These people establish contacts with local newspapers and radio stations and actually write the articles and comments that, if acceptable by the media, appear in the news sections. Small stores employ the services of free-lance writers or public relations agencies for this purpose.

Newspapers and other media are well aware of the fact that their audience, particularly women, is interested in news concerning merchandise. Newspaper editors are constantly on the lookout for stories that supplement their advertising pages. Such information as the opening of a new season's fashions is important to readers, and editors are pleased to accept stories and photographs concerning such events. Many newspapers appoint special editors and writers to cover fashion events and report such news as a regular feature.

Studies have shown that there is a direct relationship between the amount of advertising space a company buys and the amount of free publicity it receives. This is probably due, in part, to the newspaper's willingness to please their good customers. It is also likely that a store with a large advertising budget probably engages in many newsworthy promotional activities.

SMALL STORE ADAPTATION

Without question, the advertising and sales promotional budget of the small retailer is often so limited, or nonexistent, that many of those businesses do little or no promotional activity. Whether it is in advertising or the promotion of a special event, the small retailer must do all that is possible to make the consumer public aware of its existence. Even on the most limited budget, much can be accomplished.

Most localities publish shopping publications, or local newspapers have advertising rates that are compatible with even the smallest budgets. Professionals will verify that shopping publications are religiously read by those in a well-defined trading area and are a good source for potential customers. Their popularity is also attributed to the fact that they are often free and are mailed or delivered directly to consumers' homes.

To extend or stretch the advertising dollar to its fullest, small retailers could avail themselves of the same opportunity afforded the large store. By making use of cooperative advertising, half the cost of the ad is paid for by the vendor or merchandise supplier. For those retailers that extend charge accounts to their customers, simple enclosures announcing sales or some other event of interest could be included in monthly customer statements. Since postage is already being spent, the direct-mail piece requires only the cost of printing.

Major promotions are out of the reach of small, individual businesses. This, however, does not eliminate their ability to participate in promotions. Charity or benefit fashion shows that employ those organizations' members as models without cost and their meeting rooms as presentation places without a rental fee are excellent promotions. To motivate purchasing, the store could donate a small percentage of all purchases to the charity. Another event to encourage customer buying is to run a campaign by using window and in-store signs to announce that for a particular period of time, 10 percent, say, of all sales will be given to a charitable organization, a school, or other worthy cause.

It is not necessary to spend large sums on notifying customers that your store is alive and well. Merely think creatively and spend carefully for positive results.

CAREER OPPORTUNITIES

The career path for those interested in advertising and sales promotion is unlike the route for merchandising and management. Individuals who usually enter into this field have taken special courses in school that are not necessarily retail-oriented, and have an artistic or creative flair. Those with the ability to capture the attention of the consumer through imaginative and motivational writing and/or are capable of visually presenting ideas through drawing or photography would be prepared for a career in this area.

One need only examine consumer newspapers, magazines, direct-mail brochures, television and radio, and the numerous special promotions and store events that are presented everyday to comprehend the enormity of the advertising and sales promotional responsibilities of retailing. A quick look at the organization chart for most large retailers would show such job titles as copywriter, typographer, proofreader, layout artist, merchandise artist, advertising manager, special events director, fashion director, publicity manager, and so forth. In order to meet and beat the competition, stores must employ large staffs of people to make their advertising and promotional messages reach the marketplace and motivate purchasing.

With particular emphasis for most retailers today on direct mail, to appeal to the individual who doesn't have time to visit the store, there is expansion of advertising departments. Couple this with the projection of the U.S. Labor Department's Bureau of Statistics for advertising positions to increase over the next five years at a growth rate of 42.4 percent, the field seems a good choice for qualified individuals.

It should be noted that those seeking these creative-oriented positions often need more than a positive interview. Whereas all of the other retailing divisions may base their selection of personnel on interviews, testing, references, past experience, or any combination of these factors, the selection of an advertising trainee or individual seeking any level of employment in that area, also calls for a portfolio of work. This must include a variety of materials indicative of the candidate's ability: writing, layouts, drawings, photography, special event creations, and so on. Anyone pursuing such a career should carefully prepare the presentation under the direction of a professional, since this, more than likely, will be the key to employment.

KEY POINTS IN THE CHAPTER

1. In most large retail organizations there is a separate sales promotion division with responsibility for advertising, display, special events, and publicity.

2. Small retailers plan their advertisements with the assistance of advertising agencies, vendors, free-lancers, and media services.

3. The responsibility in large stores for initiating the advertising procedure rests with the buyer.

4. Basically there are two types of retail advertisements: promotional and institutional. Promotional advertisements sell products, whereas institutional advertisements sell image.

5. The newspaper is the most important of the media available to retailers. Space is sold on a line basis, with premiums for special positions.

6. Retailers stretch their advertising budgets through cooperative advertising, an arrangement in which the vendor shares the cost of the ad with the store.

7. The bait-and-switch ploy lures customers to the store with ads of low-priced goods and then tries to sell high-priced goods instead. It is an illegal practice.

8. A melding of advertising, displays, and special events constitutes the multimedia concept.

9. Special events take place on a limited basis. Parades, anniversary sales, grand openings, and fashion shows are examples of special events.

10. Publicity is something a store receives "free" as a result of something it does. It may be favorable or unfavorable.

Worksheet 6

COMPLETE THE FOLLOWING STATEMENTS

1. The sales promotion division is usually made up of advertising, publicity,

    display, and _____.

2. In large retail organizations, advertising is divided into the copy section,

    artwork, and _____.

3. Aside from using advertising agencies and wholesalers and manufacturers for advertising assistance, the retailer can go directly to the

    _____ for preparation of its advertisements.

4. Before an advertisement is run in a newspaper or magazine, a

    _____ is prepared for the buyer's approval.

5. The style of type is known as its _____.

6. An advertisement that shows goodwill is said to be _____ in nature.

7. Newspaper space is sold on a _____ rate.

8. Through their _____ editions, magazine publishers enable retailers to reach a narrower market.

9. Nationally, direct mail is the _____ largest of the advertising media.

10. An arrangement where the retailer and supplier share the cost of the advertise-

    ment is called _____ advertising.

11. A melding of advertising, display, and special events is commonly known as

    the _____ concept.

12. It is the duty of the promotion manager to achieve as much free

    _____ as possible to extol the store's virtues.

TRUE OR FALSE

_____ 1. The sales promotion division usually includes the selling respon-sibility.

_____ 2. Free publicity comes as a result of something a store does that is newsworthy.

_____ 3. Most retailers have their own advertising departments.

_____ 4. In most department stores the creation of an advertisement is initiated by the advertising manager.

_____ 5. Pica is a unit of measurement describing the width of type.

_____ 6. Newspapers' offerings are so diversified that they appeal to the retailer for advertising purposes.

_____ 7. The milline rate is used to determine the true value of the money spent on newspaper space.

_____ 8. Fashion show costs are so prohibitive that retailers are refraining from using them.

_____ 9. The purpose of holding special classes in stores is to bring traffic to the stores for the purpose of purchasing merchandise.

_____ 10. Grand opening promotions are being toned down by stores because they are too expensive.

MULTIPLE CHOICE

_____ 1. The multimedia concept is concerned with
   (a) advertising
   (b) display
   (c) special events
   (d) all of the above

_____ 2. Small stores run ads with the assistance of
   (a) advertising agencies
   (b) free-lancers
   (c) manufacturers
   (d) all of the above

_____ 3. A paper composition printing plate is called a
   (a) proof
   (b) tear sheet
   (c) mat
   (d) plate

_____ 4. An advertising unit of measurement for height is
   (a) pica
   (b) point
   (c) typeface
   (d) none of the above

5. Advertising space is sold on the basis of
   (a) ROP
   (b) preferred position
   (c) regular position
   (d) all of the above

6. The milline rate and the line rate are
   (a) synonomous terms
   (b) opposite terms
   (c) similar terms
   (d) none of the above

7. Magazine advertising is used by
   (a) large, prestige fashion retailers
   (b) giant retailers with national organizations
   (c) a and b
   (d) neither a nor b

8. Car cards are purchased in designations called
   (a) portions
   (b) locations
   (c) runs
   (d) spaces

9. Small retailers can inexpensively promote through
   (a) fashion shows
   (b) charity sales
   (c) manufacturer demonstrations
   (d) all of the above

10. Publicity may come as a result to a store because of
    (a) great promotions
    (b) celebrity appearances
    (c) price-fixing practices
    (d) all of the above

DISCUSSION QUESTIONS

1. Describe the structure of a typical large store's promotion department.

CASE PROBLEM 1

The Caryn Shop, retailer of children's wear, is located in a suburban shopping center. It has been in business for five years and has averaged $350,000 in sales in each of the past three years. The shop's promotion consists of a window display and periodic advertising in the local newspaper. The advertising is prepared by the owner and sent to the newspaper for printing. Since sales have remained at one level for the past three years, Caryn feels that the advertising is not paying off and wishes to stop the little advertising it does. The newspaper's representative suggested that the newspaper's professional staff prepare future advertisements. The store manager feels that, although the newspaper's staff is better trained in advertising, it still is not the proper agency to rectify the problem.

1. Do you agree with the store manager? Why?
2. To what type of organization would you bring your problem? Why?
3. Which advertising medium do you believe would best serve Caryn's interests? Why?
4. Does such a small store need advertising? Why?

CASE PROBLEM 2

Jim Klar is the advertising manager for Helen's Boutique, a chain of fifteen stores located within the metropolitan area of a large eastern city. He is disturbed by one aspect of the organization's advertising policy. Although he has free rein concerning the type of ads, the newspapers in which to advertise, and the size of the ads, Klar must abide by the chain's policy of advertising placement. It is management's feeling that newspaper ads must be placed on an ROP basis. Home office management contends that the stores' merchandise offerings do not require a special advertising position, and that ROP placement would permit more lines than the other available position arrangements. Klar would like the stores' ads to appear next to the newspaper's daily fashion column every time an ad is placed. This would increase the cost of advertising, but Klar holds that such placement would result in increased sales. He is even willing to stay within the present budget and run fewer ads in the more desirable position. Management refuses to move from its policy of ROP placement.

1. What other arrangements are available in ad placement in addition to ROP?
2. With whom do you agree? Why?

CASE PROBLEM 3

Linda-Carrie Fashions has been operating as a successful high-fashion women's sportswear shop for many years. The store is located in an upper-middle-class suburb, and the clientele consists of repeat customers who have been shopping there for years. In addition to the two partners, the store employs five saleswomen. Profits for the last three years have averaged $80,000 per year before partner's drawings. The store is located in a small suburban town and can be conveniently reached by bus or train.

A large shopping mall has recently been constructed five miles from the store. Among the tenants of the new project is a branch of a high-image, well-known urban department store that caters to the same clientele as does Linda-Carrie Fashions. Linda-Carrie Fashions has never been interested in advertising and sales promotion. However, because of the new competition, it has approached an independent agency with a request for an advertising and sales promotion plan.

1. List all the types of advertising and sales promotion plans you can think of that would be suited to the store. Explain why each plan would be appropriate.
2. Give details for the operation of each plan.

PROJECT 1

Contact the advertising manager of a department store or large specialty store and interview her or him to find out the type of advertising used by the store, the media used in advertising, and the proportion spent on each in a budget period. Then determine the following for a specific newspaper advertisement:

1. Work done by the store's advertising department
2. Work done by an independent advertising agency
3. Work done by the newspaper's staff

PROJECT 2

Cut out four retail advertisements from a newspaper and follow them up to determine whether or not they are part of an overall promotional plan. Answer the questions below for each advertisement. For ease in identification, assign each a number (for example, advertisement 1—Toni's Sportswear, and so on).

1. Was there a coordinating window display?
2. Were any signs posted to direct customers to the advertised merchandise?
3. Did an interior display feature the advertised item?
4. Was the salesperson aware that the item was advertised?
5. List any other devices that were used to promote the advertised goods.

PROJECT 3

Pretend you have the responsibility of producing a fashion show at school. The merchandise to be featured is men's and women's clothing suitable for the college set. This is to be a formal fashion show production complete with theme and background. Using the following outline, indicate your preparatory plans.

1. Theme
2. Stage set (backgrounds)
3. Musical accompaniment
4. Number of models and method used for their selection
5. Devices used to promote show
6. Costs of promotion (determine cost of advertising media used from appropriate people)
7. Location of show (number of seats and so on)
8. Selection criteria for show's commentator

PROJECT 4

Get the following information from the advertising department of a large retailer in your area:

1. Types of special promotions
2. How free publicity is accomplished
3. Organization of the sales promotion department and responsibilities of each job
4. Preparation necessary for a job in retail sales promotion

Visual Merchandising and Display

MANNEQUINS ARE NOT DUMMIES

One need only examine the fashion merchandise that graces prestigious department and specialty stores to discover the significant similarities in the stores' inventories. The expert eye immediately discovers the same lines from one store to the next. Who could fault the buyers for pouring their dollars into the likes of Liz Claiborne, Perry Ellis, Norma Kamali, and other designer "names" when that's exactly what the customer wants to buy? Cover the shoppers' eyes, march them to a department, and it's likely that they wouldn't be able to tell you which store they are in.

It is imperative that each retailer portray an image that attracts, and captures, the customer's attention and dollars. But if the merchandise bears such sameness, how can one store distinguish itself from the rest?

Visual merchandisers or display designers, call them what you may, are charged with the responsibility of filling the store and its windows with the excitement necessary to generate customer enthusiasm. Many stores' displays give the impression that "commonplace" is the best descriptive term for their evaluation. Not only do the themes lack motivation, but the mannequins seem tired and overworked.

A few years ago, American stores were provided with a resource that would never again permit the word "dummy" to be synonymous with mannequin. Adel Rootstein Display Mannequins, Ltd., based in London, appeared on the fashion scene and reshaped the world of display—creating male, female, and child mannequins with such individualized uniqueness that the Rootstein forms enabled display departments to express themselves as never before. Whether it is absolute realism, as in the Joan Collins look-a-likes, or the neorealism forms, all of the figures are designed to have a long fashion future ahead of them (see Fig. 7–1).

Adel Rootstein fosters the concept that fashion is more than new clothing, new makeup, or a different hairdo. She creates her mannequins with attention paid to the way people change from one decade to another. The gestures, the shape of the bodies, the posture, and the movement are different today than yesterday. These details are translated into mannequins that truly reflect today's individual. Unlike most mannequin designers, Rootstein almost always models hers on real people. Stars of movies and television, beauty queens, international models, and even anonymous faces have served as models for the Rootstein mannequins.

With more than 300 mannequins in the collection, and new groups added periodically, visual merchandisers have been provided with an enormous selection from which to choose. It is no longer necessary for one store's display to resemble another's. The talents and imagination of visual merchandisers, coupled with the Rootstein "stars," help merchants to build a unique fashion image that the customer can easily recognize.

FIGURE 7-1

Photo courtesy of Adel Rootstein Display Mannequins Limited. Used with permission.

LEARNING OBJECTIVES

Upon completion of this chapter, the student should be able to

1. Write an essay on the three functions of a display.
2. List and discuss four types of window display.
3. Differentiate between overall lighting and highlighting, giving examples of each.
4. Explain the use of monochromatic, analogous, and complementary colors in display.
5. List five types of theme displays.
6. Discuss the importance of balance, emphasis, contrast, and space in merchandise arrangement.
7. Produce copy cards and price tags employing the C-curve and gothic stroke.

INTRODUCTION

Having made the customer aware of the store through advertising efforts and promotional campaigns, it is now the task of the display staff or visual merchandisers, as they are often called, to transform the store's interiors and windows into "silent salespersons." Creative display plays an important role in motivating the browser to become a purchaser.

Displays are executed in large organizations by professional staffs who work exclusively for their companies. The size of such staffs ranges from one or two in the branches to as many as or more than twenty-five in the giant parent stores. Some chains employ display experts to prepare displays, photograph them, and send them along with instructions for their use in the company's various units.

Small retailers have neither the need nor the budget to employ a full-time display person. In order to make certain that their windows and interiors are effective, the small store often uses the services of a free-lancer. The free-lancer is usually a person who has department or specialty store training and has decided upon self-employment. Free-lancers' fees average $50 an hour or upwards of $500 per window display. Armed with staples, hammers, glue, pins, and so on, they do the entire job.

No matter what the size of the store, a display should perform the following functions:

1. It must attract the buying public's attention. This may be achieved by the exciting use of color, dramatic lighting effects, and in-motion display. The great annual event at Lord & Taylor, New York, at Christmastime, with the dancing dolls in the window or a live Santa coming down the chimney, are examples of in-motion displays. Figure 7–2 shows an animated display created by David Hamberger, Inc., one of the largest manufacturers of animated and other displays in New York City.

FIGURE 7–2 Victorian Carolers—An Animated Display

Photo courtesy of David Hamberger Inc. Used with permission.

2. A satisfactory display must hold the individual's interest, much as a newspaper advertisement must. It is not enough to stop the passerby; it must make him or her investigate further. Interest is held by the display's timeliness, the merchandise's appeal, and the information on the accompanying show card.

3. The display must be exciting enough to arouse the desire to examine the merchandise (by asking to see it, try it on, and so forth). Retailers have long argued over whether display creates or arouses desires. The shopkeeper should settle for the awakening of the individual's desire to purchase.

Once these fundamentals are achieved, the display should sufficiently whet the prospective customer's appetite so that further merchandise investigation and close examination will take place.

SCHEDULING DISPLAYS

Stores give careful attention not only to what they will feature in their displays, but what the formats will be, when the displays will be changed, and in the case of window use, which departments will occupy specific windows for specific time periods.

Within each department's selling area, the goods to be "visually merchandised" will come from that particular department. Windows are another situation. No individual store has sufficient window space to feature all merchandise at all times. It is thus necessary for a system to be worked out that provides a sufficient amount of window time for each department, with the major departments getting the most time and the lesser getting the least. Figure 7–3 shows an excerpt from a typical display calendar, which is generally planned on a six-month basis.

WINDOW STRUCTURES

Today, with the enormity of the enclosed shopping malls, the traditional window structures are not as dominant as they once were. While many retailers still use the "closed back" window, which actually separates itself from the store, the "open back" and "window-less" windows are also very popular. The open back variety lends itself to displays on window ledges with the store's interior serving as the background. This type of format shows the prospective customer an overview of what the store is offering. The window-less window is an arrangement that uses the actual open front of the store—there is no window. A gate either rolls up, when the store is open for business, or slides into a concealed recess. This arrangement provides for the greatest amount of customer access into the store. As with open back windows, window-less windows use the store's interior as the background.

More formal windows are those that are parallel to sidewalks, arcades, corner windows, angled windows, and island windows. Each

FIGURE 7–3 Window Display Calendar

Window Schedule - January

Date	Window	Merchandise
Jan. 5	14	Avalon antron prints, Daytime Dresses
	15	Art deco print jersey, Bobbie Brooks, Juniorite, Jr. Sportswear
	16	Men's polyester knit slacks, Hagar, knit shirts (12/22)
Jan. 9	1	Furniture and Accessories
	2	"
	3	"
	4	Lamps
Jan. 12	5	Bridal Lingerie
	6	Guest at the Wedding: Chiffon costumes, Young Modes, Don Sophisticates, Gold Room
	7	Bridal Registry with Lenox
	8	Bridal gowns: Priscilla, Pandora, Bride's Boutique Collection.
	Stage	Polyester knit dresses, long torso, moving skirts, Moderate Dresses
Jan. 26.		What a Bright Idea!
	1	Crinkle patent suits & sportswear - battle jackets, skirts, Jr. Suits & Sportswear
	2	Crinkle patent handbags, gloves, Spring brights
	3	Linen coatdresses, melon, brown, Sue Brett, Colette, Jr. Dresses

type provides an arrangement that is most appropriate for particular displays.

Parallel to Sidewalk

The straight front, or parallel-to-sidewalk, window is most typical of large department stores. This type has a good deal of frontage on the street.

Arcade Windows

The arcade window extends from the building, with the store's entrance set back between two windows. This arrangement allows a store with little frontage to increase its window space. It is a popular structure for small stores (see Fig. 7–4)

FIGURE 7–4   Arcade Windows

Corner Windows

Corner windows are usually considered the most desirable by retailers. Because the window actually faces two streets, it allows for the greatest amount of converging traffic (see Fig. 7–5).

FIGURE 7–5   Corner Windows

Island Windows

Stores with very large vestibules, formed by two arcade windows facing each other, often build island windows in the center of the vestibule or lobby. These are windows, either built down to the ground or elevated, with glass on all sides. They permit shoppers to walk completely around and see the merchandise from all angles. They can, though, present the display person with problems in showing the merchandise (see Fig. 7–6).

FIGURE 7–6 Island Windows

Angled Windows

An angled window follows a slight angle from the building line of the store to the entrance, which is set back from the street. It is actually a variation of the parallel-to-sidewalk window but allows for more interesting design (see Fig. 7–7).

FIGURE 7–7 Angled Windows

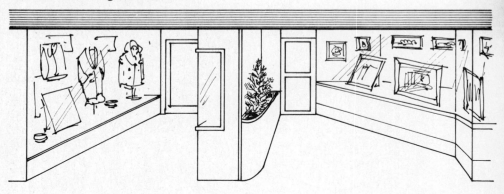

DISPLAY FIXTURES

Display fixtures are the devices on which merchandise can be shown to its best advantage. The fixtures can be either forms that simulate the human figure (mannequins) or parts of the figure or various types of stands, platforms, pedestals, and discs on which to drape and elevate the merchandise. In order to prepare a display, one must be familiar with all the various fixtures.

Human Form

Mannequins are used to display an entire outfit. Men's, women's, and children's forms are available in a variety of materials, such as plastic, plaster of paris, burlap, velvet, raffia, papier-mache, rubber, and wood. They range in design from lifelike replicas of humans, complete with imaginative hair stylings, to stylized forms, such as mannequins without facial features or with strawlike hair.

In selecting the proper mannequins for a retail store, the store's image should be kept in mind. For example, a store catering to teenagers would hardly select conventional lifelike mannequins. Similarly, the typical women's shop in a midwestern shopping center most probably wouldn't choose the stylized variety. Large department stores, some with hundreds of mannequins, often use all types: Their wide range of merchandise calls for such a variety. The retailer with a display budget that only occasionally allows for the purchase of new mannequins, and with a narrower assortment of merchandise than the department store, should select those forms that most typify the store's image.

The greatest percentage of human forms made today are plastic and lifelike. The plastic is lightweight and chip-resistant, and the lifelike variety is more easily accepted by the majority of consumers. Figure 7–8 shows an example of a mannequin head that has been inspired by the

FIGURE 7–8   New Wave Italian Mannequin Head

Photo courtesy of Adel Rootstein Display Mannequins Limited. Used with permission.

new wave Italian Memphis movement. Figure 7–9 shows an example of a high-fashion female form; and Figure 7–10, a male mannequin "working out."

FIGURE 7–9   High-Fashion Female Form

Photo courtesy of Adel Rootstein Display Mannequins Limited. Used with permission.

In addition to the full-figure mannequin, the following variations of human forms are used extensively in display. All come in the same materials as do the mannequins.

1. *Woman's torso*, or *three-quarter form*. Used for bathing suits, jackets, suits, lingerie, blouses, and skirts.
2. *Man's suit form*. Used for suits and sports jackets. Traditionally, this form is used a great deal more than a full-figure mannequin.
3. *Woman's shoulder-head form*. Used for millinery, scarves, jewelry, and hair ornaments. Usually these forms are abstract or stylized.
4. *Woman's blouse form*. Used for blouses, sweaters, and lingerie.

FIGURE 7–10 Male Mannequin "Working Out"

Photo courtesy of Adel Rootstein Display Mannequins Limited.
Used with permission.

5. *Woman's hand.* Used for gloves, jewelry, scarves, and watches. It is also extensively used to drape merchandise such as blouses, skirts, slacks, and sweaters.
6. *Hosiery legs.* Used for hosiery and socks.
7. *Shoe form.* Used for shoes and slippers.

Adjustable Stands

These stands are devices that can be adjusted to various heights and to which several attachments can be secured for displaying dresses, blouses, lingerie, hosiery, textiles, table linens, and so on. The stands come in several sizes and can be adjusted as follows:

   9-inch adjusts up to 18 inches
12-inch adjusts up to 24 inches
24-inch adjusts up to 48 inches
36-inch adjusts up to 72 inches

The most frequently used attachment for these stands is the T-rod. When used in combination, it is called a T-stand. Blouse forms and display hangers are also used for display with these stands.

Pedestals and Platforms

To achieve a variety of heights, pedestals and platforms in various sizes and shapes are used. These devices elevate the merchandise to the desired height to enable the merchandise to be shown to advantage. The pedestals are generally available in clear plastic, wrought iron, wood, chrome, and brass. The majority of platforms (the fixture used atop the pedestal) are made of glass or clear plastic.

A complete understanding of the many display fixtures and of their infinite variety of combinations is of utmost importance in display. Not only are the stands adaptable to different devices (hangers, "T" bars, and so on) but mannequins' arms can also be interchanged, positions can be adjusted, wigs can be changed to fit the merchandise, and so forth. One need only to go to the local department store and watch the display people preparing a new display to realize the many ways in which these fixtures can be used.

Most important in interior display is that the featured merchandise be available for purchase. Windows often cannot be changed to coincide with the sale of all of the displayed items, but interiors can be changed more frequently. Department managers, assistants, and sales personnel can easily make the changes as needed. A simple knowledge of the workings of such display properties as mannequins, stands, pedestals, and other props can make almost any store employee adept at interior display. Featuring merchandise that is no longer available is a waste of valuable display space.

LIGHTING

To prepare carefully the most beautiful merchandise, display fixtures, and background materials and then not pay attention to proper lighting is to completely destroy a display. Without lighting effects, the theater could never achieve the desired moods. Similarly, displays are not complete without good lighting.

Overall Lighting

To add general light (overall light) to a display satisfactorily, either incandescent or fluorescent lighting may be used. In both cases, the fixtures should be recessed into the ceiling. These lights should be used both in daylight and evening hours. In addition to illuminating the display, the overall lighting can overcome any glare. This general lighting should use only white bulbs. Colored lighting effects is achieved through highlighting with adjustable spotlights, but such special effects must always be used with extreme care to get proper results.

Highlighting

Spotlights, either mounted behind a valance or frame in a window or placed on the floor, are used to highlight the focal point of the display. This will set the mood and bring attention to an explanatory show card. For the novice, white spotlights are best. They throw a direct, bright, colorless, narrow beam.

Color, while most effective in display, can be disastrous if used incorrectly. For example, in the theater, purposely staged, lighting is used to change the colors of costumes many times. For theatrical effects, this is useful. However, a customer asking for the color seen in the window should find that same color.

The important rule to remember when using colored light (achieved by using colored bulbs or, more commonly, by attaching colored gels or colored transparent sheets over white bulbs) is to use only lights of the same color as that of the merchandise being highlighted. A red light on a red dress will intensify the color; a different light will change the color.

With attention paid to these simple lighting fundamentals, a display can be well lighted and exciting enough to attract customers. With some experience and experimentation, more dramatic effects can be achieved. And drama is an attention-getter.

COLOR

Whether you are preparing to display merchandise in a showcase, on a countertop, or in a window, the correct color coordination of merchandise is necessary for an eye-catching presentation. In addition, the colors selected for the copy card (a poster giving pertinent information that accompanies the display) must be those easiest to read.

An intensive survey of color is not intended in this book. Our discussion is limited to just enough information to permit the department manager or buyer to select the appropriate color combinations for use in the display. It is the individual department's responsibility to select the merchandise; the display department's job is to show it to its best advantage.

Basically there are six colors, plus the neutrals—black, brown, and white. Three are primary colors: yellow, red, and blue. Orange, violet, and green are secondary colors. Unlimited color combinations can be achieved with these colors, but the novice attempting to create an attractive display should stay with the simpler color combinations.

Monochromatic Color

Monochromatic (mono, meaning "one," and chroma, signifying "color") arrangements center around the use of one color. The merchandise would consist of all yellows or all reds, for example; for interest and variety, different values (lights or darks of the one color) and different intensities (brightest to dullest tones of the same color) are used. Thus, a manager might select a wide range of blue merchandise, avoiding monotony by choosing light blues, dark blues, dull blues, and bright blues. Blacks, browns, and whites, technically not colors, can also be used, still maintaining a monochromatic scheme. In seasons where there is a particular, universally accepted "fashion color," the monochromatic arrangement is perfect in a display.

Analogous Color

Use of more than one color can be achieved by selecting colors that are analogous (next to each other on the color wheel). For example, yellow and orange is an analogous color scheme; likewise, blue and green, green and yellow, and so on. As is true in monochromatic arrangements, different values and intensities, plus black, brown, and white, are added for interest and variety. An entire display might be worked around a two-color printed piece of merchandise (blue and violet, as an example) as a central or focal point in a window, with various other pieces in blues and violets. In this way, prints, if popular, done in analogous combinations (artists' designs and color sections are often based on the same arrangements taken from the color wheel) can be attractively displayed in both window and interior displays.

Complementary Color

Again, one must go back to the basic color wheel. By definition, complementary colors are direct opposites on the wheel. Yellow and violet, blue and orange, and red and green are complementary colors.

There are many, many other combinations, both usual and unusual, that can be used. The department manager who knows the job will automatically select creative combinations. Until that time, staying within the simple guidelines will allow for safe color combinations for merchandise displays.

MATERIALS AND PROPS

The materials selected and the props used are important in enhancing merchandise. Window floors and platforms are covered in a variety of fabrics, carpets, paper, stones, plastics, simulated grass, sand, and other materials, and backgrounds employ the simplest to the most elaborate papers, wood, or fabrics, depending on the nature or theme of the display. A visit to the local display center will show the enormous variety of available materials.

Props can vary from simple household articles, such as chairs, ladders, and room divider screens, to elaborate displays built by the store's display department. Displays are also available, either by purchase or lease, from display houses. One need only visit a display house when planning a Christmas presentation to see the wondrous creations for use in windows and interiors. Santas, fully moving, dancing elves, and skating children are just a few of the props available.

The selection of the display materials and props without the assistance of a professional display person is often difficult. Keeping in mind the message you are trying to project, plus the merchandise you are planning to sell, will help you select the right materials. Aid is always available at the display houses. The modern retailer wishing to keep abreast of what is current and available in display should read the National Retail Merchants Association's *Stores*, which continuously features innovative window and interior displays executed by the country's leading retailers.

SELECTING A THEME

The selection of a theme or topic for a display is generally a simple task. The approaching season, a local event, a president's birthday, the opening of school—these are just a few examples. Generally, themes of displays are usually one of the following types.

Seasonal Display

A seasonal display requires the arrangement of merchandise in a seasonal setting. The use of snow to emphasize winter, with a display of winter jackets, ski pants, skis, and bulky sweaters, is typical of a seasonal display. Figure 7–11 represents the Christmas season with the "Van Deer" family and Santa Claus.

Ensemble Display

Some stores choose to include complete outfits in their displays. For example, Figure 7–12 shows an ensemble display of men's evening wear and another depicting country horsemen.

Unit Window Display

To emphasize its importance, an item is shown in abundance, alone in a window—for example, twenty-five one-gallon cans of paint, many colors of the same shoe, or many patterns of textured hosiery.

Theme Display

Any theme can be chosen: a beach scene featuring swimwear, a camp scene showing campers' needs, or a church scene with a bridal party.

FIGURE 7–11   The "Van Deer" Family at Christmas

Photo courtesy of David Hamberger Inc. Used with permission.

FIGURE 7–12   Ensemble Displays

Photo courtesy of Adel Rootstein Display
Mannequins Limited. Used with permission.

FIGURE 7–13   Children at Play

Photo courtesy of Adel Rootstein Display
Mannequins Limited. Used with permission.

Figure 7–13 features two children in playclothes, appropriate for picnics or camping.

General Display

A general display presents unrelated merchandise. This arrangement is becoming less frequently used by display people today.

Institutional Display

Institutional display is used periodically by retail stores to sell the stores' image rather than merchandise. A window devoted to "Boy Scouts of America in Action" or "The Heart Fund" or some other event of public interest tends to show that the store is dedicated to the good of the community. Many retailers agree that the occasional use of institutional displays, void of merchandise, often brings more customers into a store than conventional displays. It should be understood that any display bearing a message that features neither merchandise nor direct merchandise copy is considered institutional. Figure 7–14 is such a display.

EXECUTION OF A DISPLAY

An orderly plan should be followed in preparing a window or interior display. Generally, a window display is a more difficult task, but the suggestions previously discussed should be kept in mind when preparating any display.

FIGURE 7–14 Institutional Christmas Display

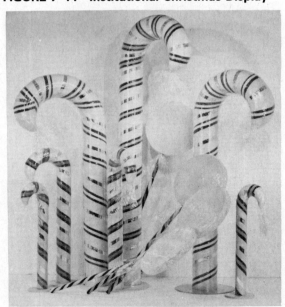

Photo courtesy of David Hamberger Inc. Used with permission.

Selecting Merchandise

Although a great deal of emphasis is placed on background materials and props, the merchandise to be displayed is the most important consideration. Too often the display person overpowers the merchandise by paying too much attention to the nonmerchandise factors. The merchandise should be timely, clean, carefully pressed (if this applies), and desirable in every way.

A limitation of display often ignored by some retailers is the fact that display does not sell unwanted merchandise—but it does help to sell greater quantities of desirable merchandise. So select those goods that will make the customer come through the door to purchase.

Selecting Display Materials and Props

For floor coverings, fabric is easier to handle than paper and they have a longer useful life. Stores frequently invest in neutral carpeting for windows and interior platforms, eliminating the necessity of frequent change. Whatever floor covering is used, care should be taken to eliminate wrinkles and creases and to conceal staples.

Walls can be painted or covered with paper, fabric, or other material. The most important consideration in the selection of floor and wall coverings is that they must not overpower the merchandise, but enhance it. With attention paid to careful color selection in background materials as well as the merchandise, there will be color harmony.

Props should be consistent with the theme selected. For example, a back-to-school display might make use of chalkboards, desks, rulers, erasers, and so on. A beach scene might employ sun umbrellas, lifeguard chairs, beach chairs, and water wings. Props are important in setting the stage on which the merchandise is to be presented. Consequently, they should be carefully selected.

Some props are functional in addition to being decorative and permit an interesting display of merchandise. A dress draped over a settee, clothing suspended from a clothesline, and shoes arranged on a ladder are imaginative ideas from a creative display designer.

Selecting Fixtures

Mannequins, T-stands, blouse forms, and other fixtures should be selected next. If a wide choice of mannequins (or changeable wigs) is available, select those that best fit the merchandise. The youthful-looking, casual, standing female mannequin with a long, simple hairstyle is certainly better in a swimsuit window than is a sophisticated one with an elegant hairstyle.

If the props selected provide for the display of merchandise, fewer fixtures will be needed. The reverse is also true.

An overcrowded display leads to confusion. Select only those fixtures appropriate to the merchandise. Fight the tendency to include even one more than is absolutely necessary.

Preparation of Component Parts

The preparation of the physical parts of the actual display centers around a program of "cleaning." In a store window, glass should be carefully washed before each display is executed. A film settles after a while on the inside of the glass because of gases, soot from heating devices, and so forth. Anything that distorts the viewer's ability to clearly observe the display must be eliminated. Care should be exercised in avoiding streaks from washing; handprints, often left by display people on the inside glass, should be removed.

The floors and walls of the window should be cleared of staples, nails, wire, and soil marks left from the previous displays. All fixtures, including mannequins, should be cleaned. This not only guarantees a perfect picture for the customer but also avoids soiling the new merchandise being displayed.

Light bulbs should be replaced where burned out. A display window is worthless without lighting. Colored bulbs or gels used to change white bulbs to color should be prepared if they are to be used in the display.

Planning the Merchandise Arrangement

Perhaps the most difficult task for a person with little or no display experience is where and how to place the merchandise in an interesting and attractive arrangement. Following are some of the most important factors to consider in arranging the merchandise.

Balance

There are basically two types of balance in display, symmetrical and asymmetrical. The symmetrical is frequently referred to as formal balance. This is an arrangement in which, if the window were divided down the center, each side would have equal weight (see Fig. 7–15). This balance often tends to be dull, unoriginal, and monotonous to the viewer. An asymmetrical or informal balance is achieved by placing merchandise arrangements without a central axis. These displays are more difficult to execute and, while more exciting, should be left for later attempts. An example of an asymmetrical display is shown in Figure 7–16.

Emphasis

Each display should have a point of emphasis, or focal point. This can be achieved through using a spotlight, setting the main item apart from the rest, featuring one item in a contrasting color and the rest of the display in another color, and many other methods. Experience teaches different ways to achieve emphasis.

Contrast

Contrast can be achieved by use of more than one color, various sizes and shapes of merchandise and fixtures, and so on.

FIGURE 7–15 Symmetrical Balance

Photo courtesy of David Hamberger Inc. Used with permission.

FIGURE 7–16 Asymmetrical Balance

Photo courtesy of David Hamberger Inc. Used with permission.

Space

Avoid overcrowding a display. Separating the various pieces in a window is important. If one piece of merchandise overlaps another, without being part of an ensemble, the eye doesn't know which belongs with which. The eye is incapable of absorbing very large segments. By allowing visible floor space between objects, the eye can outline each piece of merchandise separately. Raising merchandise from the floor, on pedestals, can help achieve separation and add interest to the display.

Preparation of a Graphic Plan

In order to save the costs of large display staffs and to aid managers in executing window displays, large retail organizations with many separate units prepare graphic presentations of proposed windows, for distribution. Planning in advance on paper saves time and labor in the installation. For those who must plan a display without professional help, a similar plan should be used. Although different procedures may be used, the following one should be satisfactory for organizing most window displays.

1. Prepare on graph paper the floor of your window. A 1-inch to 1-foot scale is suggested. However, any other scale suited to your needs would be adequate.
2. Indicate, to scale, the position of props, mannequins, and other fixtures, keeping in mind the importance of balance.
3. Attach to the plan, or indicate in writing, the floor covering and wall materials to be used.
4. Show the position of display cards. Figure 7–17 shows an example of a window planned to scale on graph paper.

FIGURE 7–17 Window Plan on Graph Paper, to Scale

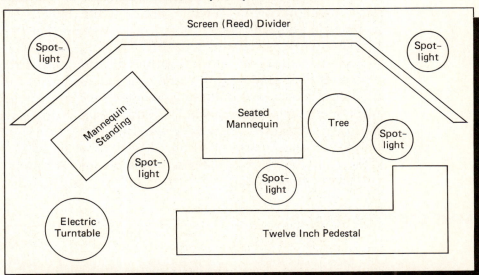

Trimming the Window

At this point, the actual arrangement of merchandise on the floor, stands, platforms, pedestals, and mannequins takes place. Proper planning, with attention paid to all of the points discussed, should result in an attractive, well-coordinated window. An additional basic principle, which can be practiced by the display person only while actually "trimming" rather than being indicated on a layout plan, is the placement of various items. Small items should be placed up front. They will not be seen in the rear of the window. Generally, merchandise is arranged with the smallest in the front and the largest in the rear. Naturally, mannequins should not be placed in front of other displayed merchandise.

The actual draping, pinning, and folding of window merchandise cannot be mastered by reading about it. This ability comes with the understanding of materials, shapes, and forms. A trip to a large store's display department to watch how it's done, or instruction in this area, will show how simple this part of display is.

Preparing Price Tags and Copy Cards

Attractive merchandise in the proper setting will surely get a customer's attention. In the case of window displays, the store wants to bring the right customer inside to make a purchase. Since few consumers are knowledgeable enough to determine the prices and pertinent facts about the merchandise, the written part of the display is important. Without the price, at least, departments could become overcrowded with consumers who are not real prospects. In today's world of retailing only the inexperienced retailer avoids the use of prices and copy cards to accompany their displays.

Before the preparation of the written material, the colors to be used for this purpose should be carefully selected. A safe choice, appropriate for any display, is black lettering on white stock. This combination is neutral and easy to read. Other easy-to-read color arrangements are black on yellow, green on white, red on white, blue on white, and white on blue. In choosing these colors, make certain that they do not clash with the display's color scheme.

After selecting the stock (cardboard, oaktag, construction board, or other material) and the ink to be used, execution of the message and price tags takes place. Lettering, while a highly specialized job, can be simply performed. The practice of three simple strokes will enable even the most untalented artist to create a written card. Figure 7–18 shows samples of two C-curves and one single gothic stroke. From these three strokes, any letter or number can be achieved. A few hours of practice will enable anyone to prepare price tags and copy cards.

SMALL STORE ADAPTATION

One need only look at store windows and interior displays to appreciate the efforts invested in visual merchandising. Attention to any store's

FIGURE 7–18 Samples of C-curves and Gothic Strokes

CO ccccccccc
ciacddeeq̇cjg̣iu
acdeqg acdeqg cc
ooo bbjophhnnm
abcdefghijklmnco
pqrsstuvwxyyz
AaBBbCcDdEFG
HIJjKkLIMNOP
QRSTUuVWXYZ
ABCDEFGHIJKLMNOPQRSTU
VWXYZ SINGLE STROKE GOTHIC

Courtesy of Ellen Diamond. Used with permission.

display that indicates a comprehension of timeliness will show that the company fully understands the value of display and its effect on sales. While large stores make certain that the Christmas window is removed right after Christmas Day, small stores often permit their valuable display space to continue to house presentations that are no longer of value. This is an important lesson for the small retailer, whose inexperience in visual merchandising often results in this oversight.

Small companies rarely have the specialist to create displays, nor do they have necessary capital for extravagant visuals. This by no means eliminates the independent retailer from putting the best foot forward in windows, counters, and interiors. Creative and exciting displays can be accomplished in any number of ways. If the store's owner or manager or salesperson is artistically talented, then meaningful visual presentations could be easily achieved. Since the execution of these displays will not incur any additional salary, the only expense will be for props and supplies. Carefully used and stored, they can be effectively adjusted time and time again through fresh paint and cleaning. Some small retailers employ free-lancers to create displays for each season. Props may be used for the entire season, with a store employee making weekly merchandise changes, following the format of the professional display person. Through distinct color changes, each week's window will have a new look.

Where none of these approaches is appealing, the store could build a permanent background that would complement any display. For example, a women's country boutique might have a parquet wooden floor, with neutral painted walls, and props such as a spinning wheel or easel for display of the merchandise. The same parquet floor and neutral walls could be used for a formalwear display; only the props need be changed. By using a minimum of items in the window, changes can be easily accomplished.

Through continuous investigation of the larger store's displays, the small retailer could become educated in the inexpensive aspects of display and adapt them for small store and interior usage.

CAREER OPPORTUNITIES

Display personnel, or visual merchandisers as they are more commonly called in retail circles, have the job of showing the store and its merchandise to the best possible advantage. Whetting the customer's appetite is the sum total of the visual merchandiser's task.

A career in display is not a typical goal for one who sets out for a life in retailing. While a knowledge of the store organization and its merchandising classifications is helpful, it is not one of the chief requirements for the display person hopeful. Of paramount importance to such a career is a working knowledge of color theory and coordination, lighting techniques, the specifics of balance, special arrangements, and so forth. In essence, those seeking opportunities in visual merchandising should be artistically oriented.

There are a number of different paths to follow in visual merchandising. One is to work for a major retail organization that has its own display department. Apprentice positions that require individuals to prepare windows for displays, dress mannequins, and refresh "tired" display props are often available in these stores. The size of the retail operation and its commitment to display dictate the number of different types of available positions for visual merchandisers. Some companies have specialists in a particular narrow area, whereas others prefer jacks and jills of all trades. For example, the very large retailer will employ an individual expressly for the purpose of preparing display copy cards, or one whose sole responsibility is to change interior counter displays. At the head of the visual merchandising department is the display manager, who usually reports to the director of publicity or sales promotion. It is these two individuals who have the ultimate responsibility for setting the tone and image of the store's window and interior displays. Their subordinates create backgrounds, change mannequins, "dress" windows, prepare copy, and so on.

Another route to take for display-oriented people is that of freelancing. Whereas major stores employ their own staffs, small retailers have neither the funds or need to do so. These organizations routinely call upon a free-lancer to create window and interior displays whenever necessary. The free-lancer is self-employed and sells his or her services to the company. Anyone wishing for self-employment and who possesses creative visual merchandising ability will find this career path both artistically and financially rewarding.

KEY POINTS IN THE CHAPTER

1. An effective display attracts attention, holds interest, and arouses the desire to further examine the merchandise.

2. In order to make certain that departments get their fair share of window display space, schedules are arranged as much as six months in advance.

3. Stores have a variety of window structures, ranging from "closed back" windows to the "window-less" windows.

4. Display fixtures run the gamut from human form mannequins to a variety of other forms, stands, pedestals, and platforms—all in an enormous variety of materials and styles.

5. When using lighting in a window, it is important to use only the same colored lighting as that of the merchandise or the color will look different.

6. Color schemes are most frequently arranged employing schemes that are monochromatic, analogous, or complementary.

7. Themes used in display are seasonal, general, thematic, institutional, or ensemble. Selecting the appropriate type is dependent on the message to be conveyed.

8. Structurally, a good display has balance, symmetrical or asymmetrical, and emphasis and contrast. It avoids overcrowding.

9. Graphic plans enable displays to be copied by store personnel. In many chains, this procedure is used so that store personnel, not display people, will be able to build a display.

10. Price tags and copy cards can be easily prepared with the use of two simple C-curves and a single gothic stroke.

Worksheet 7

COMPLETE THE FOLLOWING STATEMENTS

1. When using color lighting, you must use the same color light as the

   _____ to be displayed.

2. A color arrangement centering around one color is said to be a

   _____ color scheme.

3. There are basically two types of balance in display, _____ and

   _____.

4. Each display should have a point of interest known as a

   _____ point.

5. Large stores prepare _____ that indicate important
   dates, days for display presentations, and so on.

6. Window schedules are planned as far as _____ months in advance.

TRUE OR FALSE

_____ 1. The corner window permits viewing of a window from all angles.

_____ 2. In the giant enclosed malls, there is a tendency to eliminate the
   formal window structure.

_____ 3. For general window lighting, it is best to use white bulbs.

_____ 4. Yellow and violet are complementary colors.

_____ 5. The promotional display is used to promote the store's image.

_____ 6. In enclosed malls, the interior of the store is often the window.

MULTIPLE CHOICE

_____ 1. The window structure that allows a store with limited frontage to
   increase its window space is the
   (a) parallel-to-sidewalk window
   (b) arcade window
   (c) corner window
   (d) island window

_____ **2.** Human form fixtures best suited for display are constructed of
  - **(a)** plaster
  - **(b)** plastic
  - **(c)** papier-mache
  - **(d)** all of the above

_____ **3.** When using a colored light to accent a piece of merchandise, the color of the light should be
  - **(a)** the same as the merchandise
  - **(b)** an analogous color of the merchandise
  - **(c)** the direct opposite color of the item
  - **(d)** none of the above

_____ **4.** Display emphasizing one item is
  - **(a)** theme display
  - **(b)** general display
  - **(c)** unit window display
  - **(d)** seasonal display

_____ **5.** Included among display elements is
  - **(a)** balance
  - **(b)** emphasis
  - **(c)** contrast
  - **(d)** all of the above

DISCUSSION QUESTIONS

1. What is a "silent salesperson"?

2. How does the small retailer overcome the disadvantage of not having a display staff or department?

3. In addition to location, what is the main difference between window display and interior display?

4. What is the major difference between the parallel-to-sidewalk window and the angled window? Which one allows for more interesting design?

5. How does a stylized mannequin differ from a conventional mannequin? Give some examples of stylized forms.

6. Why are pedestals and platforms used in display? What materials are they made of?

7. Compare overall lighting with highlighting. Explain the different functions of each type.

8. What color light should be used on a red dress, a blue sky (background), a sunny sky (background)?

9. List two types of color arrangements that employ two colors. How do these arrangements differ?

10. Where can one find window props without incurring expense?

11. Which type of display does the supermarket manager use most successfully?

12. What is a limitation of display not often understood by inexperienced or uninformed retailers?

13. Although paper used as flooring in windows is inexpensive, some display people avoid using it. Why?

14. What is the most frequently used stand in display? How can it be manipulated?

15. To what details in the actual window structure must attention be paid before the merchandise is arranged?

16. What are other names for formal balance and informal balance? How do they differ?

17. How can a display person achieve contrast in a display? Why is contrast important?

18. What is the purpose of preparing a graph of a proposed window?

19. In addition to knowing the copy-card colors that are easy for customers to read, what must the display person keep in mind when selecting colors that are to be used in a particular display?

20. What is a window schedule, and why do stores prepare them?

CASE PROBLEM 1

Richlord's is the major department store in a small city in the northeastern United States. Sales have remained relatively constant for the past three years. This has distressed management, since overall retail sales have increased nationally.

Many suggestions have been offered to rectify the situation. One, which seems to be upsetting the department managers, is to alter the display program at the store. Departments have traditionally been assigned window display space on a priority basis. Each department would then select the merchandise to be displayed in the windows. The new plan would take some display space away from the individual departments and use this space for institutional displays. Top management feels that this type of display would eventually bring more business to the entire store. The department managers argue that with less display space for the actual presentation of each department's merchandise the amount of goods sold would decrease.

1. Do you agree with top management's new display plan? Defend your position with sound reasoning.

2. Do you think institutional display should receive as much space as regular merchandise displays? Why?

CASE PROBLEM 2

The Value-Rite Supermarkets traditionally display their goods in the usual unexciting manner most supermarkets do. Cans and boxes of special items are stacked either in the window or on the selling floor in pyramids.

The new store manager wants to change the interior look of the stores so that it might motivate customers to buy more merchandise. He feels that more attention to interior display might do the job. Some of his plans include the use of such items as in-motion displays, turntables, and large, colorful posters. He would also take some of the display space away from the food items and use it for nonfood items.

1. Are there any dangers in changing from the traditional type of supermarket display? Defend your position.
2. Is display necessary in supermarkets, or are newspaper advertisements and signs in the windows announcing specials sufficient? Defend your answer.

PROJECT 1

Complete a window calendar for a large store selling men's, women's, and children's clothing. Make certain that only the dates that are important to the store's business are included. In addition, suggest the traditional colors that might be used in the window's background and some props that might be employed. Also, place an asterisk next to those events the store must pay most attention to in planning and spending.

Window Calendar

Date	Day	Colors	Props

PROJECT 2

Prepare layouts on graph paper for the following displays:

1. A unit window (parallel-to-sidewalk variety, 8 feet wide by 2 feet deep) for a supermarket introducing latex wall paint in its nonfood department.
2. An angled window 10 feet wide by 6 feet deep, tapering to 4 feet at the store's entrance, displaying back-to-school preteen clothing.
3. An island window 4 feet square displaying menswear.

A scale of 1 inch equals 1 foot is suggested. However, any more convenient scale may be used. To clarify the layout further, include notes on the reverse side of the graph paper. For ease in adjusting and readjusting layouts, cardboard templates (shapes to represent platforms, stands, mannequins) might be cut to scale and traced onto the graph paper.

PROJECT 3

Using the strokes and curves described in the chapter, prepare rough layouts of copy to accompany the following displays. Suggest the colors to be used on the copy cards.

1. A nautical display showing men's swimwear selling at $20 in the men's shop on the main floor
2. A display of a kitchen featuring a yellow refrigerator ($650), range ($500), and dishwasher ($475); merchandise is located in the basement
3. A display of the latest in Paris imports available exclusively in the boutique department at Penrod's Department Store

After completing the rough layouts for each, carefully prepare one with the appropriate colors on 18-by-24-inch construction board, as it might appear in an actual window.

PROJECT 4

Take a black-and-white photograph of a window display featuring men's, women's, or children's clothing. Attach three copies of the same photo to the places indicated and suggest colors that coordinate properly in monochromatic, analogous, and complementary color schemes. Indicate the color for each piece of merchandise displayed, as well as background colors that will best complement the merchandise. Label each piece of merchandise with a number, and list the colors you have assigned.

Photograph

	Monochromatic Color Scheme *Merchandise Colors*

1.
2.
3.
4.
5.
6.
7.
8.
9.
10.

Background Colors

1.
2.
3.
4.
5.
6.
7.
8.
9.
10.

Photograph

Analogous Color Scheme
Merchandise Colors

1.
2.
3.
4.
5.
6.
7.
8.
9.
10.

Background Colors

1.
2.
3.
4.
5.
6.
7.
8.
9.
10.

Photograph   _Complementary Color Scheme_
                                                  Merchandise Colors

1.
2.
3.
4.
5.
6.
7.
8.
9.
10.

Background Colors

1.
2.
3.
4.
5.
6.
7.
8.
9.
10.

PROJECT 5

Divide the class into groups of four or five. Each group is to prepare a model of a window display for presentation before the class. The group may divide its responsibilities any number of ways. For example, one might be the display director with overall responsibility for coordination, another might be assigned to prepare the copy, and another might be responsible for lighting plans. An actual three-dimensional display in miniature should be executed and presented for criticism. The goods to be displayed can be of any variety and of any theme. This is an opportunity for creativity of the part of each group.

A suggested rating form for use in criticizing each group's display follows. Other categories might be added. Place an X in the appropriate space for each category below.

	Excellent	_Very Good_	_Average_	_Fair_	_Poor_
Originality of idea					
General appearance					
Material and props					
Lighting					
Emphasis (focal point)					
Color					
Balance					
Cleanliness					
Copywork					

Consumer Behavior and Personal Selling

TAKE "CARE" AND INCREASE SALES

Too many merchants constantly blame a host of reasons for declining sales and profits, from "The economy is bad" to "The off-price retailers are getting all the business." To some degree, both reasons may be instrumental in creating bleak times, but it isn't wise to sit around and wait for bad times to get worse. Often, unattended problems *do* get worse.

Although the Gimbel's stores are no longer in business, one device that organization used effectively was good, old-fashioned personal selling. Gimbel's, like most retail organizations, had lost sight of the fact that the principal function of the sales staff is to sell merchandise. How often have you sought the assistance of a salesperson only to find he or she is "taking markdowns," preparing inventory counts, or working on "internal transfers"? This seems to have become the rule rather than the exception.

On a one-day trial arrangement, Gimbel's offered $5 to any salesperson who made just one sale more than for the previous period in the prior year. The results were impressive in that sales, for the day, almost doubled. This prompted management to embark on a program to return the salesperson to the customer. In order to make certain that the new direction was appropriate, Gimbel's hired Senn-Delaney & Associates, a research company, to survey and make suggestions about the selling situation.

Supported with information from the research that confirmed the belief that the salesperson's role should be one of a total commitment to selling, Gimbel's embarked on a "CARE" program—*customers are really everything.* The store held CARE seminars and CARE committees and orientation programs, all of which emphasized the philosophy that the customer is most important.

After two years of the program, management revealed that the efforts of CARE were successful. By taking "care," Gimbel's increased its sales.

LEARNING OBJECTIVES

Upon completion of this chapter, the student should be able to

1. Discuss the psychological steps involved in decision making.
2. Write a short essay on learning, including the importance of drive, cues, response, and reinforcement.
3. Differentiate between rational and emotional motives.
4. Discuss attitudes and habits, giving examples of each.
5. Discuss five personal characteristics essential to a successful salesperson.
6. List five areas of merchandise with which a salesperson must be familiar.
7. Write a brief paragraph on the selling of additional merchandise after a sale has been made, including at least three methods.

INTRODUCTION

All of the functions of retailing must be aimed at satisfying the needs of the customer. Thus, the more the retailer knows about the customer, the greater the chances for sales. Sophisticated retailing requires that consumer behavior be studied. It is no longer appropriate for stores to take a haphazard approach in terms of selling. Most retailers used to rely on the premise that once a customer enters the store, purchasing is sure to follow. Today, the educated retailer finds out what makes the customer tick—through consumer psychology, motivation, and habits—and trains the sales force to use this information.

This chapter focuses on the various aspects of understanding consumer behavior, and how retailers sell to their customers.

CONSUMER BEHAVIOR

The study of human behavior is probably older than retailing. In recent years, however, there are two reasons for this: First, greatly increased competition has forced retailers to look for an extra "edge," and second, the success of certain retailing giants has resulted in funds being available for the necessary research.

Those stores that are best able to satisfy customers will make the sales. Consumers who are satisfied with their purchases are likely to become loyal repeat customers.

Decision Making

Consumer buying is a matter of decision making. Therefore, it is important to understand the internal workings of the decision-making process. This process involves the following steps: stimulus and problem recognition, information gathering and selection, and purchase and evaluation. An understanding of each of these steps and their application to successful retailing is necessary.

Stimulus and Problem Recognition

Decision making, like all problem solving, starts with an awareness of the problem. Some stimulus is necessary to bring the problem to the attention of the future buyer. The initiation of the idea can come from a variety of sources, each of which will turn the consumer's thoughts toward resolving the problem. For example:

Self: "I have a headache, I need an aspirin."
Friend: "Let's see a movie tonight."
Business Advertisement: "All designer jeans 10% off."

Whatever the source of the stimulation, it begins the decision-making process by focusing attention on a need. Of particular interest to retailers is the fact that advertising and other promotional devices, such as counter and window displays, can provide the stimulus if they are properly conceived.

Of course, the stimulus will not lead to a problem until a need arises. For example, the person with the headache who needs an aspirin will take one if it is available, and, thus, the decision about whether or not to buy is hastened. If, on the other hand the response to the stimulus "I have a headache, I need an aspirin" is "I took the last one in the bottle last week," then the problem is recognized and the decision-making process goes on. Similarly, if the response to the friend's suggestion is "I have too much homework," or to the advertisement, "I have all of the jeans I need," then there is no problem. If, however, the response to the stimulus is positive, then the decision-making process continues.

Information Gathering

In the event that the problem recognized is of sufficient importance to the consumer to require a solution, the next step in the decision-making process is to gather information and make the selection. Even in the simplest case, many decisions must be made: "Shall I buy an advertised, popular brand of aspirin or the generic brand, which is cheaper and, I'm told, just as good?" "Shall I buy the one advertised on TV as stronger or my own brand?" "Shall I stop in the next drugstore I come to or wait until I get to my neighborhood drugstore?"

As the intended purchase becomes more expensive and complicated, the information gathering becomes more intensive. For example, a person needing a new car must first decide on standard size, compact, or subcompact. Then, having decided on a compact, two-door or four-door? Blue or gray? Automatic or shift? Which maker? The list is endless, and the complications so great that outside help is frequently needed. For such expensive purchases, people usually visit many showrooms, have discussions with friends who have made similar purchases, and consult literature such as *Consumer Reports* magazine before making a decision.

Retailers, in order to turn the information-gathering phase of the decision-making process to their best advantage, must be prime providers of information. Advertising, displays, and knowledgeable sales personnel are of great importance in getting the message across. The consumers, after all, are faced with alternatives and must be convinced that one retailer's product is more likely to satisfy their needs than is the product of a competitor.

Purchase and Evaluation

After the prospective purchaser has evaluated the information that has been gathered, the next step in the decision-making process is the actual purchase. It is at this point that the retailer's involvement is most intense, because the decision to purchase a specific product involves the selection of the specific store from which the purchase is to be made. The buying decision may have had as a stimulus an advertisement stating, "All designer jeans 10% off," but that does not mean that the purchase will be made from that particular advertisement. All that the ad did was to start a reaction that resulted in a consumer's decision to buy a pair of jeans. Among the information gathered were: Is a 10 percent deduction enough, or is another store offering more? What is the store's image? Convenience? Return policy?

The availability of the required merchandise is another important factor to the retailer. Once the decision to purchase a particular item is made, the purchaser wants the goods to be available in the selected store. If the merchandising of that particular store has not anticipated the customer's desire, not only will the sale be lost, but also the selection of that particular store in the future is jeopardized.

The decision-making process does not end with the purchase. There is still the problem of satisfaction. The satisfied purchaser may be an immediate customer for accessories. The shirt buyer may select a tie; the woman who bought a handbag may be interested in matching shoes. In addition, the contented customer may become a loyal repeater, and that is the bottom line of successful retailing.

On the other hand, a dissatisfied customer can be a serious problem. Not only is the future business of the dissatisfied customer lost; also endangered is the business of friends who may hear the story. How does a retailer guard against dissatisfaction? For one thing, no high-pressure selling; for another, follow-up calls or letters on expensive items such as automobiles and high-priced appliances help. Honest advertising and liberal merchandise return policies are steps in the right direction. Finally, money-back guarantees if the consumer is not satisfied are offered by many large retailers, recognizing that a satisfied customer is worth more than a lost sale.

Learning

Basically, decision making is a learning process. Having made the buying decision by the steps indicated above and having achieved satisfaction, the consumer is likely to repeat the purchase when the need arises again. Decision making, then, is a response to a stimulus.

Some years ago Ivan Pavlov, a Russian psychologist, found that, with the proper conditioning, he could teach a subject to respond in a particular way to a given stimulus. In other words, he could guide the learning procedure. His work was simple: Each time he fed a dog, he would ring a bell. After repeated trials, the dog would salivate at the sound of the bell, without the presence of food. He had taught the dog to salivate on cue.

Pavlov's work is the foundation of learning theory and provides the basis of much of today's retail advertising and sales promotion. Modern behavioral scientists have refined Pavlov's work by breaking it down into four steps: drive, cues, response, and reinforcement.

Drive

The first step in the learning process is a drive. By definition, a drive is an individual's awareness of an internal tension that is caused by a need from within. Basic drives may be to satisfy needs for humor, shelter, or warmth. Other drives may be to obtain a new tie, hairstyle, or sweater. The drive creates a tension in the individual, which will only be appeased by taking action. If the drive is strong enough, the individual will seek to satisfy it.

Cues

The manner in which an individual responds to the drive depends on cues that individual has been made aware of. These are ideas and other bits of information that have been stored in memory. Advertising is an example of an important generator of cues. An individual who is interested in buying a pair of slacks may remember a recent advertisement for just the sort of merchandise that will be suitable. Another, anxious to satisfy a drive for food, may remember a Chinese restaurant or fast-food place nearby. Advertising, window displays, conversations with friends, and store decor are all cues of sorts.

Response

A positive action taken, as a result of cues, to satisfy a drive is called a response. This is the actual making of the purchase that will ease the tension caused by the drive. Purchasing the slacks or ordering the food are examples of responses.

Reinforcement

When the response to the drive proves satisfying, reinforcement occurs. When a similar need arises again, the reinforced response is likely to return as an important cue for future satisfaction. Those who enjoy McDonald's hamburgers return again and again. Popular brands are established through positive reinforcement, as is store loyalty.

It may seem a long jump between Pavlov's dogs and successful retailing, but consider the worker who glances at a clock at 12 noon and becomes hungry for lunch. Is that response unlike the salivating dogs? How about the person who is deluged by television commercials for designer jeans? Isn't that an effective way to start a drive and suggest a brand name as a cue?

Buying Motives

The more retailers know about their customers, the more likely they are to satisfy the customers' needs. One major piece of information is why people buy and what motivates them. Different people buy for different reasons. Consider this: An individual decides to buy a car. The alternatives from which the selection is to be made are enormous. To understand the reason for a particular choice, we must first understand why the decision to buy the car was made in the first place. Has the old car broken down? Does it look tacky? Is it in the repair shop too often? Is it a gas-guzzler? If we can understand the motivation for the purchase, we can direct our total sales pitch, including advertising, merchandising, personal selling, and other promotion, in that direction.

Rational versus Emotional Motivation

One common way of classifying motives is by differentiating between rational and emotional buyers.

Rational buyers do their homework. In the case of the car buyer, comparative information will be obtained on the cost of the automobile, gas mileage, frequency of repair, estimated life, and so on. The actual purchase will be based on the outcome of a careful study.

In contrast, the emotional buyer bases the buying decision on style, pride of ownership, romance, and so on. For example, any jacket will provide warmth. The rational buyer will select the product that provides the best construction, durability, and economy. The emotional buyer will buy the high-fashion, designer-label jacket that looks best. It should be pointed out that we are discussing buying motives, not intelligence. The rational buyer may gather the wrong information, interpret it incorrectly, and for any of a number of reasons make a totally irrational purchase.

The borderline between rational and emotional motives is frequently crossed. That is, some individuals, usually rational buyers, take an occasional flyer for an emotional product that strikes their fancy. Moreover, an individual who buys clothing on an emotional basis might put considerable research into the purchase of a lawn mower.

The point for retailers is that when selling products that appeal to emotional purchasers, use an emotional sales pitch. Do not, for example, use the same advertising and sales promotion for a Cadillac as for a Chevette. Also, alert retailers must change their message as their products move from one category to another. Consider Volkswagen advertising over the years. Originally the automobiles were offered as a low-cost, efficiently operating machine, ideally suited to the rational buyer. In recent years, costs have increased, styling has improved, and the stripped-down version is hard to find. The down-to-earth advertising has changed to one with snob appeal. The cars now appear outside mansions, fancy country clubs, and expensive art galleries. The ads are peopled by cultured, well-spoken individuals who can well afford a Cadillac or Mercedes-Benz. The focus is no longer targeted to the down-to-earth rational buyer, but to the status-seeking, prestige-conscious, emotional buyer.

Attitudes

An attitude is an individual's feeling toward a particular object. These preconceived opinions are often crucial to a store's success. Attitudes are learned; they are the result of, for example, an individual's experience, conversations with friends, and reactions to advertising and sales promotion. To illustrate the importance of attitude to retailing success, consider an individual who has several friends who have had negative experiences with the return policies of a particular store. As a result, that person may never try the store. A positive attitude can result if the experiences with a particular retailer are good. Attitudes can be shaped from a wide variety of sources. Even such information as the personal life of the store's owner can have an effect on a prospective customer toward a store.

Rarely can attitudes be changed. For example, the perception of Sears has always been that of an organization that gives value, and the store's emphasis has been on hardware, housewares, and appliances. An ongoing attempt to include fashion clothing as part of the store's image has met with only fair success. Or consider the perception that small, independently owned retailers do not accept returned goods easily. It is doubtful that a small retailer that advertises a liberal return policy would change many consumer perceptions.

A retailer's image—the way it is perceived by customers and potential customers—is vital, and difficult to alter. Consequently, every effort must be made to minimize customer discontent. The slogan "The Customer Is Always Right" has a more beneficial effect on the store than it does on the customer.

Habits

Another important factor in consumer behavior is the buying habits of the retailer's market. When, where, and how much will be purchased are pieces of information that the successful retailer must blend effectively if customer satisfaction is to be achieved.

Conforming to the consumer's "time" habit, that is, when the consumer buys, requires that the retailer have the merchandise on hand, the staff available, and the advertising geared to consumer wants. Christmas tree ornaments must be available in December, and bathing suits, in the spring and early summer. Advertising must inform customers of the availability of the goods, and the store's operation must be geared to handle peak loads whenever necessary. In the case of supermarkets, whose peak day is Friday, advertising usually appears in the Thursday newspapers and the shelves are fully stocked by Friday morning.

Satisfying the "time" habit is usually learned quickly and conformed to easily. It is not a habit that can easily be changed. The "where" habit, the store from which a consumer buys a particular item, is another matter. In recent years, this habit has been changed. Supermarkets now carry a line of nonprescription drugs, large drugstores display housewares and small appliances, and prestigious men's shops carry women's ready-to-wear. This is not to indicate that the "where" habit is easily changed. It requires a considerable investment in inventory and promotion and patience. But it can be done.

The quantity habit is easily adjusted to. It depends on the area that the retailer services. In suburban areas, where shoppers travel by automobile, supermarket shoppers buy in huge quantity. Not so in urban areas, where supermarket purchasers must hand-carry the goods. They shop more frequently and buy smaller quantities. Similarly, in economically deprived areas, food marketers must be prepared to sell eggs individually rather than by the dozen.

Conforming to customers' behavioral habits is relatively easy. However, many retailers do not seem to realize that these habits are in a constant state of change and that frequent adjustments may be necessary. For example, the growing number of working women has been changing buying habits. For one thing, because shoppers who work are not able to shop during the day, evenings and Sundays have become increasingly important for shopping. A resultant change is the increased number of men shoppers for goods that traditionally had been the responsibility of women. Promotional displays, merchandise, and sales presentations that had been successful with women must be adjusted to this new breed of customer.

Where people shop is another changing habit. For example, the success and continued growth of the flea market has been causing serious problems to traditional retailers. As more people get into the habit of buying at these low-overhead, cut-price retailers, the competition is forced to adjust to this new threat by means such as carrying different lines of merchandise or lowering prices.

PERSONAL SELLING

Having learned about consumer buying motives, attitudes, and habits, a salesperson could now approach the customer with more insight and understanding. By applying this knowledge to selling, closing a sale is bound to be an easier task to accomplish.

Comprehension of consumer behavior alone, though, is not a guarantee for successful selling. Salespersons must also possess certain qualities in order to do the job well, must know the merchandise, should understand the proper techniques for approaching the customer, and, finally, must be trained to close the sale.

Essentials for Effective Selling

Too much emphasis cannot be placed on the importance of the salesperson's ability. The image of the store is directly affected by the impression that that person makes on the prospective customer. It is important to remember that until the shopper actually makes a purchase, that individual can only be considered a prospect. Personal selling ability, more than any other type of selling aids, is the main activity in retailing that builds or destroys the shopper's confidence.

To the public, the salesperson *is* the store, and many times a customer purchases or does not purchase because of him or her. Often when a shopper states, "I don't like that store," she or he is referring to the sales force. With the enormous amount of competition facing the retailer, the store's main liaison with the public, the salesperson, must be properly prepared.

Appearance

Before helping shoppers with their purchases, the salesperson must make an impression that is conducive to purchasing. The first impression is the salesperson's appearance. The prospective customer isn't apt to be receptive to the advice of someone who isn't appropriately attired.

In small stores, dress regulations are not as stringent as they are in the larger organizations. Most small storekeepers deal with only a few salespeople and can supervise their dress habits informally. In some larger stores, where management often deals with several hundred salespeople, a uniform dress code is established. For example, such colors as black, brown, navy blue, and gray may be prescribed. The main reason for this regulation, often frowned on by employees, is that it ensures that the salesperson's attire will not detract from the merchandise, and that shocking colors and patterns will be avoided.

The simple statement that "employees should dress in good taste" is not adequate. Taste is too personal to be left to chance. The salesperson should avoid wearing any type of outfit that might be offensive and could discourage a customer from asking for sales help. For example, the younger employee working in a conservative men's shop should avoid wearing "way-out" styles. If salespersons choose to dress in a manner unlike the atmosphere of the store, the potential customers might not seek their advice.

Salespeople at Abraham & Straus, a department store with branches in New York State and New Jersey, receive a booklet called "Your Appearance Counts," which serves as a guide in the selection of appropriate styles and colors for business use. The following questions are posed in the booklet, which, when answered affirmatively, contribute to proper appearance:

Ladies . . .

Is your hair neatly combed?
Is your skin clear?
Are your hands clean and well manicured?
Makeup just right . . . not too heavy . . . not too light?
No runs in your stockings?
Are you wearing neat, well-heeled (and comfortable) shoes?
Is your attire businesslike and fresh looking?

Gentlemen . . .

Is your hair trim and clean?
Do you shave daily?
Hands well scrubbed . . . nails clipped and clean?
Are your shoes well shined?
Is your shirt or uniform clean and pressed?
Are your collar and shirt fresh?

Enthusiasm

Enthusiasm does not mean that a salesperson should be overly aggressive and should "come on strong." Being too aggressive may lead to overpowering the customers and convincing them to buy items they might not really want. An enthusiastic salesperson is one who shows a real feeling for the merchandise and stimulates the customer's emotions. If the salesperson discusses the merchandise enthusiastically, the enthusiasm may transfer to the customer. Too often, shoppers are helped by lethargic salespeople who encourage a poor frame of mind.

Voice and Speech

An audible voice and proper diction are important to successful selling. Salespersons do not, by any means, need theatrical training to make a clear presentation to customers, but they should exercise care in the manner in which they speak and in their choice of words. The salesperson who speaks properly will more easily establish rapport with the shopper.

Tact

Being tactful is essential to selling in the retail store. The salesperson's job is to help satisfy the customer's needs. Should the salesperson allow the customer to purchase something that the salesperson knows is wrong, even though the customer wants to make the purchase? Allowing this purchase to be made might lead to criticism (by the customer's friends) and eventual return of the goods. On the other hand, the salesperson's suggestion that the shopper's choice is a poor one might be an affront. For example, if a stout woman would like to purchase a dress that accentuates her figure in the wrong places, extreme care must be taken not to offend the customer, but to direct her tactfully to something more appropriate. Tactfulness is something that comes only with extreme caution and experience.

Self-Control

It is unlikely that even the most even-tempered salesperson hasn't had the desire to punch a customer in the eye. A salesperson who is to be successful must keep in mind that "the customer is always right" and must control emotions even when following this rule seems intolerable. Abusing the customer will only lead to the loss of sales. A person who is easily excited by the shortcomings of others shouldn't pursue a sales job, or for that matter, any career in retailing.

A prospective salesperson should show initiative and sincerity, and be cheerful, knowledgeable, and resourceful. It may be unusual for one person to have all these qualities, but the more that are possessed, the greater are the chances for success in a sales position.

How to Sell

Perhaps the most difficult job to learn from a textbook is how to sell. Selling can be improved by many techniques, such as role playing, but there are basic steps in the selling process that should be learned before refinement can take place.

Know the Merchandise

Salespeople who say that they can sell anything without knowledge of the product are either naive or do not have an understanding of good selling methods. The ability to sell merchandise in a way that will gain the customers' confidence and satisfy their shopping needs requires an understanding of the merchandise for sale. The inability to answer the shoppers' specific product questions tends to make salespeople bluff or avoid the queries. Using proper techniques may result not only in an immediate sale; it may also lead to future customer purchases.

While it is not possible for a salesperson to be completely knowledgeable in all areas of hard goods and soft goods, it is important to have some fundamental information about the merchandise. Complete unfamiliarity with the goods (in the case of a new employee or a transfer from another department) necessitates getting the necessary product information. The following areas should be completely familiar to the salesperson.

Merchandise location.   Not all merchandise is arranged in shelves or on racks that are easily accessible. Some goods are kept in reserve (under counters or in stockrooms, for example), and the knowledge of their location is important. The need to search for merchandise detains customers and wastes time. Even for merchandise that is on the selling floor, it is important to know the exact location.

Merchandise uses.   While it is obvious what purpose a dress or a suit serves, some goods have less obvious uses or even numerous uses. For example, a vacuum cleaner, in addition to cleaning rugs, may be adapted for upholstery and drapery cleaning and perhaps even for spray painting. Even in soft goods some items might be adapted for various uses. With a different blouse, an outfit can be used for daytime or evening wear.

Styles.   The shapes of things—their styles—vary from season to season. Besides knowing which styles are fashionable or suitable for a particular purpose, salespeople should know the appropriate styles for their customers. For example, the lines of a double-breasted jacket are arranged in such a manner that they somewhat conceal a bulging midsection. Knowledge of styles and their uses can help in closing a sale more quickly. Style is not limited to soft goods. Refrigerators, ranges, dining room tables, and chairs are examples of other types of merchandise available in a variety of styles. It is important for a salesperson who sells refrigerators to have sufficient knowledge of that department's various models and their advantages to satisfy the most discriminating customer. For example, a customer might want to know the advantages of a double-door refrigerator-freezer as compared with a conventional model.

Sizes.   In addition to clothing and accessories, other merchandise comes in a variety of sizes. Sofas, chairs, dishwashers, television sets, and pool tables, just to mention a few, come in different sizes. Salespersons should have an understanding of such sizes so they can quickly help customers choose the right items. Some years ago a person selling women's clothing was concerned only with misses' and junior sizes. In an attempt to approximate the female figure more closely and eliminate costly alterations, manufacturers have introduced many new size ranges. In addition to the two mentioned, sales personnel must know the differences among junior petites, misses' petites, diminutive, half sizes, junior plenty, and women's sizes (see Fig. 8–1) Sizes for the male figure run an equally wide gamut.

FIGURE 8–1   Size Range Chart

TYPICAL SIZE RANGES FEMALE FIGURE									
Department	Special Information	Sizes							
Junior	Short waisted, narrow figure	3	5	7	9	11	13	15	
Junior Petite	5'2" and under	3	5	7	9	11	13		
Missy	Average female figure	8	10	12	14	16	18	20	
Missy Petite	5'5" and under	8	10	12	14	16			
Half Sizes	Full figure, short waisted	14½	16½	18½	20½	22½	24½	26½	
Womens	Full figure, average height	38	40	42	44	46	48	50	

Price and quality.   Aside from remembering the prices, a salesperson must often justify them. Remembering the prices without consulting the price tags gives a customer the impression that the salesperson is familiar with the merchandise. This knowledge, while it might seem insignificant, often establishes confidence. In those areas where prices vary according to changes (the use of one fabric instead of another on a chair), it is less likely that a salesperson will remember all the prices.

Justifying the price requires a knowledge of quality and being able to talk about a product's salient features. Quality can be impressed upon the customer with an intelligent discussion of such information as materials ("this is linen, which is one of the costlier fibers"), construction ("this glove is made with an outseam, which eliminates stitches on the inside and allows for maximum comfort"), guarantees ("this refrigerator is unconditionally guaranteed for three years"), and craft ("the lapel is handsewn, which provides for a neater look").

Care of merchandise.   The special care or the ease in caring for an item is important to good selling. Noting that a suit is unconditionally washable and dries without wrinkles just about convinces the travel-minded customer to buy. Similarly, the customer purchasing a garment that requires special attention, such as a suede coat, is apt to receive longer wear if he or she is familiar with the care of the coat. The salesperson should be absolutely certain about how to care for such goods because mistakes can lead to unnecessary returns and customer dissatisfaction.

Approaching the Customer

After becoming familiar with the merchandise, the salesperson is ready to greet prospective customers. Customers should be met with a friendly smile. The words used to begin a conversation are important. Do not begin with a question that might bring a negative response. For example, asking, "May I help you?" might bring a reply of "no." Although such openings are typical of retail store selling, it is a poor way to begin a sales presentation. Preferably, begin by saying, "Good morning, I'm Mr. Smith. I'd like to help you with your purchasing needs." Another desirable approach is to strike up a conversation regarding an article of merchandise that a shopper is examining—for example, "That chair is as comfortable as it is good-looking. Try sitting in it."

When a customer approaches a salesperson for help, the greeting is less difficult because the customer is seeking assistance. A mere "Good afternoon" is sufficient. Even "May I help you?" is acceptable, since in this situation it will not bring the possibility of a "no" response.

At this early point in the sales demonstration, it is time to determine the shopper's needs. Certainly, approaching the customer who is examining an item gives the salesperson an idea of what is desired. In cases where the customer isn't studying the merchandise, determining what is needed is a little more difficult. Some brief questions (which become second nature with experience) pertaining to style, color, size (if applicable), and so on will guide the salesperson in the selection of appropriate merchandise. Keeping in mind what the store has available for sale, the salesperson is now ready to show the merchandise to the customer.

Presenting the merchandise. In telling the customer about the merchandise, the salesperson should include all of those features that make it distinctive. Such factors as construction, materials, and uses are generally discussed. To make the item more desirable to the customer, an outstanding feature should be stressed. For example, the mention of the name of the designer would probably be more meaningful to a fashion-minded customer than any other information. Similarly, to shoppers who are interested in easing their household chores, the mention of "wash and wear" should be most meaningful. It is beneficial to invite the customer to "try" the merchandise. A piece of jewelry becomes more exciting if it is tried on rather than being viewed on a counter. The person interested in a lounge chair should be invited to sit in it rather than merely admire it. The comfort achieved (if it is comfortable) will help close the sale. How many suits and coats would a man purchase if he didn't try them on? Whatever the item, the customer's involvement is extremely important for closing the sale.

If an item can be demonstrated, it should be. What could be more convincing than the demonstration of a vacuum cleaner in action? Would stores sell as many color television sets without showing them in operation? Some other examples of the power of demonstration are the purposeful dropping of an unbreakable dish or the crushing of a wrinkleproof blouse. Very few types of merchandise do not lend themselves to customer involvement or demonstration.

Handling objections. There are many hints that indicate when a customer is getting ready to purchase. These hints are usually questions. "How much does it cost?" "Does it come in other colors?" "Are alterations included in the price?" "How soon can it be delivered?" "Is the installation cost included in the price?" These are but a few of the signals that a customer might be ready to purchase. But even after spending time considering a purchase, the shopper might hesitate and raise objections. These objections might be excuses telling the salesperson that he or she isn't going to buy, or they might be sincere objections that need further reassurance. Whatever the reason for the objections, the salesperson must overcome them to close the sale.

Some of the more common objections are those involving price, the product's features, inadequate guarantees, the delivery time, and poor fit. Even the salesperson's attitude might deter buying. The experienced salesperson is prepared to handle these objections and does so in a number of ways. One technique is to agree with the customer but then to offer another selling point. For example, Mrs. Jones shows interest in the dress she is trying on but declares, "The price is high." The salesperson might reply, "Yes, but the fit is so perfect that the cost generally involved in alterations will be eliminated." Aside from the use of "yes, but" to handle objections, these phrases may also be used:

I agree with you, sir, but another factor to consider . . .

You're right, Mr. Peter, however, . . .

One of my customers felt exactly as you do, but she finally made the purchase because . . .

It certainly is a long time to wait for the table, Miss Adams, but . . .

Another technique employed in handling objections is to ask the customer questions. In this way, a salesperson can separate excuses for not buying from real objections. Here are some examples of questions to use:

What color would you prefer?

Why do you object to the style of this refrigerator?

What would you consider an appropriate price for a sofa?

Still another technique to be used, but with caution, is to deny the objection. Salespersons must be absolutely certain of their information when employing this method.

Customer's Objection	Salesperson's Response
I think the fabric will shrink.	Oh, no, madam, the shirt has been preshrunk.
The Elite Shoppe sells it for $5 less than your price.	Our store always sells that item at a price lower than the Elite Shoppe.
I don't think the rug will be delivered in time for the party.	I guarantee the delivery date, Mrs. Reihing.

If the salesperson uses this method but doesn't provide truthful information, the customer will be dissatisfied on learning the truth and probably will never again trust the store's sales personnel.

Closing the sale. After answering all the customer's questions and overcoming any objections, the salesperson should try to close the sale. Knowing when to close comes with experience. The seasoned salesperson looks for signals that indicate that the prospect is about to become a customer. Only the naive or inexperienced salesperson expects to hear from the customer something like, "O.K., I'm ready to buy." Some of the closing signals are

How long will it take for the alteration to be completed?
Can I charge this purchase?
When can I expect the merchandise to be delivered?
Are these items exchangeable?
Is the guarantee for one year?

The salesperson who recognizes what he or she believes to be the opportune moment should then proceed to close the sale. Choosing the right words at this time might seem difficult to the student of retailing. Using the question "Are you ready to buy?" is certainly not the correct approach. The use of questions and statements such as these are more effective:

Shall I gift-wrap it for you?
Would you like to wear the shoes out of the store?
Which would you like, the blue one or the brown one?
Will that be cash or charge?
Would you like it delivered, or will you take it with you?
After today this item goes back to its original price.
This is the last one in stock; a special order will take four weeks.

Even the most experienced salespersons sometimes find that they have not chosen the appropriate time to close the sale. It may take several attempts before a sale is finalized. Retailing students should keep in mind that not everyone is really a customer, and also that not every shopper can be satisfied with the store's offerings. The customer's words in refusing to buy should be evaluated. For example, a definite "no" might indicate that the customer can't be satisfied. Reactions such as "I'd like to see another style" or "No, I'm still uncertain about the fit of this garment" are signals that perhaps more selling effort is necessary. Whatever the degree of negativism, a salesperson should not give up after the first attempt. How many attempts should be made? Too few might let the customer slip away. Too many tries might tend to make shoppers feel they are being high-pressured. The right number of times before one gives up will eventually be perceived through experience.

After making an unsuccessful attempt, a salesperson must be able to proceed again to a point that will result in success. In order to do this, the salesperson must keep some information in reserve that will perhaps whet the customer's appetite. For example

> If you purchase today, you will be entitled to buy a second pair at a 20 percent reduction.
>
> This is the last day of our special sale; tomorrow the price will increase by 10 percent.
>
> Did you know that these shoes are *wear-dated* and are guaranteed, under normal use, for one year?

If consecutive attempts to close are unsuccessful and it is felt that the customer still might purchase the product, some salespeople resort to what is called a TO, or turnover. This technique involves turning the customer over to a more prestigious department member, such as the manager or buyer. Customers might respond more affirmatively to these people and thus the department will benefit.

It is important to keep in mind that even a customer who does not make a purchase is still a prospect for future business. Courtesy is extremely important to guarantee that the customer will return. A disagreeable or disgruntled salesperson can bring disastrous results.

Suggesting Additional Merchandise

Although the salesperson should be pleased with having closed the sale, it is at this point that the experienced employee tries to tempt the customer with additional merchandise. The customer is in a buying frame of mind, and with some expert selling effort it might be possible to build the sale. Suggestion selling should in no way be considered high pressure, but rather as a way of assisting the customer. There are a number of ways in which this can be accomplished.

1. *The suggestion of accessories to be used in conjunction with the purchase.* For example, an alert salesperson having sold a customer a suit could suggest coordinated shirts and ties. Instead of asking whether the customer is interested in these other items, the creative salesperson selects the accessories that are most appropriate and demonstrates to the customer how perfectly they blend. Even if the shopper has no intention of purchasing a shirt and tie, their display might be tempting.

Accessories need not be limited to soft goods. At the close of a vacuum cleaner sale, attachments and disposable bags might be suggested. Similarly, the sale of a phonograph might result in a larger total purchase if records and record cases are suggested to the customer.

2. *The suggestion of more than one of the items sold.* For example, a customer having selected one pair of stockings might consider buying additional pairs if the salesperson can offer an advantage of the multiple purchase. In practice, you can convince a customer to buy a second pair

of stockings by saying, "If you buy a single pair and one stocking bcomes damaged, you'll have to dispose of the other. By buying two pairs, you will still be left with one pair even if a stocking from the second pair is destroyed." Similarly, upon completing a carpet sale, you might suggest additional yardage for stress areas (stairs) that might wear before the rest of the carpet.

3. *The suggestion of a special offer*. Very often purchasing one item may entitle the customer to take advantage of another item at a reduced price. In a dollar sale, a customer who purchases one item at the regular price may buy a second item for an additional dollar. Service contracts are offered to customers having just purchased an appliance, at a price less than the customary price.

Suggestions to Promote Future Business

Although completing the sale is extremely important, once having done so, the resourceful salesperson takes the opportunity to guarantee the customer's return for future purchases. Retailers seek to establish a reputation that will encourage other transactions. Spending a few extra moments with the customer at this time will promote goodwill and encourage him or her to return. Some suggestions for achieving these ends:

> Here's my card, Mrs. Bennett. It has been a pleasure helping you with your purchases. I'd like to do so again in the near future.
>
> Mr. Avidon, I'd like your telephone number in case something special comes in that I feel would be appropriate for you.

Rushing to the next customer without first extending these courtesies is not as important as the few moments used to solidify a customer relationship. This is time well spent that might establish a rapport that the customer will recall when ready to shop again.

SMALL STORE ADAPTATION

Unlike most large retail organizations, which seem to be short on personal selling and rely on other things to motivate purchasing, the small retailer can make the most of attending to the wants and needs of every customer entering the store. Despite the vast number of people who venture into large retail stores, it is quite obvious that the percentage who actually buy is often less than at the small store. The smaller retailer can ill afford losing large numbers of sales.

The small retailer should learn as much as possible about the particular market his or her store caters to through observation on the selling floor, conversations with customers, and the writings of behavioral scientists. The next step is to make certain that the prospective customer's desires are satisfied.

Where the large organization often fails, it is in the small store that expertise in selling can be and is generally realized. Many customers of small boutiques and specialty stores who regularly frequent these shops do so because of the personal sales assistance offered. In shops of this size, it is not uncommon for customers to request a particular salesperson.

Under the watchful eye of the owner or manager, the small store salesperson can learn the "terms of the trade" and turn shoppers into customers. It is at this level where customer loyalty, often the result of efficient selling, is the reason for the store's success.

CAREER OPPORTUNITIES

It has been said that a career as a professional seller is one that is both personally and financially rewarding. That comment is generally meant for sales at the manufacturer's or wholesaler's level and not at the retail level of business. Not that retail sales cannot be personally satisfying, but the dollars earned are generally less than most aggressive individuals would be willing to accept.

There are other reasons for individuals to consider selling in a retail organization. One, it offers the individual who seeks part-time employment a job that is readily available with hours that can often be adjusted to satisfy the seller's and employee's needs. This sales position is usually low-paying and often a dead-end situation. Two, it provides a place for someone who wants to reenter the job market but has few skills for other positions. This often enables the taker to gain confidence and demonstrate his or her ability. Three, it is often a starting place for those who lack the experience or required degree for entrance into an executive training program. By proving oneself in sales, the door may be opened for management positions as sales manager, department managers, or sales supervisers or merchandising-oriented careers.

As noted, retail sellers are generally poorly compensated and their motivation is for upward mobility. There are retail salespersons, however, who are both happy with careers as sellers and are financially rewarded for their efforts. These individuals usually are sellers of high-ticket items, such as major appliances, furs, expensive clothing, and furniture, where compensation is based on commissions, bonuses, and incentive plans, in addition to regular or guaranteed salaries. In these cases, the sales personnel are those totally committed to sales careers, and not to other levels of retail employment.

Whatever the situation, most retailers agree that selling on the floor enables individuals to learn retailing from the bottom up and to explore all of the activities of a retail organization. It should also be noted, that there is rarely, if ever, a salary distinction between women and men in retail selling.

1. Consumer behavior is a matter of decision making and involves the steps of stimulus and problem recognition, information gathering, and learning.

2. Buying motives are either rational or emotional. Rational purchases are based on careful thought and reasoning; emotional purchases are based on appeals to the senses, status, prestige, fear, and so on.

3. Habits refer to when, where, and how customers make their purchases; the "why" habit refers to motivation.

4. The salesperson's appearance is extremely important. The first impression made on the customer is generally influenced by the seller's appearance.

5. In order to sell effectively, knowledge of the merchandise is a must. Understanding merchandise uses, styles, sizes, price, quality and care are some of the facts needed for successful selling.

6. The correct approach is a must. By asking the typical "May I help you," the more than likely negative response may result in losing the customer.

7. It is not unusual for a customer to raise objections. Through the proper handling of objections, an effective salesperson may convince the customer to buy.

8. Closing attempts must continuously be tried to motivate purchasing. In some stores, a TO system is used when the seller believes everything has been tried but the sale has not been made.

9 Through the suggestions of additional merchandise, the size of the average sale could increase. Many customers need a little "suggesting" to purchase more.

10. Repeat business is the key to successful retailing. The use of a calling card indicates interest in the customer's future business.

Worksheet 8

COMPLETE THE FOLLOWING STATEMENTS

1. The process of _____ involves stimulus and problem recognition, information gathering, and purchase and evaluation.

2. _____, a Russian psychologist, found that with
   proper conditioning he could teach a subject to respond in a particular way to a
   given stimulus.

3. Behavioral scientists have refined the above-mentioned psychologist's work

   into four steps: _____, _____,

   _____, and _____.

4. The _____ buyer is one who bases the buying decision on
   style, pride of ownership, and romance.

5. For the salesperson, the justification of a higher price is the

   _____ of the merchandise.

6. The most common, but incorrect, approach to a customer are the words

   _____.

7. When a salesperson fails to close a sale and elects to ask a supervisor to try and

   close the sale, he or she is using the _____ technique.

8. _____ selling is a method used to increase the amount of
   the sale.

TRUE OR FALSE

_____ 1. Most successful retailers make consumer decisions based on
              intuition.

_____ 2. Decision making begins with stimulus and problem recognition.

_____ 3. Pavlov's work involved guiding the learning procedure.

_____ 4. The emotional buyer makes the decision to buy based on careful
              study of the facts.

_____ 5. Pavlov proposed the order for needs fulfillment known as the
              hierarchy of needs.

_____ 6. An attitude is an individual's feeling toward a particular object.

_____ 7. In contemporary retailing the emphasis on the salesperson's appearance is no longer important.

_____ 8. "Good morning" is a satisfactory customer approach.

_____ 9. Unlike selling on the wholesale level, where several closing attempts are made, the retail salesperson should attempt to close only once.

_____ 10. Suggesting accessories to a customer who has purchased a suit is annoying and shouldn't be attempted.

MULTIPLE CHOICE

_____ 1. Decision making involves

    (a) problem recognition
    (b) information gathering
    (c) evaluation
    (d) none of the above

_____ 2. Basically, decision making

    (a) is a learning process
    (b) cannot be learned
    (c) is inborn
    (d) is inappropriate to the above

_____ 3. Buying motives are

    (a) rational
    (b) emotional
    (c) rational or emotional
    (d) neither rational nor emotional

_____ 4. Essential for selling is

    (a) proper appearance
    (b) tact
    (c) enthusiasm
    (d) all of the above

_____ 5. "The customer is always right" is

    (a) no longer taught to salesperson
    (b) still the rule
    (c) unimportant in today's retailing
    (d) none of the above

_____ 6. "May I help you?" is considered

    (a) a poor opening
    (b) perfect for greeting the customer
    (c) satisfactory when selling inexpensive merchandise
    (d) bad taste

_____ **7.** If a customer objects to the merchandise, you should
  (a) use the "yes, but" technique
  (b) ask questions
  (c) deny the objection
  (d) use any of the above

DISCUSSION QUESTIONS _____

1. If most retailers make their decisions based on intuition, how do you account for their success?

2. To be successful, the retailer must be a provider of customer information. How is this accomplished?

3. Should the retailer make certain there is an adequate supply of merchandise on hand before it is advertised?

4. Define the term "cue" in Pavlov's work.

5. What does the word "response" mean in the learning process?

6. Differentiate between the two types of motivations.

7. Differentiate between habits and motives.

8. Is enthusiasm a dangerous quality for a salesperson to possess? Defend your position.

9. Discuss self-discipline and its importance in effective selling.

10. Do you agree or disagree that a good salesperson can sell anything, even without appropriate knowledge of the product? Why?

11. How important is it for salespeople to know the exact location of all the merchandise sold in their department?

12. State a proper greeting to be used in a retail men's store. Why is it better than "May I help you"?

13. When selling a "soothing skin preparation," how can a salespserson effectively convince the customer to purchase it?

14. Should the salesperson ever disagree with a customer's objection for not buying? What precautions must be taken in doing this?

15. How might you overcome an objection to price?

16. List three sentences that might be used to close a sale.

17. How many times might a salesperson try to close before conceding defeat? Why?

18. Define TO. When is it used?

19. How can a salesperson try to close again if he has already been unsuccessful at previous attempts?

20. Why do retailers continuously stress suggestion selling?

CASE PROBLEM 1

Carynsher is a prestigious women's clothing store that prides itself on quality. For the past ten years it has grown from an unknown fledgling retail operation to one of the Midwest's finest and best known. Its hallmark has always been high-quality, expensive clothing and accessories.

In the last year management has noticed a steady increase in the number of requests for designer merchandise. Always aware of the "customer is queen" philosophy, management has decided to offer more and more of this type of clothing to its clientele.

While the decision has been made to adjust the inventory to include the new lines, the advertising campaigns have not changed to promote the new goods properly. Because the store features quality, the advertisements reflect that aspect. You might say that the appeal used was rational in nature. Mr. Kane, manager of advertising, has suggested to top management that the appeal to customers should be more emotionally oriented. The messages should now include such "catch words" as prestigious and status. Although the change was initiated in merchandising, management is resisting in that Carynsher's "quality" image might be lost and business might suffer.

1. Is Kane's suggestion valid?
2. Does management have a valid point?
3. What would your solution be?

CASE PROBLEM 2

Harvey Miller is an automobile salesman. For the past hour he has been unsuccessfully trying to close a deal on a convertible. He has not given up at this point because he still believes the customer might buy. Some of the objections raised by the customer have been answered as follows:

Customer's Objections	Miller's Responses
The price seems too high.	You can check; we are priced lower than any other dealer.
The roof appears as though it will fall apart.	The fabric is vinyl-coated and carries a three-year replacement guarantee if it is damaged under normal use.
The radio sounds "tinny."	The radio is manufactured by Brand X, the finest in its field.

After another fifteen minutes, Miller decides to give up and bids the customer farewell.

1. What might Miller have attempted to still convince the customer? (No, the price could not be lowered.)
2. Assuming that after Miller's trying every tactic the customer was still not ready to purchase, how should Miller have parted company?

CASE PROBLEM 3

The Chic Shoppe, an established medium-sized women's specialty store, is located in a downtown shopping area. The store's competition was almost nonexistent until last year when a discounter opened about a mile from the shop. Although not all of the new store's merchandise is the same as Chic's, some of the items are identical. The discounter, able to sell at a lower price because of a "plain pipe rack" atmosphere and self-selection policy, has caused customers to complain about Chic's prices. The management at Chic's has been discussing the problem and is undecided about what to do. Some key personnel feel the answer is self-service. The manager of the selling force believes that more effective sales techniques can eliminate the problem. To make certain that the Chic Shoppe does not eliminate their jobs, the sales force has decided to meet and outline as many selling points as possible to counter the higher price objection.

1. Do you agree or disagree that self-selection is the answer to the problem? Defend your position.

2. Pretend that you are a salesperson on the store's staff. Make a list of all the points that salespeople could use to overcome the price objection.

PROJECT 1

Select six retail advertisements. Two ads should appeal to the emotional buyer, two to the rational buyer, and two should have a combination appeal. Key words indicating emotional motivation should be circled and marked emotional, with rational words treated similarly.

PROJECT 2

Prepare a one-page selling aid for new salespeople to help them with their sales presentation. Pretend that the store you represent sells men's, women's, and children's clothing and grosses $5 million annually. The store offers all the services of the conventional higher priced department stores. At peak periods salespeople number 50. Be sure to include, in the proper order, the steps necessary for effective selling.

PROJECT 3

Visit two stores, similar in merchandise offerings and services, and compare the effectiveness of a salesperson in each, evaluating the following areas:

	Salesperson: Name of Store and Department	Salesperson: Name of Store and Department
Appearance		
Courtesy		
Knowlege of product		
Helpfulness		
Voice		
Enthusiasm		
Other areas of concentration (list them)		

PROJECT 4

Visit or write two department stores and ask for information concerning the training of sales personnel. Evaluate the two in terms of how much they offer and the quality of their training procedure. List below the salient features of each store and indicate which you believe does the superior job. Include with this evaluation any printed material you receive. Defend your choice knowledgeably.

Name of Store	*Name of Store*

After completing the comparison, indicate what you feel might still improve the training of the better store's sales personnel.

CHAPTER **9**

Customer Services

AN M.B.A. OF A DIFFERENT BREED

More women than ever before are in the work force. Whether it is because of a financial need caused by the ever-increasing cost of living, a by-product of the women's movement, or a personal desire to make a productive contribution outside the home, women are working in enormous numbers. This market has become a dominant factor in retailing: Not only have working women's buying requirements changed but so have their shopping habits.

The female shopper used to be considered one with ample time for buying her family's needs. It was estimated that about 90 percent of all purchases were made by women or were at least influenced by them. And it was generally assumed in retail circles that shopping was a favorite pastime of women. Then, with more and more women working outside the home, most retailers increased their mail and telephone order services in order to broaden their stores' appeal to working women. The consensus was that if women no longer had time to shop, the stores would take their offerings to the home. This was done by an enormous increase in stores' direct advertising campaigns. In years past, retailers generally restricted their catalogs to Christmas, with an occasional mailing at special times. Today, it is rare to find a home that isn't inundated with store catalogs and other mailings every week. So successful has been the campaign that retailers continue to use this approach.

While mail and phone orders have filled the needs of those who do not shop in person, giant retailers have recognized the fact that many customers still prefer to shop in stores rather than to buy from catalogs even though their time is limited. Merchants have tried, with varying success, to lure those customers to the store with such undertakings as longer hours and Sunday openings. Although this approach has increased sales, some retailers believe that there is still a segment of the female population that hasn't been satisfactorily reached.

In an attempt to reach the career-oriented shopper who has specific merchandise needs, many retailers have initiated personal shopper programs. One of the most ambitious is Macy's By Appointment, or M.B.A. In this personal shopper program, Macy's encourages customers to contact its M.B.A. Department to discuss with a specialist the particular needs he or she might have. For example, a caller might need a blouse, shoes, and handbag to go with a suit already in her wardrobe. The customer is questioned about preferences in fabric, color, size, price, and so forth and is given an appointment to come to the store. Meanwhile, the store specialist shops the store and assembles the appropriate merchandise for the customer to try on in the M.B.A. Department. In this way, a customer with limited time for shopping can easily choose from merchandise that has been preselected. Thus, this service not only addresses the limited time factor of busy customers but also offers professional, personalized assistance. There is no extra charge for this service, nor is there a minimum purchase requirement. Goods may be requested at any price line the store offers.

For the customer who isn't satisfied with selections from booklets, the Macy's By Appointment and other stores' similar programs seem to be appealing—and thus capturing an otherwise untapped market. It should also be noted that such programs result in higher than average sales. The qualified personal shopper who knows how to build a sale through proper suggestion of merchandise generally finds a willing and receptive consumer.

LEARNING OBJECTIVES

Upon completion of this chapter, the student should be able to

1. Discuss the various types of service and services afforded the customer.
2. Describe the concept of the executive shop.
3. List three types of credit offered by retail organizations.
4. Differentiate between store credit cards and cards offered by credit organizations.

INTRODUCTION

The past decade has witnessed significant changes in retailing. As we have seen, innovative merchants have challenged the traditionalists with merchandising techniques that have captured the attention as well as the dollars of consumers. The greatest impact in the race for the consumer's money has been made by the off-pricers. Whether their clout will continue to be felt by the conventional retailer or their methods of doing business will fade as quickly as they have appeared on the scene is not yet known. It is generally agreed that a substantial segment of the market will continue to be motivated by price. Twenty-five years ago many consumers abandoned the department store for the discount operations, and today, that same group seems to have found satisfaction at the off-price outlets.

Many retailers experienced trouble when they tried to compete with the stores that "sell for less" by also selling at lower prices. To meet competition by reducing prices, there had to be belt-tightening in terms of operational expenses. Some stores cut their sales staffs to such small numbers that shoppers had difficulty finding assistance on the selling floor. Others curtailed customer services. Neither approach seemed to be the answer.

Thus, finding it difficult to beat the off-price retailers at the game they play best, the major department stores and large specialty organizations seemed to have made a unanimous decision to return to the game that they themselves play best. The route being taken involves reemployment of services that no longer were being offered, expansion of those that are still in existence, and the development of new ones that indicate creativity and initiative of management.

SERVICE AND SERVICES

The service and services that make up a retailer's list are either free of charge or carry an extra cost. It is a commonly held belief that even those services that are "free" are actually built into the cost of the goods. Some merchants believe that it is wiser to include the service in the cost, as in the case of alterations, so that the customer won't be presented with an "add-on" at the time of purchase. Others, who charge extra costs to those who want the service, believe it should only be charged to the "taker" of the service and not to those individuals who don't require it.

Whatever the store's philosophy, the services provided vary from company to company.

The Executive Shop

In an attempt to go one step farther than providing personal shoppers, as does Macy's in its M.B.A. program, stores have begun to service the needs of the shopper with little time in another manner. Of this often rushed, ever-growing group of customers is the woman executive who is usually affluent, has specific merchandise needs, and lacks the time typically necessary to tackle the crowds and enormous square footage in the stores.

The answer seems to be to create a separate shop in the store with unique features that is suitable for the woman executive. Such an operation requires the department store to set aside space and offer one-stop shopping to satisfy this customer's needs. Carson Pirie Scott, a Chicago-based department store, has transformed the basement of the parent store into the "Corporate Level," a shop that caters to the successful career woman. The operation has been so successful that the company has added branches of the department to two suburban units. Besides offering a total merchandise mix of clothing, accessories, shoes, intimate apparel, giftware, cosmetics, and so on, the Corporate Level features a wide assortment of services especially designed with this customer in mind. Among them are the following:

- Each customer is assigned a specific personal fashion consultant who assists with purchases.
- Taste and sizes are recorded on a computer for easy access to enable phone orders to be handled more quickly and appropriately.
- For a $50 fee, enrollees in the "Corporate Level Club" receive free twenty-four hour alterations; semiannual free, at home, wardrobe consultations; choice of a free haircut, manicure, or facial; reminder service of birthdays and anniversaries; a free leather portfolio, "CL" inscribed; a garment bag; free "CL" giftwrap; free refreshments while shopping; free use of the "Board Room" for meetings; prior notification of sales; and a flower ordering service.
- A separate entrance to the store that permits shopping from 7:30 A.M. to 7:30 P.M.

Personal Shopping

Many merchants, especially those that cater to the affluent, have initiated personal shopping services or have expanded those already offered. Marshall Field, Chicago, for example, is once again emphasizing the training of personal shoppers. Instead of the self-service approach, which many retailers, including Marshall Field, resorted to, the path being followed is for better personal shopping to help the customer who wants assistance in making a decision.

Most stores make the public aware of their personal shopping service through advertising and promotion. In its "White Carnation" campaign, Marshall Field notified newspaper readers of 1,000 executives and managers who would be available as personal shoppers for a certain period of time. So successful was the campaign that the store, again through advertising, notified customers to seek out hosts and hostesses, who would be wearing white carnations, for regular personal attention.

Lord & Taylor regularly advertises its personal fashion advisory shopping service, which features the fashion adviser and staff for every shopping need. Most retailers agree that personal shopping is a service that produces greater sales volume.

Gift Registry

People are frequently faced with the problem of gift selection, as in the case of a friend or relative getting married. It is difficult to know if the newlyweds will enjoy it or will keep it in a closet, only to be brought out when you visit them.

Many department stores offer bridal registry services to help with this problem. It works this way: The prospective bride and groom visit the store and pick out items that they would like, such as flatware, tableware, linens, and so on, at a wide assortment of prices. The gift givers are made aware of this. When they go to the store, they are given a list of the chosen merchandise from which they can select an item that fits their budget with the confidence that it will be wanted and that there will be no duplication. The store keeps track of the purchases and constantly deletes the items purchased from the list.

This works well for certain types of expensive gifts. For example, if the couple wants a service for eight in a particular pattern of expensive silverware, gifts can be bought as service for one by eight different people. As soon as these eight individual services have been bought, silverware is removed from the registry listing. Registry is good for the newlyweds because they get what they want, good for the purchaser because it eliminates gift-selection problems, and good for the store because it generates business.

Dayton's, Strawbridge and Clothier, and Jordan Marsh have taken registry a step farther: They have begun a registry for newborns. New parents complete a form indicating date of birth, sex of the baby, and quantity, color, and size of the newborn's needs, including clothing, bedding, nursery, bath, and so forth. Dayton's calls its baby registry the Stork Club. Prospective buyers are given a listing from which to make selections. Each purchase is deleted from the list. The list is maintained for two years after the baby's birth and is used for direct-mail purposes to announce special events and sales.

Giftwrapping

Giftwrapping is provided by most stores that sell gift merchandise. Some stores, because of their unique giftwrapping, gain a clientele who could otherwise make the same purchase elsewhere. The smaller retailers of boutique items and small giftware often include the cost of giftwrapping in the price of the merchandise. It is traditional that the larger retail organizations provide a free giftwrapping service, making use of less costly materials, and offering fancy packaging for an extra charge that varies with the complexity and cost of the wrappings and decorations used.

Giftwrapping is an excellent way to advertise a store's image. It is relatively inexpensive for a large store to operate a giftwrap department or for a small store to provide free giftwrap when weighed against the enthusiasm often generated by beautifully decorated packages.

Giftwrap as a source of income is an area that has been woefully neglected. Lately, however, such stores as Diamond's, Macy's, Higbee's, Bloomingdale's, and A&S have been focusing on this area, not only as a customer service but also as an important profit source. Department store executives think of giftwrap as a growth area with better than normal margins. A&S for example, expects giftwrap to go as high as $500,000 per year, and Woodward & Lothrop expect $1 million. When you consider that Higbee's averages 2,000 packages a week (triple at Christmas) and Sanger Harris, Dallas, about a quarter of a million a year, it is easy to see the profit potential.

All of this has had a considerable effect on this long neglected growth area. Macy's, California, has gone into giftwrap in a big way. While most stores treat giftwrap as a customer service that they hope breaks even, Macy's treats it as a profit center and actually merchandises it as it does with any other profit center. Macy's designs its own paper, uses highly styled popular colors, and goes so far as to use a layered look when that look is fashionable. Its design picks up other major style themes throughout the store, and a wide assortment of dummy packages is displayed in appropriate departments. To Macy's (and others), giftwrap is a new kind of fashion merchandise and it is treated appropriately. Last year the giftwrap department did a volume of $1.5 million at higher than normal markup and it is still growing.

Restaurants

More and more retailers are offering dining services to their customers. A restaurant might not be considered a service, but some retailers offer food at lower-than-usual prices in order to dissuade the customer from leaving the store at mealtime. By retaining the customer on the premises, the store increases the chances for additional shopping. Some stores manage these restaurants themselves, while others lease space to food companies to operate the eating facilities. The service runs the gamut from snack bar to the fanciest of establishments, such as Bloomingdale's gourmet railroad dining car restaurant in its flagship store. If a customer is kept in the store for an extended period, then the use of such space for a dining facility is worthwhile.

In many stores restaurants are considered a profit center in addition to being a customer service. The problem is they are one-meal-a-day operations (lunch) and that is rarely enough to ensure a restaurant's success. At Higbee's eleven stores, restaurants account for about 3 percent of total store volume, at a profit. When you consider that 3 percent of the volume of eleven large department stores is millions of dollars, it is obvious that restaurants can make a considerable contribution.

As store hours lengthen, the number of working women increase, and the economy strengthens, in-store dining facilities are changing from tea shops into fine restaurants. Hecht's, at its Beverly Hills location, charges up to $16.50 for lunch and grosses $1.5 million in profitable business serving only lunch.

Merchandise Alterations

Clothing alterations are often referred to as a necessary evil. Many retailers confess that the service is costly and occasionally leads to complications. For example, a customer might be displeased with the alteration and refuse to pay for it, leaving an altered piece of merchandise that is potentially a complete loss.

While some stores play down the alteration service for women's clothing, it is virtually impossible to eliminate it for menswear. Men generally do not buy unless the item can be altered. They simply do not have the time or desire to go elsewhere for alterations. Most menswear retailers agree that, without the alteration shop, sales would dramatically decline. Women, on the other hand, generally are not as demanding about on-premises alterations. Those with more time often seek outside services for their needs. Some stores, though, particularly those that cater to the working woman, find that there is a need for tailoring in the store.

Whether to charge extra for tailoring or include it in the price of the garment is a problem retailers must face. Traditionally, in the store that features both men's and women's clothing, the male customer's clothing is altered free of charge while the female must pay. Recently, a female customer who discovered a charge to women for alterations and none for men on an identical item took her complaint to court on discrimination charges. As a result of this complaint, stores such as Macy's have decided to study the impact of an equal system for males and females. Whatever the decision, unless the merchandise is severely discounted, store alterations is generally one service that is esssential.

Delivery

Stores furnish customers with a service to deliver goods for a number of reasons. When offered such a service, customers will often purchase gifts to be sent to individuals who live at distances from the purchaser. Some merchandise, such as furniture and appliances, is too cumbersome to carry home. Most retailers, though, in store signs, encourage carrying home the purchase. Delivery can be costly, especially if included in the price, and unnecessary deliveries are avoided.

There are a number of delivery arrangements available to retailers. For small items, parcel post is often used. Other goods may be delivered through a store's own trucks or by a private carrier. Unless a store does a sufficient amount of business to warrant operating its own delivery system, an outside company is employed. Many of the large retailers that deal in bulk items and operate from warehouses, such as Levitz, the furniture discounter, offer the customer two prices—one including delivery and one if the merchandise is carried by the customer. In such a situation an individual has the option to save money even on the traditionally delivered item. In some cases of bulky merchandise, delivery is required. In other cases, the retailer must weigh the advantages and disadvantages of providing delivery service, and whether or not the service should carry an extra cost to the customer.

Other Services

The extent and nature of other services are directly related to the store's image, the type of business it conducts, and the clientele served. The following is a list of some of the services offered:

- Free interior design advice with furniture purchases
- Use of strollers for small children
- Foreign-speaking assistance for non-English-speaking customers
- Personal shoppers to advise on purchases
- Play areas for children
- Special shopping days or hours for particular groups, such as the handicapped
- Use of community room for organizations
- Travel service departments
- Expanded shopping hours at peak periods
- Automobile leasing with financing arrangements
- Computerized apartment rental service
- Corporate gift service
- Press-on monogramming that simulates handsewing

CREDIT

While credit is certainly a service, and can be classified along with the others already discussed, its scope and impact on retail businesses necessitate a more in-depth discussion than the others. The 1980s has seen credit purchases soar well over the $100 billion figure, with the numbers increasing every year. It is estimated that 80 percent of all American families own at least one credit card. On average, about 70 percent of traditional department and specialty stores sales are on credit, with some stores reporting a higher percentage.

Why Retailers Offer Credit

Bluntly, retailers give credit because they have to. It is expensive and time consuming and involves the use of floor space that could be put to better use. With today's buying habits, however, there is simply no other way of maintaining sales. Certainly there are side benefits, but considering the costs involved, many retailers would drop charge accounts if they could.

Customer Preferences

Customers have many reasons for demanding credit. Many simply will not patronize a store that does not offer charge accounts. Some years ago, discount retailers were enormously successful. Their operation included reduced selling prices in return for a cutback in customer services. For a while they were very successful, but with the increase in customer demand for charge accounts, they have been forced to offer this service also. This necessitated an increase in selling prices, which narrowed the difference between their offerings and those of their more conventional competitors. In other words, competitive pressures are such that a store that does not offer credit will have difficulty maintaining its share of the market.

Customer Relationships

Although it would be difficult to prove, most retailers believe that a charge customer is a loyal one. Tests have shown that charge customers are more likely to read the advertising of stores with which they have accounts. Other research indicates that the charge account buyer is a better customer, in terms of volume, than the cash buyer. It is likely that this "customer loyalty" view of charge accounts is an exaggeration. Given the present wide use of credit, most buyers carry credit cards for competing stores and are hardly "loyal" to any individual retailer.

Direct-Mail Selling

An important benefit that charge accounts bring to a store is a mailing list of persons who have shown a fondness for the store's specific type of operation. This type of list is valuable and difficult to come by. (Most commercial lists include many names of totally disinterested people.) These lists, when carefully used, may be an important source of mail-order business. This can be accomplished as direct mail or, more frequently, with enclosures that are inserted along with the monthly charge account statement. When the latter method is used, there is no additional mailing cost and the expense of printing the enclosure is frequently borne by the supplier rather than the retailer.

Kinds of Retail Credit

An important portion of the expansion of consumer credit is that offered by retail stores to their customers. There are four major types of retail credit, and individual retailers offer many variations of these basic kinds.

Charge Accounts

Charge account credit is the most important type of credit offered by department stores. Customers receive their merchandise at the time of purchase without being required to give a down payment or a pledge of collateral. Upon receipt of a monthly statement, the customer is expected to pay within thirty days. There is no charge for this kind of credit, although customers who fail to pay within the thirty-day period are charged interest or a service charge. Under this arrangement the store has no right of repossession, and collection of late accounts may require expensive legal proceedings. Such credit is expensive in terms of bad debts, collection costs, and the expenses involved in carrying customer accounts. Frequently, stores must borrow money to cover their outstanding receivables. As is the case with all other customer services, a store's markup must be sufficient to cover these expenses. Some years ago, open account credit was offered only to the most affluent customers, minimizing bad debt risks. More recently, charge account requirements have been liberalized, and at present almost anyone with a job is encouraged to open such an account.

Installment Accounts

Installment credit is much more formal than charge account credit. It has the following characteristics:

Down payment. At the time of purchase, the customer is sometimes required to make an immediate payment of a percentage of the total sale. The amount of down payment varies with the type of merchandise and the particular store.

Periodic payments. Installment account customers agree to make a specified number of equal payments over the life of the loan. These payments are usually made monthly with the number of months varying, frequently at the customer's option.

Finance charges. Unlike charge account customers, installment customers are required to pay interest and other finance charges for the extended life of their loan. These costs are frequently so high that the seller can make a larger profit on the financing costs than on the sale itself. Some retailers, such as jewelry stores, are often described as finance companies first and retailers second.

Repossession rights. Installment sellers retain, as security for their loan, the right to take back the merchandise sold, in the event of nonpayment of an installment when it comes due. In the event that the repossessed goods, when later sold, do not bring in enough money to satisfy the remaining debt, the seller may go back to the defaulted customer for the difference.

Formal contract. The installment purchaser must sign a formal contract setting forth the conditions of the sale and the rights of both parties at the time of purchase. This serves two purposes. It both clearly outlines the terms of the complicated transaction and permits the seller who so desires to get immediate cash. Installment contracts can be sold and can serve as collateral for loans.

Revolving Credit

Revolving credit is a combination of charge account and installment credit. Installment credit is usually reserved for such expensive items as jewelry, furniture, and appliances. Revolving credit permits installment paying for small purchases. It works this way: A customer is given a credit limit by the store, for example, $500. In addition, the customer has to pay $50 per month whenever there is an outstanding balance to the store until the debt is wiped out. At the same time more merchandise may be purchased whenever the debt to the store is less than $500. Like that of the installment buyer, this buyer's monthly payment is $50 (unless less is owed), and like the charge customer, this customer can freely buy on credit up to the credit limit.

Revolving credit usually carries a service charge (about 1.5 percent per month). As is the case with installment credit, revolving credit can be profitable to the store.

Option Terms

Revolving credit requires a fixed monthly payment. A variation of this permits the customer the choice of paying in full or making some minimum payment (usually one-twelfth). Most charge customers are automatically given option terms. Their monthly statement indicates the full amount due and the minimum option payment that will be acceptable if the customer prefers it. Because the option payment is a fixed fraction of the amount owed, it will vary with the size of the balance. Customers who prefer the option payment are billed service charges for the unpaid balance (usually 1.5 percent).

Revolving credit with option terms is growing in use. Stores like it because it increases interest income while reducing customer resistance to service charges. Customers like the method because they are given a choice of payments, which they can vary depending on their budget for each month.

Credit Card Organizations

In recent years, independent credit card organizations have become a major source of retail credit. Some, such as American Express, Diner's Club, and Carte Blanche, are generally restricted in use to hotels and restaurants (although American Express is attracting many retail store members). Bank credit card systems, on the other hand, are widely used in retail stores. These are systems in which banks offer credit to their consumer customers. The two principal bank credit cards are MasterCard and Visa. Their growth as a factor in retail credit has been phenomenal.

Bank credit card operations begin with the customer applying to the bank for a card. (This is sometimes done at a retail store.) After a credit check, a card is issued that is acceptable in almost all retail stores. After making a sale, the store forwards the sales slip to the credit card organization, which remits the amount of the sale to the store after deducting from 4 to 6 percent, depending on the store's volume.

The charge customer, under these plans, is the bank's customer. All of the responsibilities for credit decisions and collections belong to the bank. Banks usually allow small sales to be made without authorization. Large amounts are authorized by special telephone lines.

Bank credit is a boon to small retailers that lack the financial strength and know-how to engage in a credit business in any other way. It is widely used among large retailers also. With the growth in use of credit cards, customers prefer to carry a single card that may be used in many situations.

Retailers using bank credit card systems find that they have several disadvantages:

1. The cost of the system is considerable. If it cannot be added to the selling price (usually set by competition), it reduces profits.
2. The illegal use of lost or stolen cards is the store's responsibility. This is a serious factor in high-crime areas, and careful identification is required.
3. The close relationship between the store's credit card holder and the store is destroyed. The various advantages of store credit, such as mail-order selling and special sales, are lost, along with customer loyalty.

SMALL STORE ADAPTATION

Not too many years ago, small retailers were often shut out in the area of customer services. This was particularly true in terms of credit offerings to customers. Few had the finances necessary to offer charge accounts or the awareness of the necessity for other services to compete with the giants. Today, progressive independent retailers have made great strides in both aspects of customer services. Those that haven't as yet will probably find that it will be necessary for survival in business.

Service, as it can be offered by small stores, comes in many ways and can be a means of successfully competing with their large-scale counterparts. For example, the personal attention of the buyer is generally unavailable in large stores, but, available at the small retailer, it can give a sense of "importance" to a customer. Alterations service, whether free or included in the price, is easy to offer. Oftentimes expert alterations bring the customer back to the store again and again. Giftwrapping is another simple accomplishment. Distinctively wrapped packages often motivate people to purchase from a particular store. Delivery, extended shopping hours, and telephone ordering are still other services that make the small store appealing.

In terms of credit, the small retailer no longer need be left out in the cold. Through such credit organizations as Visa, MasterCard, American Express, and Carte Blanche, even the smallest businesses can serve the needs of those who prefer to shop with credit cards.

Unless a small retailer's method of operation is discount or off-price oriented, it is of significant importance to feature and make the customers aware of the services offered.

CAREER OPPORTUNITIES

In their efforts to combat the competition of the off-price merchants, traditional stores are significantly increasing services to attract and maintain customer loyalty. The services run the gamut from customer credit to personal shopping. These service areas offer individuals still more types of career opportunities in retailing.

Charge account customers are often the most important, in terms of dollars spent, for most large retailers. Retail credit requires a variety of tasks to be performed. The credit manager, the head of the department, is a position that requires a number of years at lower levels involving credit. Staff in this department have such responsibilities as interviewing prospective charge customers, approving loans, setting limits on customer accounts, keeping credit records, and billing and collecting unpaid debts. The tasks are, for the most part, clerical.

Stores employ individuals whose primary responsibility is to make shopping easier and to satisfy customers' needs. The service manager is usually called on to handle the complaints or problems of customers that haven't been solved elsewhere in the store. It requires a high level of patience and the ability to make the customer feel satisfied. Personal shoppers act in a particular shopper's best interest and serve him or her in any manner to make purchasing easier. Macy's, New York, employs ''interpreters'' who are personal shoppers who cater to foreign-speaking people.

From the various services explored in this chapter, it is evident that a career choice in the service area offers experiences that are often totally customer-oriented and yet different from those in store management and merchandising.

KEY POINTS IN THE CHAPTER

1. By providing a host of services, the traditional retailer is attempting to fight the price advantage available at the off-price stores.
2. Personal shopping and specialized shops are an attempt to appeal to working women who have less time to shop.

3. Giftwrap, while considered a service, has become a revenue-producing department for many retailers.

4. Restaurants in stores have become profit centers for most retailers while at the same time they also are a service to customers.

5. Approximately 80 percent of all American families own at least one credit card, and 70 percent of traditional retail sales are made on credit.

6. Charge customers are excellent candidates for direct-mail sales. Stores, when sending monthly statements to their charge customers, generally insert direct-mail advertisements that generate a great number of orders.

7. The most important type of credit offered by retailers is the charge account. This credit enables the customer to purchase goods and pay for them in thirty days without an interest charge.

8. Installment accounts usually require a down payment at the time of purchase, with periodic payments and finance charges on a monthly basis.

9. Revolving credit, which is a combination of charge account and installment credit, permits installment paying for small purchases.

10. In recent years, independent credit card organizations such as American Express, have made an impact on retailing as have such bank cards as MasterCard and Visa.

Worksheet 9

COMPLETE THE FOLLOWING STATEMENTS

1. Corporate Level is a shop established by Carson, Pirie, Scott that caters to

   successful _____.

2. The MBA personal shopping program is the brainchild of

   _____ department store.

3. _____ credit is the most important type of credit
   offered by department stores.

4. _____ credit requires a down payment, periodic
   payments, and finance charges.

5. _____ credit is a combination of charge account
   and installment credit.

TRUE OR FALSE

_____ 1. A customer service is a service that is offered without cost to the
customer.

_____ 2. Many large stores offer merchandise at two prices for bulk items,
one if delivered and the other if taken by the customer.

_____ 3. Restaurants in stores are not considered services.

_____ 4. All major areas of retailing extend customer credit.

_____ 5. A charge account with a prestigious store is considered by some a
status symbol.

_____ 6. Many retailers would drop charge accounts if the competition
allowed.

_____ 7. A salesperson should be concerned with merchandise and not
encourage customers to open charge accounts.

MULTIPLE CHOICE

_____ 1. Customer services are offered to

    (a) fight off-price retailers
    (b) increase profits
    (c) deal with competition
    (d) all of the above

_____ 2. In order to provide personalized service, stores feature

    (a) specialized shops
    (b) personal shoppers
    (c) both a and b
    (d) neither a nor b

_____ 3. Giftwrapping is

    (a) free of charge
    (b) an extra cost to customers
    (c) often profitable for the store
    (d) all of the above

_____ 4. Among customer motives for buying on credit is

    (a) convenience
    (b) cash is unnecessary
    (c) simplified home bookkeeping
    (d) all of these

_____ 5. Debts that are repaid by equal periodic payments are called

    (a) installment accounts
    (b) charge accounts
    (c) revolving credit
    (d) revolving credit-option terms

DISCUSSION QUESTIONS

1. What current retailing force has motivated traditional stores to increase their customer service offerings?

2. Describe Carson Pirie Scott's Corporate Level shop.

3. Discuss the operation of a gift registry and the market to which it caters.

4. How can a store afford to offer free giftwrapping?

5. Is the store restaurant a service? Defend your answer.

6. Discuss customer motives for not owning credit cards.

7. Why do retailers give credit?

8. Define charge account.

9. Explain the advantages to the retailer of revolving credit with option terms.

10. Describe option terms.

CASE PROBLEM

The Man's World Corp. operates a chain of twenty medium-sized men's apparel stores in the suburban area of a large urban center. The business was begun forty years ago as a single unit, and as the exodus from the city to the suburbs grew, the operation prospered and additional stores were opened. The organization is family-operated, and thanks to their skill and aggressiveness, the stores generate a handsome profit and the financial base is very sound.

At present, the suburban area in which the stores are located is densely populated, and the only expansion possibilities would require the relocation of several members of the family. Since this is distasteful to them, any increase in profits will have to come from the existing stores.

The chain extends credit to its customers through banks and other independent credit card organizations, at a considerable cost to the organization. Management reasons that since the store has the required financial strength, it could take over this operation at a considerable cost savings since the independent credit card companies' profits would be eliminated.

The success of Man's World has been due in large part to the fact that it does its homework before making any important decisions. The problem has been broken down into several parts, and individuals have been asked to submit reports on the various areas.

1. Describe the types of credit that you think should be offered and the reasons for your choice.
2. Give the reasons for and against the continued use of independent credit cards after the company has issued its own.

PROJECT 1

Visit two major department stores and determine the various types of services they offer and whether or not they are free.

Store 1 Services	(check if free)

Store 2 Services	(check if free)

At which store would you like to shop? Why?

PROJECT 2

Interview the credit manager of a retail store in your area. Prepare a report indicating the types of credit offered. If possible, get examples of the forms used by the store for opening charge accounts.

CHAPTER 10

Resident Buying Offices and Other Retail Advisory Organizations

A NEWS BUREAU THAT DOESN'T REPORT ON CRIME

Every retailer, regardless of size, is bent on stocking its shelves with merchandise that's "sure to sell" and thus bring a profit to the company. Capable buyers and merchandising managers learn very quickly that if the bottom line doesn't show the projected profit, they could certainly be scanning the classified ads for positions with other companies.

Sources of information, external to the store, have become more important every year as competition increases. Retailers cannot rely only on the expertise of in-house personnel. While it is usually agreed that store employees better understand their own company's image, policies, merchandising concepts and goals, none would argue the value of the advisory service. Unlike resident buying offices, which are either independently owned and represent a store for a fee or a part of a retailer's organizational structure, advisory services are independent bodies that strictly provide retail information to subscribers.

One of the leading reporting services in the United States is the Retail News Bureau, a fashion-oriented company. For a monthly fee, based on the volume and size of the retail organization, the bureau provides a wealth of information about merchandise: what is selling well, where it is selling, and from which vendor it is available. No matter how carefully a buyer plans purchases, it is rare that a hot item won't be welcome to charge a department with excitement and generate sales.

The mode of operation of the Retail News Bureau encompasses several activities done on a daily basis: "Scouts" shop retailers to determine which items are receiving the greatest amount of attention in terms of displays, floor space, and customer activity. Advertisements by stores that are considered to be market barometers are carefully scanned to see what is being promoted and to what extent. (Since stores don't usually advertise slow-moving items, those appearing in the newspapers can be expected to be winners.) Shopping the wholesale market is another approach the Retail News Bureau takes to uncover important vendor sources. Finally, the organization gets information from buyers who regularly cover the market about trends, items of interest, and the like.

Retailers generally rely on the reports of the Retail News Bureau because the company has a reputation for unbiased, confidential reporting. Whereas resident buying offices have been known to push the merchandise of favorite vendors, the bureau is known to report retail news as it happens, much like consumer newspapers.

The information is disseminated to member retailers via a number of reports. Among them is the *Merchant's Newsletter,* which features trends in the market, pricing outlooks, color forecasts, and so on. Also, merchandise reports concerning specific items are sent to retail subscribers whenever a particular item warrants special attention. This kind of report usually includes a copy of an ad that a store has run, customer response to the ad, how the store has displayed the item, the resource from which it is available, other stores carrying the same item, and delivery availability. Such a report enables each store buyer to compare his or her own store to the store featured in the report and the potential of the item in his or her own department's merchandise mix. *Today's Retail Headlines* is still another publication that suggests items that are expected to be hot and where they are available.

Unlike the former report, which highlights a *specific* design or style that has a proven track record, this one speaks to what type of merchandise *appears* to be important and gives a number of sources where a buyer could purchase them.

For the wealth of information it provides, most professional buyers agree the Retail News Service is a source that is to be carefully scrutinized.

LEARNING OBJECTIVES

Upon completion of this chapter, the student should be able to

1. Explain the difference between a privately owned resident buying office and an independent one.
2. Write an essay on the selection of a resident buying office, including at least four factors that should be considered.
3. List and discuss ten services performed by a resident buying office.
4. Indicate the importance of foreign resident buying offices, pointing out four services they perform.
5. Describe the operation of a reporting service.
6. Discuss the purpose of fashion forecasters.

INTRODUCTION

Throughout this book, attention has been paid to the various aspects of operating a retail organization and the roles and functions in which management and lower level employees have been involved.

In order to achieve a competitive position in its appeal to consumers and to establish itself as a profitable force, retailers seek the advice and counsel of many individuals and companies outside of their own, immediate organization. Dominant in the field are the resident buying offices, or retail marketing firms, as many prefer to call their companies. Uppermost in their goals is the assistance and advisement necessary to make the stores with which they are affiliated more profitable. Other outside organizations, such as reporting services and fashion forecasters, also play an important role in the proper direction of many store operations.

This chapter focuses on resident offices; both independent and privately owned, and the services they provide, as well as other types of retail advisory organizations.

CLASSIFICATION OF RESIDENT BUYING OFFICES

Resident buying offices are located in wholesale markets throughout the United States and abroad, with the greatest number in New York City.

Offices feature a wide range of products and offer a variety of services to the retailer. As with retail organizations, there are small and large resident buying offices, each with a specific image or personality. Another similarity to retail organizations is that the offices may be independently owned or part of a large organization.

Although resident buying offices may vary, their primary function is to provide the store buyer with *as much* assistance and advisement as the store needs to merchandise its departments successfully.

Privately Owned Offices

In the strictest sense of the word, the private office is owned by and exclusively aids a single retail organization. Since maintaining a buying office is costly, there are few private offices. Not completely private but certainly more so than the independent offices are those resident offices that are owned by a group of stores. This arrangement allows for expenses to be shared by the members of the group, much like a cooperative. The members of the group are noncompeting stores and can thus safely aid each other without fear of jeopardizing their own operations. In the completely private office this information exchange is unavailable since ownership is exclusive.

There are several group offices in New York City. One of the best known is AMC, the Associated Merchandising Corp., with such members as Abraham & Straus and Bloomingdale's, both large New York–based department stores. Others in the cooperative or corporate division of a retail organization, as most are structured, are the Allied Stores, Associated Dry Goods Corp., and Macy's Corporate Buying. Private offices are maintained by companies such as Sears and Neiman-Marcus.

Independent Offices

The independent office has as its members many different, noncompeting retail stores. These offices represent fairly small retail organizations as well as the larger retailers. The fees charged for the many services afforded customers vary according to sales volume, remuneration generally being a percentage of the sales figures. The fees also vary from office to office, depending on the services offered. Stores generally enter into contractual agreements with the resident buying offices for periods of one year. Some of the better known independent offices are Atlas Buying Corp., Independent Retailers Syndicate, Certified Buying Service, and Felix Lilienthal.

Figure 10–1 shows a listing of the major resident buying offices and their classification.

SELECTION OF AN OFFICE

Stores that do not have private, cooperative, or corporate affiliation with a resident buying office, must select an independent resident buying

FIGURE 10–1 The Major Resident Buying Offices

Buying Office	Type
Allied Stores	Corporate*
Associated Merchandising Corp. (AMC)	Cooperative
April-Marcus	Independent
Associated Dry Goods Corp.	Corporate*
Atlas Buying Corp.	Independent
Belk Stores Services, Inc.	Corporate*
Clothiers Corp.	Independent
Felix Lilienthal	Independent
Frederick Atkins	Independent
Independent Associated Distributors	Independent
Independent Retailers Syndicate	Independent
Macy's Corporate Buying	Corporate*
May Merchandising Corp.	Corporate*
Mens Fashion Guild	Independent
Neiman-Marcus	Private
Promotional Buying Exchange, Ltd.	Independent
Retailers Representatives, Inc.	Independent
Sears	Private
Specialty Stores Association	Cooperative

*Division of a retail corporation.

office for representation. Careful selection must be made to ensure that the best possible results will be realized by the store. Since New York City alone houses approximately 300 offices, the choices are plentiful, but not always a simple task. With contractual obligations for a long-term commitment, care must be exercised in making the choice. Figure 10–2 shows an example of a typical resident buying office contract.

One important point to consider in selecting an office is its size. The office must be sufficiently large to give the store adequate assistance. For example, some offices are so small that their staff members cannot specialize in any one capacity. Perhaps one individual may cover both the sportswear and the dress markets in all price ranges. This monumental task surely does not give one person enough time to investigate either of these markets thoroughly. The store cannot, then, be confident of the office's recommendation.

Other stores that deal with the resident buying office also require careful investigation. First, it is important to be certain that competitors are not members. Since the resident buying office is a great place for exchanging information with other store buyers, competition at the same office could be disastrous. Second, the other retail organizations being represented should be similar to one's own. Clientele, merchandising policies, price ranges, and image are just some areas of significance. If the other stores are unlike your own operation, the information exchange will be meaningless. Some resident offices represent a number of different types of retail operations. This is fine, as long as it is large enough to employ enough people to cater to all the different needs.

The merchandise in which an office specializes is an important factor in its being selected by a store for representation. Only the very large offices run the gamut of hard goods and soft goods. Others specialize in particular merchandise. For an operation that encompasses all types of

FIGURE 10–2 Resident Buying Office Contract

```
Gentlemen;

Confirming our understanding, we shall for the period
beginning                    through
place at your disposal the complete resident buying
facilities of our organization, and shall, on your
behalf, perform all services usually performed by
resident buyers including the placing of your orders
for merchandise and the furnishing of information
regarding market conditions.

For our service, we shall receive from you the annual
fee of $        payable in advance in equal monthly
installments of $          each, plus postage.

Unless either you or we shall give the other written
notice to the contrary at least 60 days before the
annual expiration date, we shall continue our service
on your behalf for the further annual periods.

                              Very truly yours,

                              Name of Company

                              BY_____

AGREED TO:

  By: _____
```

merchandise (for example, a department store), membership would be most beneficial in an office whose offerings are more diversified. The more specialization in a store, the more specialized the chosen office should be. Both the office and the organization should be interested in the same type of retailing.

SERVICES OF AN OFFICE

Typically, all resident offices function in a similar manner. Resident office buyers or product managers, as some prefer to be called, cover both domestic and foreign markets. In addition to the all-important task of merchandise recommendation, there are a host of other services afforded the retailer. It is imperative to select the office that offers those services needed to help your operation. Very small stores, unable to afford the fees of the full-service resident offices, often join a small office that only advises about new resources and new merchandise available. Most retailers join an office for many additional services. Following are some of these.

Placing Orders

Stores often satisfy their customers by reordering out-of-stock merchandise for them or merchandise not usually carried at all. The resident office will place these "special orders" and make certain that the vendors deliver the item within the specified time period. Sometimes buyers are in need of new merchandise and are unable to visit the market. Given approximate specifications, resident buyers will make purchases for the store.

Most retailers' businesses thrive on reorders of merchandise that has sold successfully. Since the timing of receipt of reordered merchandise is extremely important, store buyers often depend on the resident office to place the reorder. With the office located in the market, the resident buyer can carefully check with the vendors to make certain that delivery promises are kept. Only the retailer that has run a newspaper advertisement and not received the merchandise when promised can appreciate this responsibility that is undertaken by the resident offices.

A typical order form used by resident buying offices to place store orders is shown in Figure 10–3.

In order to maintain appropriate lines of communication between the resident buyer and the store buyer, concerning the placement of orders, a form similar to the one in Figure 10–4 is used. With such a form, the retailer has a memo for recordkeeping containing all of the information pertinent to the merchandise purchased through the resident office.

On occasion, a retailer will cancel an order with a vendor. The store might have found better merchandise at a more affordable price, or it could be overstocked. Such cancellations might be done through the resident office. Figure 10–5 shows an example of a typical cancellation notice.

Arranging Adjustments

It is not unusual for a store buyer who has carefully ordered merchandise, paying strict attention to style, color, and size selection, to receive unwanted goods. Receiving a garment made in a completely different fabric from that in the sample merchandise is not uncommon. Handling these adjustments through a resident office is much wiser for the retailer. Vendors are unlikely to ignore the resident buyer's complaints as they might an individual small retailer, since the resident offices are so influential through their recommendations.

Sometimes the buying office can convince a vendor to accept a return of merchandise that has been ordered but is not selling satisfactorily. In this case, a retailer handling the situation alone usually doesn't stand a chance. Other adjustment situations include poor fit, inferior quality, and poor wearability.

Market Forecasting

In order to give the retail merchandisers and buyers an inside look at the market before any new major purchase plans are made, the buying office scouts the market and prepares literature that would be helpful to the store. This forecast might include such vital information as price changes, fabric, silhouettes, and so on. Independent Retailers Syndicate

FIGURE 10–3 Purchase Order Form

INDEPENDENT RETAILERS SYNDICATE, Inc.
33 WEST 34th ST. NEW YORK, N. Y. 10001
212 564-4900

DATE | 226700
STORE ORDER NO. | DEPT. NO.

ABOVE STORE ORDER AND DEPT. NUMBERS MUST APPEAR ON ALL INVOICES & PACKAGES

SHIP AND BILL TO

TERMS | F.O.B. | INSURED YES ☐ NO ☐

SHIP VIA

PURCHASED FROM

WHEN SHIP | CANCELLATION DATE

ALL MDSE. SHIPPED AFTER THE 25th OF ANY MONTH MUST BE INVOICED AS OF THE 1st OF FOLLOWING MONTH

STYLE NO.	DESCRIPTION	INSERT SIZE HERE	QUAN.	PCS. DOZ.	COST	UNIT RETAIL

No merchandise is to be charged to Independent Retailers Syndicate, Inc. unless authorized in writing by an officer of the company. The store to whose account it is specified that the order shall be charged is the purchaser, and not Independent Retailers Syndicate, Inc., which acts only as agent for such store in placing the order.

In Accepting Order Vendor Specifically Agrees and/or Warrants: (See Other Side of This Sheet)

BUYER

If any changes are necessary on this order advise IRS immediately.

VENDOR COPY

NET AMT. OF ORDER
$

MEMBER OF THE ASSOCIATION OF BUYING OFFICES

Courtesy of Independent Retailers Syndicate, Inc. Used with permission.

periodically prepares such a report, *State of the Market*, for its member stores. Figure 10–6 features an excerpt of such a notice.

Foreign Market Information

In both hard goods and soft goods, foreign markets are becoming increasingly important. A tremendous amount of merchandise is being imported each year at prices below those found in the United States. Large resident buying offices have branches in many foreign countries. Because few stores can send their buyers abroad, the information about the merchandise available is an extremely important service.

FIGURE 10–4 Placement Notice

 NOTICE OF PLACEMENT OF YOUR ORDERS

DATE _____

STORE _____ DEPT. _____

CITY _____ STATE _____

Orders listed below have been checked and placed   Any changes noted below

STORE ORDER #	MANUFACTURER	DELIVERY DATE	REMARKS ON CHANGES	AMOUNT OF ORDER

INDEPENDENT RETAILERS SYNDICATE, Inc.

Per _____

Courtesy of Independent Retailers Syndicate, Inc. Used with permission.

FIGURE 10–5 Cancellation Notice

VENDOR COPY

INDEPENDENT RETAILERS SYNDICATE, INC.

33 WEST 34TH STREET • NEW YORK 1, N. Y. • LOngacre 4-4900

CANCELLATION NOTICE

_____ 19

Resource _____

_____

Kindly cancel the following order for:

Store _____

City _____ Dept. No. _____

_____

Date of Order _____ Order No. _____

Style No. _____

Acknowledged by: IRS Buyer _____

Mfr. _____

Per _____

IR.-F. 118 5M 10-50

Courtesy of Independent Retailers Syndicate, Inc. Used with permission.

FIGURE 10–6 An Excerpt from State of the Market

DEPT.: JR. SPORTSWEAR
NUMBER: 4-7620-0
DATE: 1/28/85   amw

STATE OF THE MARKET

Junior departments for Spring/Summer '85 are looking for a turn-a-round from 84's poor performance. Understanding the junior customer, buying closer to time of need and reserving open to buy for items as they develop are basic merchandising techniques that must be followed.
Understanding todays Jr. revolves around 2 distinct customers:

    A. Young - trendy
    B. Sophisticated Career

Each area must be catered to individually.

Must items are:

Career - Sophisticated

* Linen type pants & skirts
* Challis print skirts
* French canvas pants
* Career styled pants & skirts in sheeting & twill
* Camp shirts
* Cotton sweaters
* Linen look skirtings

Young - trendy

* Stirrup pants
* Print/pattern pants & skirts
* Mini skirts
* Stretch pants
* Shorts boxer - trouser - solids & patterns
* Camp shirts - solids & prints
* Novelty "T" shirts
* Cartoon character T-shirts
* Tanks
* Crop tops

JOYCE ABOLAFIA - Buyer
Bottoms, Swimwear

APRIL RINGE - Buyer
Tops

BILL FRIEDMAN
Div. Mdse. Mgr.

(OVER PLEASE)

© 1985 INDEPENDENT RETAILERS SYNDICATE INC.

Courtesy of Independent Retailers Syndicate, Inc. Used with permission.

Locating New Resources

Retailers are always looking for new resources. Since many vendors begin on a small scale with little sales help and advertising, it is difficult for stores away from the market to hear about the newcomers. Through the resident offices (every new firm tries desperately to be recommended by them) retailers are made aware of new resources.

Recommending New Items

Buyers purchase sufficient goods prior to each selling season to complete their opening inventories. They generally visit their markets, either alone or assisted by the resident buyer, to select the goods they desire. During the season, when store buyers are involved in duties at the store, they may find that they need new merchandise to spruce up the inventory. The resident office will scout the market and suggest merchandise to fit the bill. Often this recommendation by the resident buyer turns out to be a hot item.

Figure 10–7 shows an example of a format often used by resident offices to notify the stores of what is new. It not only tells about specific items, but where they are available, price lines, and why they are considered hot.

FIGURE 10–7   Hot Items Report

ladies sportswear flash report

Week of <u>January 21, 1985</u>

WHAT DID WE SEE	WHO HAS IT	WHAT DOES IT COST	WHY IS IT EXCITING	REPORTED BY:
Disney: Mickey Mouse & his Friends; Donald Duck, Minnie Mouse, Betty Boop and Bluto. T-Shirts, cover-ups, crop tops, tank tops and bowling shirts.	1) Sunday Comics 1407 Broadway 2) America's Favorites 1407 Broadway N.Y.C., N.Y. 3) Mickey & Co. 485 7th Ave. N.Y.C., N.Y. 10018	$11.75-$14.50 $6.00-$8.50 $6.00-$22.50	These cartoon characters add fun and excitement to any junior department. Display on mannequins and T-Shirts.	April Ringe
Swimsuits and Cover-ups.	4) Dotty 1407 Broadway	$14.00-$19.00		Joyce Abolafia
Looney Tunes: Bugs Bunny, Tweetie Bird & Sylvester in T-Shirts, Crop Tops and Tank Tops.	1) B.J. Frog 1407 Broadway N.Y.C., N.Y. 10008 2) Sunday Comics 1407 Broadway N.Y.C., N.Y. 10018	$3.75-$4.50 $11.75-$14.50		April Ringe

© 1985 INDEPENDENT RETAILERS SYNDICATE INC.

Courtesy of Independent Retailers Syndicate, Inc. Used with permission.

Preparing Displays and Promotional Materials

In large stores, the display department is charged with the responsibility of creating dramatic, timely windows and interior displays. The small shop either engages a free-lance display person or trims its own windows. Catchy ideas are always being sought by store buyers. Many resident offices arrange displays in typical window-size settings so that the retailer can copy them. This gives retailers new ideas to bring back to their stores. Similarly, copy for advertisements is prepared. Some offices even provide mats (paper composition printing plates of complete advertisements) to which the store's name is added, for newspaper advertisements.

Preparing Fashion Shows

Resident buying offices typically present fashion shows to their member stores during "market week," a time when most buyers visit the market to begin purchasing for a new season. In addition to these shows, many of the offices prepare complete fashion show packages for retailers to present at their stores. These packages include such important elements as the commentary, suggested musical selections, and background recommendations. These prescribed plans make the presentation of a fashion show a routine job.

Training Salespeople

Some offices aid in the training of salepeople, providing such training materials as booklets, brochures, and recordings. In addition, some may send counselors to the store. By using this service, the buyer makes certain that once the purchases arrive at the store, the salepeople will be sufficiently knowledgeable about the merchandise.

Preparing for the Store Buyer's Visit

The frequency of visits a store buyer makes to the market varies from store to store. Distance from the market, size of the department, and the store's need for the buyer's presence on the selling floor are just some factors that help determine how often the market is visited. Whenever the buyer does decide to come to the market, the resident buying office goes to work to make certain that the trip will be fruitful and that as much as possible can be condensed into that brief period. The office's preparation includes the following:

1. Locating the most desirable merchandise.
2. Publishing the "buyer's arrival" in such papers as the *New York Times* and the appropriate trade papers. This notifies all interested vendors about the buyers that are in town, the length of their stay,

and their temporary residence. In this way advance appointments can be made through the offices.

3. Arranging hotel accommodations.
4. Providing work space for buyers at the resident office to study their purchasing plans and to see salespersons and their merchandise.
5. Assigning a resident buyer to accompany the store buyer to market to help with the selection of merchandise.

Market Week Preparations

Although the resident offices must have their services available to the retail store members at all times, it is during the regular visits to the market that the resident buyers are busiest serving the store buyer's needs. These periodic visits are generally made during "market weeks," when the manufacturers of particular industries open and show their lines to the store buyers. Because the period is extremely hectic, and the store buyer's time away from the store is generally limited to a week, the resident office's planning must be perfectly organized. It is for this period that the preparations for the store buyer's visit must be made.

Making Available Private Brands

A private brand is one that bears either the store's label or the resident buying office's name. Private brand merchandise permits the store to gain a high markup without the fear of price-cutting by competitors, because exact comparison shopping is impossible. Few retailers are large enough to market private brands by themselves. By joining a buying office, small individual orders can be consolidated into large orders. To obtain large orders, manufacturers will gladly produce merchandise to specification and attach private labels. This merchandise usually costs less because of the great quantities manufactured. In this way, the store makes a better profit and the customer gets good value.

More and more resident buying offices are busier than ever in their private label or private brand endeavors. Most report that their retail clients are continuously increasing the proportion of the "exclusive" lines of their total inventories. In Figure 10–8, the *Private Brands Bulletin* featuring the Pedals label of Independent Retailers Syndicate shows a very complete picture of how profitable such merchandising could be for the stores. Markups, as indicated, of from 57.5 to 59 percent are considered excellent.

Figure 10–9 displays a typical order form that features the Pedals line. Not only does the buying office make these specialized items available, but also merchandises the styles in terms of quantities, colors, and sizes to fit specific retailer requirements. These illustrations clearly indicate that, in terms of private labels or brands, the store buyers have little decision making to do and can thus concentrate on purchases of nationally advertised goods.

FIGURE 10–8 *Private Brands Bulletin*; Featuring the Pedals Label

Private Brands

 ... <u>LOGO TENNIS APPAREL</u>

Based on the success of the Pedals private label fleece program, we are now going forward with a new and exciting private label woman's (year round in stock) tennis group. This program includes: an elastic side, fly front basic tennis <u>short</u> in a 65% poly/35% cotton tennis twill, a 100% cotton pique 4 button placket tennis <u>polo</u> and a 100% acrylic traditional <u>tennis cardigan</u> with 2 patch pockets. All garments will have the "Pedals" logo & label.

This program will once again be exclusive to IRS member stores and will afford stores the opportunity for exclusivity and additional mark-up on basic tennis items for functional activewear departments.

The contractor selected for this program is Fred Perry/Loomtogs, one of the most highly reputable Tennis Manufacturers in the industry with an excellent selling record.

The first delivery for Pedals Tennis Basics is 4/30 Complete.

Private Label program prices are as follows:

Style #	Perry Logo Line	Pedals Logo I. R. S. Store Cost	Sugg. Retail	M.U.
3228 - Twill Tennis Short	$14.50	* $12.65	$29.00	57-1/2% approx.
5602 - Cotton Pique Mesh Polo	12.00	* 10.56	24.00	56-1/2% approx.
3508 - 100% Acrylic Tennis Cardigan (less 2%)	18.00	* 14.80	36.00	59% approx.

DEPT	Sportswear
MERCHANDISE	Functional Active
RESOURCE	PEDALS PRIVATE LABEL
TERMS	2/10
DELIVERY	4/30
F.O.B	PA
DEPT HEAD	Fran Levy
BUYER	Marti Unger
NUMBER	3-5-6571-0
DATE	January 9, 1984 mm

NOTE: Attachment (1)

(OVER PLEASE)

FIGURE 10–9   Private Brands Order Form

IRS   INDEPENDENT RETAILERS SYNDICATE, Inc.
33 WEST 34th ST.   NEW YORK, N. Y. 10001
212 564-4900

SHIP AND
BILL TO

DATE	ORDER NO.
F.O.B. Summitt-ville Pa.	DEPT. NO.
TERMS 2/10ROM	ABOVE STORE ORDER AND DEPT. NUMBERS MUST APPEAR ON ALL INVOICES & PACKAGES
SHIP VIA	

PURCHASED FROM   **PEDALS** Tennis
33 W. 34th
N.Y. N.Y.

	INSURED YES☐ NO☐
WHEN SHIP AIR	CANCELLATION DATE 4/30C

ALL MDSE. SHIPPED AFTER THE 25th OF ANY MONTH MUST BE INVOICED AS OF THE 1st OF FOLLOWING MONTH

STYLE NO.	DESCRIPTION	6	8	10	12	14	16	QUAN.	PCS. DOZ.	COST	
3228	Poly/cotton Tennis twill short W/elastic sides and 2 pockets									12	65
	Crimson	1	1	1	1	1	1	6			
	White	2	3	4	4	3	2	18			
	Navy	2	2	2	2	2	2	12			
									36		
5602	100% cotton pique 4 button placket polo shirt	P	S	M	L					10	56
	crimson	2	4	4	2			12			
	White	2	4	4	2			12			
	Navy	2	4	4	4			12			
		34	36	38	40				36		
3508	100% acrylic traditional Tennis Cardigan w/tiping and 2 patch pockets	4	8	8	4				36	14	80
	White w/Red + Navy Tiping										

Active Private Label
Tennis Program

No merchandise is to be charged to Independent Retailers Syndicate, Inc. unless authorized in writing by an officer of the company. The store to whose account it is specified that the order shall be charged is the purchaser, and not Independent Retailers Syndicate, Inc., which acts only as agent for such store in placing the order.

BUYER
Marti Unger

If any changes are necessary on this order advise IRS immediately.

NET AMT. OF ORDER
$

Pooling Orders

Since small retailers can't economically place large orders, they are eliminated from quantity discounts. Buying offices often assemble or pool individual retail orders and place one large order, which could qualify for a quantity discount. In this way, the small store could more effectively compete in terms of price.

FOREIGN RESIDENT BUYING OFFICES

Since only the very large retail organizations will invest in trips abroad for purposes of purchasing, other methods are employed by smaller entrepreneurs for importing goods.

Similar to those resident offices operating in the United States are the resident buying offices located in foreign countries. Some of the offices, called commissionaires, are completely independent and are designed to service buyers from other countries. Still other offices are affiliated with the U.S. buying offices, and their services are available to member stores. Whichever type of office represents the U.S. retailer, the services afforded the buyer are the same. Some of the services offered are the following:

1. *The purchase of new merchandise.* Purchasing in this manner is somewhat risky for the store because the foreign office must use its judgment and the store must accept what has been purchased. Sometimes, if time is available, photographs or samples of goods are sent to the United States for approval. This eliminates some of the risk.
2. *The placement of reorders.* Much the same as U.S. resident buying offices, those in foreign countries place orders and follow up reorders. Even though the office facilitates purchasing in foreign countries, the reordering of merchandise must be done with caution. Shipping delays, strikes, and so forth can cause merchandise to be delivered too late to be meaningful in terms of sales.
3. *The arrangement for shipment of the merchandise.*
4. *Assistance to those wishing to visit the foreign markets.* They arrange such things as hotel accommodations and appointments with vendors.

For their services, the commissionaires are paid a commission based on the cost of the merchandise. The commission is approximately 7 percent of the foreign cost.

Although the cost of goods in foreign countries may be considered less than comparable domestic goods, there are additional costs that must be considered before a purchase is completed. An example of the computation involved in determining the true, or landed, cost, as it is technically called, follows:

Initial cost 5 sweaters @ 30,000 lire each	150,000
10 sweaters @ 60,000 lire each	600,000
Total initial cost	750,000
Less 3% discount	22,500
	727,500
Packing charge	22,700
7% commission (on initial cost)	52,500
Shipping charge	55,200
	857,900
Duty 30% (estimated) on goods purchased plus packing charge	225,060
	1,082,960
Other expenses (storage, etc.)	91,000
Total landed cost	1,173,960

The 1,173,960 figure is then translated into U.S. dollars.

As has been discussed, several forces necessitate the purchase of merchandise abroad. Whether the purchase is achieved directly through negotiation between the store buyer and supplier or arranged through a commissionaire, a number of factors must be considered to ensure that a profit will be possible.

There has always been a fluctuation of foreign currency in relation to the U.S. dollar, and today the situation is even less stable. Each day the worth of the U.S. dollar on foreign markets fluctuates, sometimes considerably. The buyer must make certain that the terms of purchase include language that provides for protection of price. That is, if the cost due to dollar devaluation presents a risk to profit once the merchandise is delivered, the buyer should insist on some protection. Such caution is significantly needed where there is a wide time gap between purchase, production, and eventual delivery. The inexperienced could lose a great deal if these price considerations aren't carefully explored.

While the initial price might seem low, the bonded cost should always be figured to determine the real cost to the store. Such factors as packing charges and duty charges must be carefully examined to ensure that the product is worth the real cost.

Merchandise from abroad frequently includes selling features not found in domestic goods. Similarly, the merchandise might bring with it quality features that are detrimental to the merchandise. For example, European fit might be narrower than that which is appropriate for Americans. Often, the sample and the delivered goods bear little resemblance to each other. A buyer prone to purchase imported merchandise must be careful to set guidelines for the merchandise. Returns are difficult and time consuming, and subquality goods could present problems.

Although it is generally conceded that goods from abroad are necessary to many merchandising plans, care must be exercised in their purchase. The foreign resident representative must be completely instructed as to the requirements of the purchase. Although dollars are important, other factors might prevent successful sale of the goods.

Many stores need to get as much input as possible before they make merchandising decisions. While most agree that their most valuable outside resource is the resident buying office, many subscribe to other agencies for additional information.

Reporting Services

The reporting services, of which the Retail News Bureau is a major force, offer considerable market information for a monthly fee. Often referred to as "clipping" services, because much of the information they send to their clients is in the form of store advertisements taken directly from newspapers, they regularly communicate their information via merchandise reports, market studies, customer reactions to specific items, and so on. They differ from the buying offices in that they do not make purchases or provide private lines.

Fashion Forecasters

Different from the reporting services, which inform retailers of current merchandising trends, are the fashion forecasters. Fashion forecasters, of which Promostyl, a Paris-based company with branches all over the world, including the United States, is a prime example, make predictions on fashion trends before the manufacturers' lines are available for inspection. They forecast the styles, fabrics, and fashion trends that buyers will ultimately set in their favorite lines. This service enables the retail buyer to formulate future concepts and receive insight into the fashion future.

SMALL STORE ADAPTATION

It is the exception rather than the rule that the small retailer can operate successfully without the assistance of outside sources of information and advisory services. For what amounts to a nominal fee in return for invaluable information, the small retailer can feel the pulse of the wholesale market and be continuously informed of the environment of the marketplace.

The independent resident buying office, the major retail advisory service, is the counterpart of the independent retailer. Making the time-consuming and costly trips to the market for its members, the resident office acts, through its buyers, as the stores' representative. Small stores can quickly learn about new resources and hot items, avail themselves of private label merchandise, and receive expert advice and assistance on any merchandising matter. For those needing additional informational sources, or for the small retailer that needs only current, general merchandise information, there are information bureaus, reporting companies, and clipping services that provide such information for a fee.

It is imperative that the small retailer be kept abreast of market conditions. It is through these sources that the small store can understand changes that could affect business and can more favorably compete with the larger stores.

CAREER OPPORTUNITIES

Those who study retailing and fashion should be aware that enormous opportunity lies in areas that serve the retailer but are not directly part of the retail organization. The most significant of these employers are the independent resident buying offices. Their job titles are numerous, and the roles the individuals play are often preparatory for careers in management positions in stores.

Resident buying offices rarely require a baccalaureate degree for employment, thus giving the holders of an associate degree or a certificate opportunity for exciting careers. Typically, the entry-level position is at the assistant buyer level, with promotion to buyer achievable as quickly as the individual's performance merits. Often, the movement from assignment to buyer usually takes two to three years. As in retailing, the next level is divisional merchandise manager and ultimately merchandising vice president. One particular advantage of careers in resident buying offices is the work schedule. Unlike retailing, where hours include evenings and weekends, the resident office typically operates from 9 to 5 on a Monday through Friday schedule.

Reporting services, clipping services, fashion consulting companies, and the like are other organizations where careers are available. Like the resident offices, there are regular business hours and the requirements for employment are generally less stringent than in retail management. It should be understood, however, that the number of these companies are considerably fewer than the resident buying offices and thus, there is less chance for career potential.

Finally, both resident buying offices and the other retail advisory services employ more women than men. It is certainly a field of equal opportunity employment.

KEY POINTS IN THE CHAPTER

1. Resident buying offices are classified as private or independent. Private are owned by the retail giants, whereas the independent service the needs of smaller retail organizations for a fee.

2. In selecting membership in an independent resident buying office, the retailer should consider the size of the office, the other member stores, and the services offered.

3. In addition to placing orders, most of which are reorders or special orders, resident buying offices arrange adjustments, forecast trends, locate new resources, recommend new items, prepare promotional

programs, and do everything to assist the store buyer to be more productive.

4. The resident buyers play a major role in helping retailers during market week, a period when major purchases are made.

5. Private label merchandise is becoming an important part of the resident buyer office's responsibility. It enables the small retailer to obtain merchandise, under a private label, that otherwise would be available only to the large-scale retail organizations.

6. Foreign resident buying offices, known as commissionaires, help American buyers with the purchase of imports.

7. When purchasing imports through the commissionaires, it is important to determine the landed cost of the goods to make certain that they are priced in line with the store's policy.

8. Many retailers employ the services of reporting services and fashion forecasters, which supply additional information on which stores base their decision making.

Worksheet 10

Name _____

COMPLETE THE FOLLOWING STATEMENTS

1. There are two major types of resident buying offices: the

   _____ office and the _____ office.

2. Regular visits are made by buyers to the vendors during periods called

   _____.

3. A _____ brand is one that bears either the store's label or the resident buying office's name.

4. When purchasing merchandise abroad, the true cost is also known as the

   _____ cost.

5. Foreign resident buying offices are commonly called _____.

6. Reporting services are often known as _____ services to people in the retail industry.

7. Companies that predict fashion trends in advance of the season are technically

   known as _____.

TRUE OR FALSE

_____ 1. The independent resident buying office is owned by and exclusively represents a single retail organization.

_____ 2. It is important to select a resident buying office that has noncompeting retailers as members.

_____ 3. Some resident buying offices prepare displays and promotional materials for their members.

_____ 4. Market week occurs once a year.

_____ 5. Most items purchased abroad carry additional charges in the form of packing fees, duty, and storage.

_____ 6. If a store has resident office representation, it doesn't use the services of a reporting service.

MULTIPLE CHOICE

_____ 1. The services of a resident buying office
  (a) vary from office to office
  (b) are similar to every other office
  (c) are very limited
  (d) cost too much to appeal to most stores

_____ 2. Market week refers to
  (a) the time salespeople visit stores to sell to buyers
  (b) the period just prior to the buyer's visit to the wholesale market
  (c) the time the buyer spends scouting the market at the beginning of a season
  (d) none of the above

_____ 3. Resident buying office membership affords the store
  (a) private brand merchandise
  (b) information about hot items
  (c) sales personnel training
  (d) all of the above

_____ 4. Commissionaires are
  (a) independent resident buying offices
  (b) resident offices that belong to U.S. companies
  (c) a and b
  (d) neither a nor b

_____ 5. Private resident buying offices are
  (a) established for the retailing giants
  (b) disappearing from the retailing world
  (c) too expensive to operate
  (d) both a and b

DISCUSSION QUESTIONS

1. Is the trend to open more branches for resident buying offices increasing or decreasing? Why?

2. What are the principal advantages of belonging to a resident buying office?

3. On what basis is the fee paid to the resident buying office calculated?

4. Justify the cost of belonging to a resident buying office for the small retail operation.

5. Is the size of the resident buying office significant to prospective members? Defend your position.

6. In addition to placing reorders, do resident office buyers actually make purchases? In what instances?

7. Define a special order. Is there a danger to stores in becoming too occupied with this type of transaction?

8. Why are vendors more likely to make adjustments for members of resident buying offices than for nonmembers?

9. Why is it advantageous for resident buying offices to prepare advertising copy for member stores?

10. For what purpose do some large resident buying offices offer sales training aids to store personnel?

11. What advantage is there in pooling orders for retail stores? What type of merchandise orders are pooled?

12. Can retailers purchase foreign goods through resident buying offices? Discuss.

13. Describe the operation of reporting services.

14. In what way does a fashion forecaster help the retailer?

CASE PROBLEM 1

Helen Klar is a retailing major about to graduate from a New England college. As usual, the college has invited many leading business organizations to visit the campus for the purpose of recruitment. Klar has attended a number of these sessions and was interviewed by two organizations that were pleased with her ⌐tions. Each one offered a full-time position with its company. Briefly, the ⌐ere

1. $12,000 a year, with $500 annual increments for two years, as an assistant buyer in a resident buying office in New York City. At the end of a two- to four-year period (with a satisfactory evaluation), she could become a buyer in a small department at about $20,000.
2. $14,000 a year as an assistant buyer in one of her hometown's two department stores. The store grosses $14 million annually. She would be evaluated every three months and could possibly become a buyer within five years.

Keeping in mind that Helen is a bright, attractive, and ambitious twenty-year-old, answer the following questions:

1. On what basis would you evaluate the two offers? Discuss fully.
2. Which job would you suggest that she select? Why?

CASE PROBLEM 2

Jim Avidon owns and operates two women's specialty shops. Their combined volume for the past year was $500,000. Avidon, in addition to managing the larger unit, is responsible for all purchasing.

Another location is being considered for a third unit in the chain. After considerable research, it appears to be suited for a successful operation. The problem confronting Avidon at this time is how to continue the small chain's growth without ruining its efficiency. A third unit means additional managerial problems and more involved merchandising. He feels that it will be impossible for him to handle all of his old responsibilities and those brought about by the expansion.

There seems to be two obvious solutions to his problem. One is to join a resident buying office to alleviate his burden. The other is to hire a buyer to share the purchasing responsibilities.

1. Develop criteria by which to evaluate the two courses of action.
2. Compare each plan against the established criteria.
3. Is there another course of action possible? If so, discuss its merits.
4. Which plan would you tell Avidon to follow? Why?

PROJECT 1

Visit or write to two independent resident buying offices and compare the information received from each one. The following is just a sample of some of the areas you might investigate:

1. Fees
2. Merchandise specialization
3. Services offered
4. Market locations

5. Type of clientele represented

6. Size of staff

Incorporate the information into the chart below for easy comparison.

Name of Office

1.
2.
3.
4.
5.
6.
7.
8.
9.
10.

Name of Office

1.
2.
3.
4.
5.
6.
7.
8.
9.
10.

PROJECT 2

You are charged with the responsibility of preparing for a store buyer's visit for the spring market week. He is a children's wear buyer from Washington, D.C., and expects to stay in the New York market for the full week. Plan all the arrangements and advance preparations necessary to ensure the buyer a successful and fruitful visit. Prepare your work in outline form.

Index